I0626111

CROSSING THE WILD PACIFIC

Captain's Log of the Yacht Argo

ROBERT R. TISCH

Books Academy LLC
112 SW H K Dodgen Loop,
Temple, Texas 76504
Hotline: (254) 800-1189

Ordering Information:
Quantity sales. Special discounts are available on quantity purchases by corporations, associations, and others. For details, contact the publisher at the address above.

Printed in the United States of America.

ISBN-13: Softcover   978-1-964929-72-9
          Hardcover   978-1-964929-73-6
          eBook   978-1-964929-74-3

Library of Congress Control Number: 2024923911

"This is a lovely book, and many of the passages are so well written the reader is transported to another place. It is also a realistic tale and paints well the challenges, and the rewards, of such a grand activity."

Editor, BookBaby

"Many people dream about undertaking an ambitious voyage but few do. Captain Tisch realized his dream and shares his evocative and well-written account. I was fortunate to be a small part of this voyage but enjoyed experiencing its entirety through his book – I know you will too."

Capt. Curtis Hoff, PhD
- Cruisers' Net.net

"The pages ahead give not only valuable technical information on how they accomplished their goals but give good insight too to the incredible people they met and exotic places they called upon during their ocean voyage of a lifetime."

Jim Leishman, Co-Founder
Nordhavn Yachts

"Crossing the Wild Pacific is a must read for those who are adventurous and willing to go beyond the beaten path."

Gus Gialamas M.D., Chair,
Operation Rainbow

"Randy Tisch has written a comprehensive do-it-yourself guide to bluewater cruising in offshore yachts. The book describes the cruises, preparation, and challenges that he and Rebecca faced in short-handed ocean passages. Randy's accounts of their cruising experiences in the Atlantic and Caribbean, including preparation and crossing of the Pacific to New Zealand, are fun to read, enlightening, and most helpful. This is a good read for any sailor, whether thinking about going offshore or reclining in a comfortable chair."

Bill Martin, Sailing Hall of Fame Honoree
and Past President of the U.S.
Sailing Association

To Rebecca:

life mate, love mate, ship mate ....

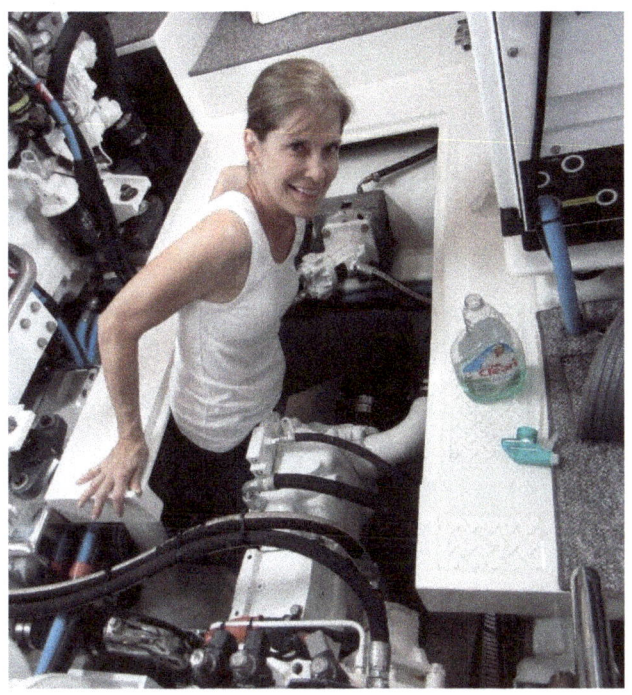

Rebecca was hands-on in every way
and did everything including standing
watches, piloting the yacht, throwing
lines and climbing into places too
small for me.

The deeps have music soft and low
When winds awake the airy spry
It lures me, lures me to go
And see the land were corals lie
The land, the land were corals lie.

Excerpted from "Where the Corals Lie",a
poem by Richard Garnett (1835- 1906)

TABLE OF CONTENTS

I once wrote that cruising of the serious variety is an activity most people pursue as a fulfillment of a dream. They seek adventure, travel and challenge, and in today's complex, controlled and densely populated world a high-quality experience that's unique and really special is not as easy to find as it once was. The sea has tremendous appeal. It is vast, challenging, ever changing, and perpetually beautiful. The allure of ocean voyaging and of destinations that are unlimited in number and variety is truly what dreams are made of cruising on one's own yacht offers an experience and adventure that is unrivaled.

For over 40 years I have helped create almost one thousand ocean going yachts that have collectively cruised over eight million miles across the world's oceans. Randy and Rebecca Tisch have owned two of our Nordhavn Long Range Cruisers and within these pages the story of cruising the Pacific aboard their 68-foot Argo is told.

I recall a late-night phone call I received from Randy as he approached New Zealand in very rough conditions. They were having some difficulty with a hydraulic cooling pump and wanted to turn down swell for a more comfortable ride while sorting the problem. I was asked how the turn should be made in the large breaking seas and with little valuable advice offered Randy turned his storm-tossed yacht around 180 degrees and calmly told me the turn was easy, and the motion had dramatically eased. I said goodnight and wished him good luck, but as I drifted back to sleep in the security of my own bed I knew Randy had hours of discomfort and stress ahead and was greatly relieved the next day to learn that all was well and Argo had arrived safely in New Zealand.

It's very satisfying for me to see the success of Argo's adventures. I'm sure Randy and Rebecca will remember their Pacific crossing as a rewarding chapter of their lives and the pages ahead give not only valuable technical information on how they accomplished their goals but give good insight too to the incredible people they met and exotic places they called upon during their ocean voyage of a lifetime.

Jim Leishman, Co-founder and Owner,
Nordhavn Yachts Author: *Voyaging Underpower II*
Dana Point – September 2017

"Go confidently in the direction of your dreams. Live the life you imagined."

Henry David Thoreau

I have always dreamed of accomplishing a grand physical adventure, like sailing across an ocean, climbing Mount Everest, or cycling across the continent. Fortunately, I am married to a wonderful lady, Rebecca, who shares my dreams and works hard to help make them come true. Our dream was to cross the wild Pacific Ocean, as the first leg of a longer cruise. I am not sure when the idea first germinated in me, perhaps as a little boy growing up on the Great Lakes and watching the huge steamers delivering tons of iron ore and coal to the steel mills of Gary and Cleveland.

Rebecca and I started boating on the Great Lakes more than 20 years ago, and I thought that navigation and seamanship would be the biggest challenges. We took courses to educate ourselves as much as possible before venturing out onto big waters. As important as those skills are, just keeping boats operating is at least half the battle. The doggone things are always breaking down in one way or another, so mechanical aptitude is a very important skill. I suppose I developed some of those skills as a boy growing up in Detroit in the 1950's and 60's when boys were always messing about with cars, much like kids today do with computers and cell phones. We were learning the mechanics of things, and while cars were not terribly reliable then, they were built without robots or computers, so it was easier to dig inside one and get your hands dirty figuring out how to make the machine work. Many of us acquired a clunker to fix up. Changing spark plugs and setting valve tolerances were commonplace. I even took the engine and transmission apart on a '54 Ford Victoria, although I don't remember if I ever got it back together again. Winter brought special challenges in the form of flooded engines.

This required an application of ether in the form of a spray administered directly into the carburetor's barrels, then a crank of the engine, and, as it started, a belch of fire! All of this playing around with mechanics has been a big help in boating. However, as much as I enjoyed cars, and although our family never owned a boat while I was growing up, boats always captured my imagination, and my mechanical know-how with cars certainly helped with our various boats.

When I graduated from high school, my father took me down to the local armed forces recruiting office, and I joined the Navy. The Navy trained me as a radar and cryptographic technician. After technical school at Treasure Island in the middle of San Francisco Bay, I spent three years aboard the USS Currituck, a sea plane tender (whose class is now extinct). We made four crossings of the Pacific and two Westpac tours including months on station in Vietnam. I loved life aboard ship. I remember one afternoon, as we were steaming past Luzon Island in the Philippines, wondering where life might take me and if I would ever return to these waters. That memory was a partial motivation for our journey in 2014 and 2015.

USS Currituck AV7 lying Hong Kong 1965

Shortly after returning to the States from my last Westpac tour my enlistment came to an end, and, unfortunately, I was discharged a few days before the 1967 Detroit riots began. Shortly after my return, Metropolitan Airport was placed under martial law, as was the entire Detroit area. I was shocked to see tanks and soldiers with guns on the streets of my hometown, the former Arsenal of Democracy. It was too much like the Vietnam I had recently left.

As the years went by, I graduated from college, settled in Ann Arbor, started a business, and met Rebecca. She was an ophthalmology resident at the University of Michigan Medical School and was an adventurous soul who also loved water sports and boats. After we were married, we worked for years building our family and professions. Then, when we had the time and money, we started our boating career on the Great Lakes. We bought a twin diesel motor yacht and named it *Currituck* after my Navy ship. We took Power Squadron courses in the winter and cruised the Great Lakes on weekends and vacations during the summer. We circumnavigated Lake Superior, Lake Michigan, and Lake Huron. We loved our time spent together in the Georgian Bay and the North Channel; Isle Royale was a special delight. Although the Great Lakes offers some of the best cruising we have ever experienced, after 6 years of boating we decided to pursue other adventures. It wasn't until several years had gone by and we were nearing retirement that we realized that some of our best memories were aboard our boat. No other pastime for us surpassed the adventure and beauty of boating. So, we started evaluating boats and the type of cruising we wanted to do in the future.

In 2009, I sold my investment management firm, and Rebecca closed her medical practice. My mechanical and electrical aptitude combined with Rebecca's medical skills were perfect for our intended undertaking. We bought *Odyssey*, a Nordhavn 55-footer, and on her maiden voyage we cruised from California to Mexico under the tutelage of a captain and other Nordhavn owners. I began studying for my own USCG captain's license. The next year we headed north to Alaska. When we returned to Dana Point, California, and Nordhavn's home office, they made us an attractive offer and we decided to build a 68-footer. We sailed *Odyssey* through the Canal and up to Rhode Island, sold her there, and spent most of the following year building *Argo* and planning our voyages. During the building process, we visited the shipyard in Taiwan, which was a wonderful experience, to customize our boat to suit my 6'5" frame. After *Argo* was delivered in Florida, we took her to the Bahamas for a brief break-in cruise (where we encountered a hellacious storm crossing the Gulf Stream). Following minor adjustments, we headed north up the east coast to Newfoundland. After returning to Florida in early fall, we provisioned and set off for New Zealand in February.

The following pages are in large part our log of the trip—a personal travel log that we sent to friends and posted on the internet during our voyage. We hope you enjoy it.

Passing Through the Gatun Lock of The Panama Canal

THANK YOU

Rebecca and I would like to thank the many people who inspired, taught, and led us to the realization of our 50,000-mile sojourn. Although many people contributed to our success, James Leishman (son of Jim and co-founder of Nordhavn Yachts) helped us design our yachts, taught us how to operate them, and answered every phone call day and night to help us sort out the many problems we encountered. We couldn't have done it without him. He did a fantastic job, as did the entire Nordhavn organization, who helped us every inch of the way all around the world. They demonstrated that the dream of ocean voyaging under power is possible, safe, and doable by ordinary people. Thank you!

We would also like to thank Scott and Mary Flanders for writing their colorful and inspiring blogs from aboard Egret, their 46-foot Nordhavn, as they traveled around the world. They showed us how to do it.

Everywhere we moored or dropped anchor, sailors of every stripe helped us with advice or directions on interesting places to visit, maintenance tips, shopping, and introductions to local resources. Whenever we came upon other Nordhavn owners, like Mary Rose and Peter van Cuylenburg, we had instant friends who shared yachting and local information with us. We met so many wonderful people, which was the real joy of our adventure.

We would also like to thank our many friends who encouraged us to take the risk and get underway, or visited us and brought with them the warmth of home as well as parts. Reid Sherard, Frank Gordon, and Captain Curtis and Melanie Hoff in particular offered special encouragement as we got started. Thanks to Gus and Lyle Gialamas for their friendship and help along the way. Hugs and kisses to our daughter Kathryn, who's infectious excitement and optimism made everything a lot more fun. Finally, a big thank you to Professor Kim Eagle M.D., my friend and doctor who helped me through troubled waters.

PREPARATION

Why a powerboat? Simple: Rebecca wouldn't go via a sailboat. She says she doesn't look good in yellow—as in rain slickers. She doesn't want to be outside, particularly on night watches, doesn't like life at 45 degrees, and doesn't want to live below decks, and neither do I (although I would have sailed in a bathtub if I couldn't afford a boat). As she is the copilot and indispensable in operating the boat, she needed to be satisfied, and luckily, she was very happy aboard our beautiful Nordhavn (and so was I).

Why a Nordhavn? There are a couple of reasons. While there are several manufacturers building motor yachts capable of ocean crossings, Nordhavn is by far the leader in building beautiful yachts that can be operated by a couple or small crew. They are proven veterans of world cruising, and they are also spacious enough to accommodate my 6'5" frame.

M/V Argo: our magic carpet…

Equipments

- Water - maker
- HVAC
- 3 Freezers & Subzero Refrigerator
- Washer - Dryer
- Wine Cooler
- 15 ft. Tender / Davit
- 600 ft. Chain & 350 lb. Anchor
- 500 Gal Fuel Bladder

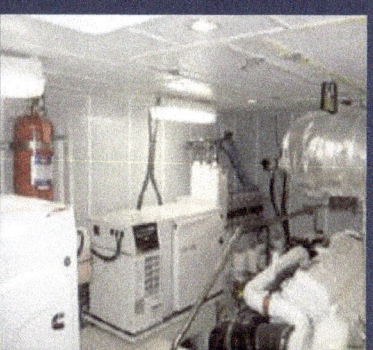

Engineering

- Single Main Engine -
  Plus a Back-Up Engine
- 2 Generators - 27.5 & 13.5 kw
- Batteries - 2200 Amp hours
- Fuel Tanks – 3,200 Gallons
- Water Tank – 500 Gallons
- Hydraulic Stabilizers / Thrusters

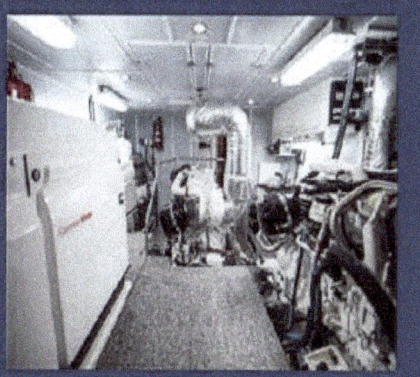

Specifications

Model: Nordhavn 68
Length: 69 ½ ft.
Draft: 7 ft.
Weight: 230,000 lbs.
Material: Fiberglass
Range: 3,200 miles
Speed: 8 - 9 knots
Flag: U.S.A.
Builder: TaShing Yard, Taiwan

ELECTRONICS

2 Radars
2 Sonars
2 Autopilots
2 Helm Stations
2 VHF Radios
2 Satellite Phones
Chart Plotter - Backup Computer
Night Vision Camera
AIS, GPS, Sat Compass
Entertainment System

Salon

Galley

Master Suite

"Boats are very space efficient. We had storage under the sofa, beds, and even in the shower compartment. I made up a master list for our provisions that included a location list, since at home we don't normally store pasta and rice in our sofas."

-Rebecca

Guest Suite

Cockpit

See YouTube video Nordhavn 68

OUR COURSE

Our route for the trip took us from Florida to the Bahamas, south along the Exhumes, past Turks and Caicos, then through the Windward Passage between Haiti and Cuba on to Port Antonio on the northeast tip of Jamaica. This took 10 days. From there we crossed the Caribbean to Santa Marta, which lies on the northern coast of Colombia. Then on to Cartagena, the Rosario Islands, Panama, and a canal transit. Once through the canal we headed 1,000 miles west for the Galapagos Islands where we spent 3 weeks exploring before heading to the Marquesas Islands 3,169 miles to the southwest. This was the longest leg of the trip, requiring 2 ½ weeks at sea. From the Marquesas, we headed south through the Tuamotu Atolls, then to Tahiti and famed Bora Bora, Raiatea, and Moorea. After a few weeks, we headed northwest to the Independent State of Samoa, Vava'U, Tonga, and then sailed 1,200 miles south to New Zealand where we were welcomed by a force 10 gale. After spending almost a year in New Zealand, we headed north to Fiji and spent nearly 2 months in those lovely islands.

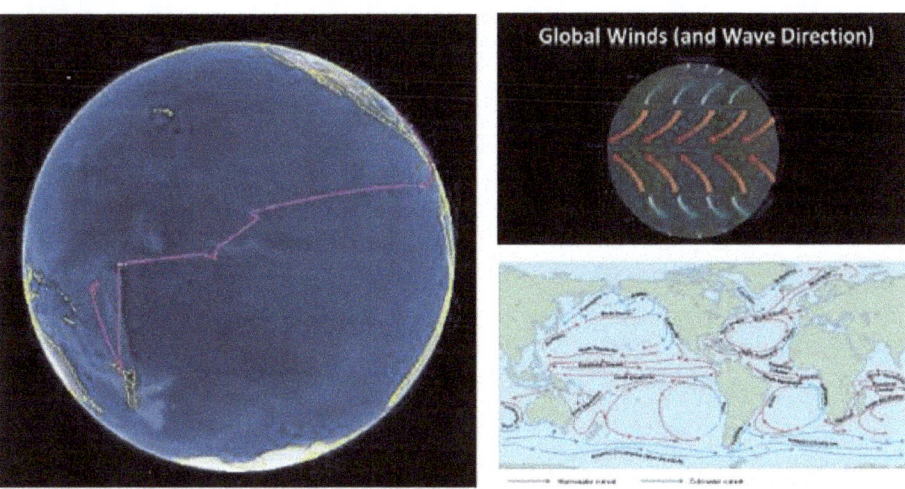

Weather conditions played a critical role in the scheduling of our voyage. For example, the waters from Florida to Cuba can be very difficult when winter storms blow across North America. These winds meet water flowing from the south, creating mountainous waves. Further south the Christmas trades blow across the Atlantic. When they reach the Andes Mountains near Colombia, they bounce off the mountains as katabatic winds of tremendous force, creating havoc far out to sea, often making the Caribbean a nasty body of water. Likewise, we needed to make it to the Galapagos in early April in order to avoid adverse winds off the coast of Central America. Every step of the way and the scheduling of each port of call were determined by the weather.

HOW DO WE PLAN A PASSAGE ?

Tentative Course Layout and Planning
Books, Charts, & Software
Personal Safety

Fine Tune based on Seasonal Wind, Waves, Storms, Currents
South Equatorial Current/ Cyclones
Christmas Trades, El Nino
Navigational Hazards, Anchorages, Harbors, Fuel

Government Regulations
FP & Tonga require a $1,500 bond PP, Visa
Agent needed? e.g. Galapagos

Insurance Company Approval

Preparation for the trip was extensive. Without going into excessive detail, I first considered single points of failure on the boat and tried to create alternative systems or at least carry spare parts. We have a special software program from Wheelhouse Technologies that contains a database of all the machinery and equipment on board as well as electronic versions of the equipment manuals. It provides in maddening detail a maintenance schedule for every piece of equipment and keeps an inventory of our spare parts as they are used. When we need parts, either Nordhavn or Wheelhouse will ship them worldwide to us wherever we are.

In determining what parts to buy, I called each of the manufacturers and asked their opinion about what parts to carry in light of our ability to repair things at sea. This step was very helpful. All of our electronic systems on the yacht were backed up with two of everything, so we didn't really need much in the way of spare electronic parts. We had two radars, three sonars, two VHF, two chart plotters, two autopilots, two engines and drive systems, two generators, two computers, and two sat-com systems (although in the South Pacific only one will work most of the time). Of course, we needed charts and cruising guides, courtesy flags, and customs information for all the places we planned to visit.

Additional 500 gal fuel in bladder - extending our range from 3,200 miles to 3,700 miles

As you might imagine, fuel was a big concern both for the 3,100-mile open ocean leg as well as the ability to obtain it in distant, remote ports. We retained a fuel broker to help us acquire fuel along the way, and we bought a 500-gallon fuel bladder to augment our fuel tanks, which hold about 3,000 usable gallons. The bladder required devising a system to secure it to the deck while at sea so that it didn't slosh around as *Argo* rolled with the waves, as well as an appropriate pump and hose system to transfer its contents to the main tanks.

Safety Planning

- Abandon Ship – Special Provisions and Raft
  - Food for 2 weeks
  - EPIRB – Sat Phone
  - Ditch Bag
- Sea anchor
- Lift bag
- Dive equipment
- Hull patch

Planning for the possibility of being shipwrecked required all sorts of other considerations. We had our life raft refitted, and we bought a waterproof ditch bag that could carry and float with 100 pounds of supplies and filled it with 20 days of rations for three people, water, a seawater desalinator, fishing gear, blankets, and a whole list of other items that other resourceful people included in their kits. In case our propeller became fouled by fishing lines or other debris encountered at sea, we carried dive and snorkeling equipment as well as two Shark Shields (devices thought to interfere with a shark's sensors and cause them to turn away) so that I could go below and cut us free. We also had onboard cable cutters to cut fishing lines. In the event of a failure of our windless system (anchor lift system), we bought a lift bag to hoist the anchor so that we wouldn't be marooned in a remote anchorage. The anchor and chain weigh about 1,200 pounds, so it is not a small consideration. Our yacht had only one hydraulic windless, which proved to be unreliable on several occasions as it turned out. We also carried an underwater hull-patching compound, so that if our hull was punctured at sea, we might be able to plug the hole ourselves right away.

Regarding our tender: one time in Mexico I was cruising about in the tender when its new Yamaha motor unexpectedly quit (later recalled for a faulty fuel pump). I was stranded, and the wind was blowing me out to sea toward

Japan. Luckily a fishing boat spotted me and towed me back to safety. Since then I equipped our tender with an electric get-home motor. Looking back, it seems the preparation list was endless.

Normally Rebecca and I were Argo's crew. We enjoy each other's company and prefer to handle the yacht ourselves. However, because this was such a long voyage we hired a young man as able crew to help with deck and maintenance work and to stand watch while underway. His name was Tom. He was a delightful person, and we enjoyed having him with us to share our adventure. Before actually crossing the Pacific Ocean, we joined The Pacific Puddle Jump. Most sailors crossing the Pacific join this or other similar groups so they can keep in touch via shortwave radio or sail together in small groups. The organization also helps provide customs and immigration information on the various ports of call. Altogether, and I don't have any hard data, we heard that about 350 boats attempt the crossing each year. Of this number, to my knowledge only two powerboats made it during the year of our crossing, the rest being sailboats of various types.

Life at Sea

- Watch Standing – Hourly ER Checks, Log Entries, Listening

  8 PM -2 AM,   2AM–8 AM,   8-12,   12-4,   4-8

- Weather File Updates 2X Daily + Emails via Satellite

- Entertainment Via TV Series, Lunch and Dinner Meals

- Fishing, Night Sky

- Sea sickness – 2 Types (Lethargy & Vomiting)

- Looking for Other Ships and Marine Life

Passage Statistics

Florida to New Zealand – 9,702 miles

Fuel = 11,325 gallons @ $3.94/gal = $44,654.23

226 Days Total
At Sea 55 days
At Anchor 109 days
Moored 62 days

Approximately 350 Vessels, 3 Motor Yachts

Planning a voyage, anticipating it, and actually getting underway is a lot of fun. Likewise, making landfall and entering a new port is quite exciting. Often, we were at sea for days and seldom saw another vessel. Because the boat was often underway day and night and usually for many days at a time, a schedule of watches was necessary to be sure that someone was always at the helm and that everyone got enough rest. We also needed food to be prepared on a normal schedule. Usually breakfast and lunch ware up to each individual to handle personally, but dinner was a hot cooked meal with salad and dessert every day at sea. A night watch snack was also generally available. Night watches are, of course, the most dangerous time, since it is dark and the watch stander has to rely on the radar and AIS (automatic identification system) to become aware of and avoid dangers. Often, we got some form of seasickness, mostly of the malaise variety, but this would pass after several days at sea. On watch, we required hourly engine room checks in calm weather, twice an hour in heavy seas. We used check sheets to make sure all the necessary things were observed, but these boiled down to looking for oil leaks and coolant leaks, monitoring temperature, and making sure that the main engine had an adequate fuel supply. This might seem strange, but Nordhavns have an isolated fuel system with a separate day tank into which carefully filtered fuel is transferred to assure that nothing clogs up the engine's injectors. This tank can run dry if not refilled periodically.

Life In Port

- Two Days in Port for Each Sea Day
- Maintenance - Hull, Thru Hulls, Cleaning/Zincs/Inspections/Oil Changes
- Tender – Deployed and Used to Go Ashore or Look About
- Land Touring / Meeting Other Sailors
- Provisioning – Farmers' Market
- Internet in Port
- Electricity Management – KW=Amps x Volts

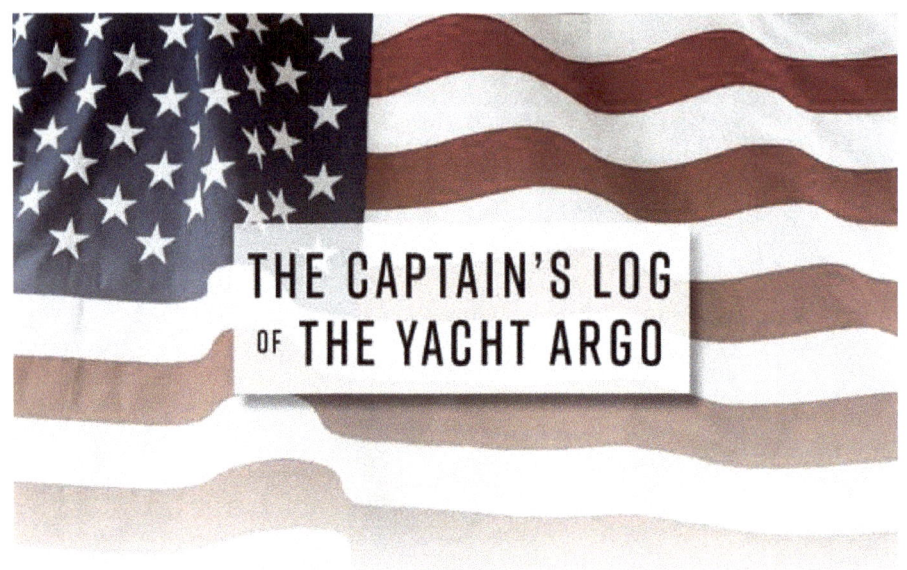

FLORIDA

February 18, 2014   **Underway from Stuart, Florida**

It is dark now. The sun has set beneath the waves in a beautiful coral-colored halo, and I am alone on the bridge. I will be on watch for a few more hours. The sea is calm, and a breeze is blowing from the east. It is completely dark outside save for the stars. The night is as black as pitch, which is disorienting since we cannot see where we are going: as the ship rolls, you feel like you did as a kid when someone put a bag over your head and spun you around. Tonight, we are bound for the Bahamas, intending to make landfall at a little island called Chub Cay. This is the same track we took on *Argo's* maiden voyage about a year ago when she was so roughly treated by the Gulf Stream, bounced around in a way that I had never experienced before.

Today is an important, or rather an auspicious, day in that we are embarking on an 8-month cruise that will take us literally halfway around the world. Ultimately, we plan to make landfall at Auckland, New Zealand, in early October, but from here to Auckland we will visit 16 countries and island groups, travel nearly 10,000 miles, and burn 11,000 gallons of diesel fuel. It is a big undertaking that has occupied a lot of our time for the past several months and our dreams for many years. It is the reason we bought *Argo*.

We got underway this morning at 10:15 and passed under the Roosevelt Bridge, which could be a metaphor for the moment: the beginning of the trip and an end to the planning and preparation phase. As we passed under it we caught a glimpse of a couple waving frantically to us: Melanie and Curtis Hoff, dear friends from Ann Arbor, surprised us by driving down from Vero Beach (where their beautiful boat is now moored) to wave goodbye and take our picture for posterity. What a wonderful gesture!

Leaving Stuart Florida 7 AM February 19, 2014

THE BAHAMAS

February 19   **Chub Cay**

Tom took the overnight watch, and I relieved him at 07:00. It was a nice clear morning, and we were still on the Mackie Bank about 20 miles east of Chub Cay. We put the fishing lines out as we neared the bank at Fleeming Channel. Apparently, no one was in the mood for breakfast even though I served up a beautiful cedar plug. About 10:30 we raised Chub Cay Marina on VHF 68 and made our way into the channel toward the docks. Chub Cay is a little limestone island that rises about 3 feet above sea level. The island is beautiful: white limestone beaches, pine trees and palms all around, and fancy homes built by the marina's developer. The homes are done in a sort of American colonial style, with brightly painted pastel colors, steel roofs, and Adirondack chairs on the porches. The marina was carved out of solid limestone rock. I can only imagine what it cost to build! Despite being beautifully equipped, it didn't seem to be doing well financially.

The marina caters mostly to the sport fishing crowd, and there were a number of them in the harbor as we pulled in. These boats are very expensive—certainly millions of dollars—with most of them having several crew members. While at the dock, crew members spend most of their time washing and polishing their boats or stringing fishing lines and preparing for the next day's expedition. The docking fees are extremely high here: $4.35/foot in season and $2.50/foot off season plus 40 cents/gallon for water and $30/night for electricity. One night at dock was $225. Because the high season began February 17, we should have paid the higher rate (about $400), but they let us off "easy."

After checking in with the dock master, Rebecca took our papers to customs and immigration located a few miles away at the dirt airstrip and paid the Bahamian $300 cruising fee. Meanwhile Tom cleaned the salt off *Argo* while I de-pickled the watermaker and got it up and running. That afternoon we went to the beach for a little while, but the ocean was only 78 degrees, a little cold for Rebecca and Tom. On our way back to the boat, an owner of a sport-fish stopped Rebecca and asked her to taste his ceviche. What a come-on! I was standing right there. Anyway, I commented on the raft of fancy reels and fishing poles bristling off the back of his boat. There must have been $50,000 worth of reels and poles, some electric and some manual, all bright and shining gold masterpieces of the sport fishing culture. To distract him from focusing on *my* wife, I asked him what he had to buy his wife in order to invest so much in all this fishing gear. That's when I heard the biggest whopper of them all: he told us that his wife doesn't particularly like jewelry, so he buys her a fishing rod or reel for Mother's Days, anniversaries, and the like. Boy, that's a fish story if ever I heard one; either that, or he has the most understanding and unselfish wife in the world!

After a delicious dinner, a la Rebecca, we all fell into bed tired and glad to have started on our voyage.

February 20 **Across Fleeming Channel and the Exuma Bank**

We got underway about 06:45 and started for a lagoon between Allen and Leaf Cay about 10 hours away. These two islands are clustered together and form one of the most beautiful places that we have been to in our travels. They are home to two species of indigenous iguanas. First, we had to cross Fleeming Channel, which is a notorious piece of water; it is often windblown and rough because the ocean breeze is channeled between the Great Abaco and Eleuthera Islands to the north and the New Providence Island to the south. Today we had 30 knots of wind and 4 to 6-foot box-wave seas, which didn't subside until we rounded the western tip of New Providence Island and moved onto the Great Bahama Bank. The depth of the water changes rapidly from the channel to the bank, going from about 1,000 feet to 20 feet or less in a very short distance. *Argo* bounced around a bit in the deep water taking the waves broadside: just a little taste of what is to come when we cross the Caribbean Sea in a couple of weeks. We made it to the bank in a couple of hours and then on to Allen and Leaf Cays, arriving around 17:14; a good run in sunny, warm weather. We anchored in sand in 15 feet of water just in time to enjoy a lovely sunset.

February 21 **On to Big Major and Staniel Cay**

The next morning, we awoke to a clear, sunny day, though breezy. Waves in the anchorage were a little rough, so we decided to pull the anchor and enjoy a 5-hour cruise down the coast to Big Major. This is one of two places where boaters congregate in large numbers to socialize and enjoy a tiny speck of civilization on Staniel Cay. Last winter we spent about 2 weeks here.

We arrived in the early afternoon and found about 50 yachts at anchor. We put out the tender and cruised around the islands, stopping in at the club for a libation. Since many cruisers come here year after year, sort of like visiting the same campground, on the way back we decided to look around for people we met last year. As we tooled about in our tender we noticed *Exodus*, a Fleming 65 with Texans Susan and Arnie on board. We met them last year and spent a fair amount of time in their delightful company. Later that evening we stopped by for cocktails and watched the sun go down. We asked about a couple (best to remain nameless) that we had met last year, and Susan told us that they had to sell their boat because neither of their mothers, both of whom are in their 90s, had died yet, so they couldn't afford to keep up the cruising lifestyle. The couple tells everyone this story and refers to themselves as trust-fund babies, so we are not really talking out of school. Apparently, the nameless couple tried to sell their boat, had a buyer, and needed to take the boat south from its location to consummate the sale. On the way, the boat unfortunately developed an engine room fire at sea. Having been aboard the boat last year, I am not sure if the fire wasn't a blessing in disguise. But, instead of letting it burn and sink, the fire was extinguished, the boat was saved and ultimately towed to shore. The buyer, of course, lost interest, and our acquaintances are now watching their mothers spend their inheritances.

Big Major Anchorage, Staniel Cay, Bahamas

February 22   **At Anchor at Big Major and Staniel Cay**

The Bahamas are spectacular: blue sky, gorgeous aqua blue water, white sand, and beautiful palm trees. The air temperature is about 80 degrees, and the water is just a few degrees less. I couldn't wait to go swimming, so we headed over to the grotto where the movie *Thunderball* was filmed. You remember the scene that drove everyone wild: Sean Connery and a voluptuous young woman diving under the rock and finding themselves all wet in a beautiful, underwater cave. Well, this was the place, and it is spectacular. There is a buoy near the underwater entrance to the grotto so visitors can tie up their dinghies. We jumped in and swam about 15 feet in aqua blue water to the edge of a small rocky island, dove under the rocks, and swam under them until we could see light from above. We came up into a domed cave about 500 feet wide with a ceiling rising about 30 feet above the water. At its azimuth were several large holes through which sunlight illuminated the grotto's interior. Across from the grotto's entrance was a second room, but it was illuminated by light from underwater reflected off the adjacent coral reef. The grotto is 20 or so feet deep, so other tourists didn't stay very long because they had to paddle with their feet to stay afloat. We had fins and snorkeling equipment, so we stayed perhaps 20 minutes. The shimmering aqua blues, golden sunlight reflecting off the lichen-colored rocky surfaces, the white sand below, and the reflected colors of the reef made our visit to the grotto among our most beautiful memories.

That afternoon Tom and I thought we should clean *Argo's* bottom. She had been sitting in the Saint Lucie River in Stuart, Florida, for several weeks, and a grassy alga had taken up residence. Growth of any kind should be removed from a vessel's bottom as it will slow the boat and decrease fuel efficiency. I had never done this sort of work before, as usually I hire a diver to clean her, but one of my boating friends does it himself, so I thought I would give it a try. In this case, we just used a washcloth and wiped the bottom as far down as we could reach, which was adequate. It can be a little unsettling to enter the water from the boat in the Bahamas as nurse sharks up to 10 feet long rest on the sandy bottom in the shadow of the boat.

That evening we took the tender on the 20-minute trip to the Staniel Cay Yacht Club. Fancy this place ain't; it's a Bahamian bar offering booze and food (mostly fried) to passing sailors. It's a fun place full of cast-off hats, flags, and other nautical and team sports memorabilia from around the world. Fishing boats and tenders are tied up at the little dock, and under the boats are a dozen or so nurse sharks milling about. They are attracted by the fishermen's fish-cleaning station, hoping to snatch an easy meal.

February 23   **Underway for Georgetown**

The next day we got up early and set out for Georgetown, about 80 miles south of Big Major. It was a beautiful day, and we planned to get out the fishing gear and see if we could put some fresh fish in the freezer. But first we had to negotiate Lumber Cay Cut, a narrow passageway through the reef that provides a path to the sea. These cuts can be very tricky as currents and wind can make them dangerous, especially since they are usually not straight passages, but curve around coral heads and rocks. Once out at sea we got out the gear and enjoyed the beautiful day. Tom took the helm, and Rebecca made breakfast. I sat on the aft deck enjoying the view—the sparse Exuma Island passing to starboard with the limestone shoreline carpeted in green. It was a fantastic morning. I put out one cedar plug, my all-time best fish attractor. On the port side, I put out a brightly colored feathered plug that I had to rig as I had never used it before. I tossed it in the water, sat back, and put my feet up, sipped some fresh coffee, and contemplated my good fortune.

After about 45 minutes I thought luck might not be with us today. Then, just as I was about to get up I scanned the waters to starboard and saw a bull dorado leap out of the water. He was about 300 yards away. As he jumped in the air he displayed a dazzlingly gorgeous neon robin's egg blue color. I never saw anything like it. I hoped he might be headed for my lure. I waited . . . then wham! Off he went with my plug in his mouth. He fought for about 15 minutes, jumping and tail walking, but unfortunately for him the die was cast; when it was over we had a nice 30 to 35 pounder in the bag. Two hours later we caught another dorado on the same bright lure, this time a 45 pounder. A beautiful fish, indeed, and an end to a great fishing day.

Around 16:00 we pulled into Stocking Harbor at Monument Hill across from Georgetown. There were about 250 boats in the harbor, mostly sailboats. Like Big Major, many people camp out here for long periods of time. They even conduct classes on the beach on all sorts of subjects. Chat & Chill is located on the beach, which is the most iconic Tiki bar I have ever seen. As we made our way carefully down the narrow fairway, we saw a familiar boat—*Pirate*—owned by Jim and Jane, a couple we met during our cruise last winter. Jim hailed us on the VHF radio and invited us to a dinner on their boat that evening. We accepted their invitation and turned

Argo around and dropped anchor next door. We went aboard *Pirate* around 18:00 that evening for a hot dog and chili cookout accompanied by a musical jam session. Jim had set up a karaoke device next to his macaw named Mackie, and two young Canadians with guitars arrived in short order. They had sailed a tiny sailboat from Ontario all the way down via the Erie Canal and Hudson River on a boat with no generator or ice maker. Despite a rough ride at times, these young men could really sing folk songs. It was a lot of fun.

February 24   **At Anchor in Georgetown**

The next morning was spectacular. Tom put out our sun shades and washed the salt off *Argo*. After completing our chores, we lowered the tender for a tour of the area and to visit some old Nordhavn friends who have a boat similar to ours. We dropped Tom off at Chat & Chill, and headed back to *Argo* for lunch on the aft deck. It was such a lovely lunch in such a beautiful place that it alone made all the work of getting the trip planned and *Argo* underway worth it.

After lunch, we returned to Chat & Chill to collect Tom and have a swim. We found Tom at the bar with new fast friends from Atlanta, Lee and Mary Ann. Lee had bought his wife a vacation at Sandals for her birthday, but they were disappointed with the resort and found their way down to Chat & Chill. Lee also found out about Gumby punches and had been buying them all afternoon for Tom. Everyone was in a very good mood by the time we arrived, and Lee insisted on buying us more of the same. It was a lot of fun.

Later in the evening we visited our Nordhavn friends George and Mary Ann aboard their yacht, which was similar to ours. It was great to see them and hear about their experiences both with the boat and their travels. They are planning a summer trip to Montreal, Quebec, Greenland, and Iceland. Sounded like a great trip to us!

February 25   **At Anchor in Georgetown**

Today is fresh vegetable day at the market in Georgetown, so off we went on a provisioning sojourn. It is a small but interesting village with only 85 inhabitants, although the Great Exuma Island has a population of around 3,000. Among other things, the town has at least three churches, two liquor stores, one grocery, a bunch of souvenir shops, a small hotel named Peace and Plenty, and the Top to Bottom hardware store, which has a little something for everyone. It's a fun little spot and much appreciated by wayfarers. That evening we hosted friends to a lovely fresh mahi-mahi dinner on *Argo*.

February 26–28   **Underway for Jamaica**

The weather has been superb and is forecasted to be perfect for the next week or so. The trip south to Port Antonio, Jamaica, is about 450 miles. This will take us almost 3 days. Our route follows the shore of Long Island (south of Exuma), past Great Inagua Island, around the eastern tip of Cuba and the Windward Passage, then a turn to starboard past Guantanamo Bay to Port Antonio in Jamaica.

February 27

At the moment, we are 27 miles north of Cuba, and the ocean is about 10,000 feet deep here. The air is 88 degrees, and the water is 83 degrees and lazily rolling under our starboard quarter. There is almost no wind (which is why we have a motor yacht with air-conditioning). *Argo* has performed beautifully. For the first day of this leg, we cruised at 1,100 rpm and used 4.2 gph and moved at 7 knots, which is 0.6 gpm. Now we are going about 8 knots at 6 gph. We are testing our fuel burn rate at different rpms so we can better plan our strategy for the Pacific crossing. We use the generator(s) between 10 and 14 hours a day to cook, charge batteries, make water, and run air-conditioning at night. The generator uses about 2 to 4 gallons an hour depending on which one we use; so, in round numbers, we are using about 160 gallons a day. With 3,200 gallons of fuel on board, we could do this for 20 days, and with our 500-gallon fuel bladder we can go along for 23 days. It should take about 15 days to cross the 3,000 miles (2,400 gallons estimated usage) from the Galapagos to the Marquesas Islands.

Around 6 p.m. on Thursday we reached the Windward Passage, which is the channel between Cuba and Haiti. We passed through it two years ago on *Odyssey,* and it was as gentle as a lamb, just like today. Lucky us!

In the morning, we passed the protection of the mountain range Massif de la Hotte, on the southern peninsula of Haiti. Here we began to feel the large swells on our beam rolling north from the Caribbean. As the sun rose, the sea changed and the wind rotated so that by afternoon the swells were much smaller and more pleasant. The day was lovely, but as time passed we became more anxious because we didn't want to reach Port Antonio after nightfall. Unfortunately, we were in an adverse current all day so our speed was limited to just over 7 knots. Later, as the sun set, Jamaica's beautiful

Blue Mountains were cast in a silhouette against the high clouds and the rose shades of the setting sun. That evening, Rebecca made us a wonderful dinner of the mahi-mahi that we caught at sea the night before.

As spectacular as the evening cruise into port was, coming into a strange harbor requires close 3attention and vigilance, particularly in a third-world country like Jamaica. At night, fishermen are often working offshore and the lights of the city present a background against which small boats, even if they have a light, are indistinguishable. Most are too small for the radar to pick up, so care and watchfulness is the order of the day (or night). The harbor's entrance can be equally hard to spot amidst the background lights. We scanned the city's waterline and spotted some red and green lights marking the fairway entrance right where the chart illustrated them to be; we checked the code blinking from them, which confirmed that we were in the right place. We slowed and proceeded in, then made a turn to starboard and entered the west harbor through a small channel. By this time, we were going very slowly as it was quite dark and there were many small boats at anchor. We looked for the marina (named Errol Flynn after its founder), but it didn't seem to be located as shown on the map. A very large four-mast sailing schooner was tied up at a pier, but in the dark, it was hard to tell its orientation or the pathway to the pier. Typical of Jamaica, the nightclubs were blasting loud, throbbing sounds, the party was in full swing, and a sweet fragrance wafted on the breeze. We inched our way toward the schooner, watching the depth and mindful of how to get out if we were in the wrong place. A couple of people on the schooner confirmed that this was indeed the marina, and so we decided to bring *Argo* to rest at a vacant portion of the dock in front of the schooner. We needed to reverse *Argo's* orientation, so in this confined space I brought her about and moved her starboard side ever-so-gently to the pier. Rebecca and Tom made sure we had adequate fenders out and that no protrusions from the pier presented a danger. As we approached, fellow sailors scrambled out of their boats to give us a hand with the lines. One fellow was still in his PJ's!

By this time, it was about 11 p.m. Within minutes, police arrived, two very nice officers. They wanted to come on board immediately, but Rebecca wanted to see their IDs. The two fumbled around trying to scrounge up their cards, but only one of them could find it. I wasn't sure if Rebecca was going to relent and let both on board. But after a minute or two of discussion, aboard they came with their shoes on, although Tom wiped the bottoms of them off. (Generally, we try not to wear shoes on the boat so as to prevent bird droppings and other dock refuse from coming aboard.)

The two officers filled out a raft of paperwork and then inspected the vessel from stem to stern; they went through the refrigerator, all the drawers, and even tossed the dirty laundry. The whole ordeal took about an hour and a half. We were then told we had three more inspections to go through: Coast Guard, Immigration, and Health. By this time, we were very tired, but not too tired to have a few Dark and Stormy's.

JAMAICA

March 1   **Moored at Port Antonio, Jamaica**

7 a.m. came early. That's when the Coast Guard came rapping on our stateroom window. They too wanted to come aboard right away. Again, two birds with heavy boots; they wanted to fill out the same paperwork we filled out the night before and they also wanted to inspect our flares. That was it.

About 10 a.m. a nice lady from the Health Department arrived. She didn't want to take her shoes off either, but complied with our wishes. She had almost nothing to say, but did fill out paperwork substantially the same as the other officials. At this point we were almost done, but we weren't allowed to leave the boat until the immigration officer made his visit and completed his paperwork. This was frustrating because we needed provisions and, as it was Saturday, the markets closed at 13:00 and would stay closed until Monday. We called the harbormaster and yacht club manager in an effort to hurry things along. They told us to go ahead and do our shopping in spite of the lack of formal permission. The immigration officer finally showed up at 5 p.m. with the same paperwork that the others had brought before, and then he demanded $38 extra payment for his overtime!

During the day, we cleaned *Argo*, reconnoitered the club, and met other sailors along the dock. That evening we had a wonderful time with three other boating couples. Our first acquaintances were Ismael and Olga from Barcelona who lived aboard the catamaran moored alongside us. She was a gorgeous young woman, and Ismael was a thin, middle-aged, athletic man who looked every bit the Castilian—like a portrait of Hernando Cortes. Both were bright, animated, and lots of fun. They have lived on a catamaran for at least 8 years, and had spent the last 3 years in Cuba, which they loved.

"Adventurous cruisers are fast friends who quickly share maps, books, stories, widgets, tools, recipes, and more. We loved the camaraderie and benefited from much of the advice. When Randy was missing, I knew to look on the docks since he loved to meet and share with other boaters."

-Rebecca

The second couple was from the United States and were named Westa and Ian; she a former teacher in Harlem, he a retired British Army officer. Lovely people. They live on a 45-foot Beneteau.

The third couple was French. He, Jean-Marie, a trauma doctor who treats sailors crossing the Pacific on French tours. He also attends drivers in famous auto races; he once treated Paul Newman at the Monaco Grand Prix. Coco, his wife, doesn't speak English, and we unfortunately don't speak French, so we didn't learn much about her except that she becomes very seasick as soon as they leave the harbor. She takes a couple of pills and goes to bed—even on long, 5-day cruises—while he stands all the watches and sleeps in 10-minute catnaps. Amazing!

Last but not least was Harry, a very energetic and affable person who had just crossed the Atlantic single-handed and was on his way home to Australia. Harry became a good friend, and we met up with him many times as we crossed the Pacific. You will hear more about him as the story unfolds.

As Harry crossed various bodies of water, he would hire hitchhiking deckhands to help run the boat and stand watch. In Port Antonio, he had a deckhand on board who was a beautiful 20-something of Asian ancestry. She was gorgeous with long, shiny black hair flowing down her back, and a great figure that she showed off in a teeny-weeny bikini. Each morning as things began to move on the dock she would make her way out of Harry's boat and take a stroll up and down the dock in her bikini and Ugg boots. At that moment, all the men's heads popped out of the cabins on their sailboats like prairie dogs looking about. It was very funny. One day she didn't show up. I asked Harry what happened to her. Apparently, he fired her because she was just an "alley cat."

March 2   **Jerk at Port Antonio, Jamaica**

For the most part, this was a welcomed day of rest. At 17:30 we had our little band of friends over for cocktails, and then we all went out for Jamaican jerk. As it was Sunday, conventional restaurants weren't open, so we headed for a beach bar not far from the marina. After a short cab ride to a seedy part of town near the ocean, we walked down a dimly lit, inclined, mud and gravel road toward an open-air circular bar covered with a tent-like roof. It was a crazy, dirty place. A few girls were hanging around looking for someone to dance with. Gigantic, loudspeakers were strategically placed and blared pulsating music at decibel levels not tolerated by the normal human ear. Not much was going on. We came there for dinner on the advice of a member of our party. Several buildings were located on the perimeter of the property near the bar. One was the kitchen shack. It was a lean-to affair with a corrugated steel roof and sides made of chicken wire. Jerk pork and chicken were being roasted on several large charcoal grills, and a pungent, spicy smoke was pouring forth. It smelled great! I could hardly wait, although Rebecca was more cautious owing to the apparent lack of sanitary conditions. At any rate, I gave it a try; jerk is very tasty and quite inexpensive. A quarter of a chicken costs about $3. However, when you order it you can't be exactly sure what you might be getting; the cook simply chops a whole chicken into finger-food-sized pieces, bones and all. Some pieces have meat, and some are mostly bone. When eating it in the dark as we did, it is a little difficult to tell what you're actually eating until it is too late! Jamaican jerk was created by the Maroons, who were runaway slaves, and local Indians who hid from the plantation owners in the Blue Mountains centuries ago. They killed and roasted feral pigs and marinated the meat with spices found in the jungle. Rather than cook during the day, the Maroons cooked the pigs overnight in pits so that their location wouldn't be detected by the rising smoke plumes from their fires.

After an hour or two of sitting on makeshift stools as far from the speakers as we could get, we tired of it all and made our way back to *Argo*. The taxi dropped us off at the yacht club's security gate, but first we walked down the street to a small park that overlooked the marina and enjoyed some ice cream.

March 3   **Blue Mountain Tour from Port Antonio, Jamaica**

Today we are off on a tour of the Blue Mountains and the coffee plantations. Our driver, Wayne Murdock, picked us up at the marina on Jamaican time, i.e., 20 minutes late. He was a former Olympian on the Jamaican bicycle team and has lived in the United States for several years, which made for interesting conversation during the drive. The Blue Mountains rise precipitously 7,500 feet from the sea on the northeast coast of Jamaica. They are steep, volcanic, and covered in a beautiful, lush rain forest. A very narrow, tortuously winding, two-lane road crawls up its slopes. The road was built by slaves in the 1700s. Terror lurks at every turn as fearless drivers speed around the curves blowing their horns to warn oncoming traffic of a possible collision, but doing almost nothing else to prevent one from occurring.

The Blue Mountains are famous for their wonderful coffee, which may be the best in the world. Our main objective was the Old Tavern Coffee Estate nestled on the slopes about 6,500 feet in the clouds. There we met Dorothy and David Twyman, mother and son who have farmed 150 acres on the mountainside for two generations. Twyman's coffee is considered the best of the best, to which we can attest (available on Amazon). They invited us to be seated on their veranda and enjoy cookies and freshly brewed coffee. A garden of orchids and tropical plants surrounded their home on terraced steps. As we relaxed and enjoyed the coffee, we marveled at the spectacular view of the steep Blue Mountains with their verdant, lush jungle carpet cascading to the sea.

After leaving the Twyman's we stopped a couple of miles down the mountain road at a Rastafarian coffee plantation. The plantation was a commune of about a dozen people farming 100 acres. We stopped to taste and perhaps buy some of their coffee. We were first introduced to their leader who didn't seem particularly interested in talking with us. He and his lady companion were dressed in African garb and had traditional dreadlocks. He explained to us that the late Emperor Haile Selassie founded Rastafarianism in Ethiopia, which he believed to be the cradle of humanity. Rastafarians espouse a life of harmony both with nature and other human beings, and apparently smoking ganja helps smooth out any wrinkles common to close habitation. It also facilitates a sense of well-being and communication with all that is. Rastafarianism isn't a religion per se, rather a philosophy of life centered on the African experience. It is particularly appealing to the descendants of former slaves who do not have direct knowledge of their ancestors or country of origin.

Overall the car trip was interesting and we saw beautiful scenery, but it was a bit taxing. After leaving the Rastafarians we headed back to Port Antonio, and I could have used some of their ganja to help mellow me out: after 5 hours in a car with no A/C, a broken window mechanism in which the window was either all the way up or down with no in-between, and springs so weak that every pothole and bump made its presence keenly felt, I was exhausted. Nonetheless, we arrived back at *Argo* in one piece and happy for the experience.

March 4   **Moored at Port Antonio, Jamaica**

Some days you just need a little quiet time, so I spent the morning working on our investment portfolio, sending emails to friends, and trying to fix the sat-phone. At lunchtime, we wandered up to the yacht club, which was a very nice little Georgian-style place, much nicer than anywhere else we had been in Port Antonio. It was run by Paul, a very affable man of English ancestry. After lunch, we walked the quarter mile or so to the downtown area, which is a shabby but interesting place. We always enjoy going to the local farmers' markets and learning what people do to make a living and what foods they enjoy. Rebecca tried shopping here one day by herself, but some of the men were rudely aggressive and the women giggled. Today I was alone, so things were different, although Jamaica has a lot of unsavory characters milling about with nothing to do and they also make me feel uneasy. Anyway, the market is wedged behind several buildings and is only accessible from an alley. It is a crowded, little, dirty affair, and seemingly disorganized with vegetables and partially butchered meat, poultry, and fish hanging from old rough-hewn wooden poles. Flies are everywhere, the people are raggedy, and everything is in shambles. The ladies sell crafts, and some of the men sell wood carvings that are surprisingly quite good. We bought a supply of vegetables and bundled it all up as best we could (they don't have bags, it's BYO) and made our way on foot back to *Argo,* hoping to avoid the spotty afternoon showers.

March 5   **Moored at Errol Flynn Marina, Port Antonio, Jamaica**

Port Antonio looks like a town out of the Wild West at the turn of the 20th century. It is situated around a large natural harbor with ships loading and unloading at the commercial docks. The portion of the town that the yacht club is near has a dirt main street with a sidewalk about 2 feet above grade; shabby lampposts with wires strung willy-nilly claiming the skyline. The buildings, except for the churches, are in a poor state of repair with very little inside to justify their existence. Old cars and small trucks ramble down the streets bellowing smoke, and the sidewalks are full of pedestrians standing about. The town is laid out in a grid and has a main square with the center occupied by a statue of an important figure. The main road leading out of town is lined with brightly painted bungalows. We decided to walk down Main Street and dine with other boaters at a little Italian pizzeria that was recommended to us. It was as shabby as everything else in town, but surprisingly the owners, who lived above the storefront restaurant, were a couple from Naples who immigrated here to make their fortune. It looked like they were hanging on by their fingernails; the husband did the cooking, and the wife waited tables while caring for her infant child. The food was very good, but one wonders how bad things must have been in Italy for a couple to seek a new life in Port Antonio.

March 6   **Kingston**

We arranged a trip to Kingston today. It was 2 hours by car across the mountains, much like the ordeal up the Blue Mountains to Twyman's coffee farm two days before. The initial part of the trip took the east coast road toward Montego Bay, then turned south across the Rio Grande River past Brule Town, then up and over the mountains to Kingston. The road was narrow with many hairpin turns. The scenery was absolutely beautiful, and again the ride was interesting. The mountains were so steep that farming was terraced and done by manual labor. Most of the farms grew coffee, but of course other crops such as bananas, cinnamon, nutmeg, and bay leaves were grown. About halfway to Kingston we stopped for a little breather at a national park high in the mountains. This gave us a chance to reflect on the splendor and lushness of this island, truly one of most beautiful places on the planet.

Kingston is home to more than 1 million people. It isn't a very pretty place nor does it have any memorable sights, save for its location at the foot of the Blue Mountains on the shore of the Caribbean. One would think it would have become a lively tourist destination with beautiful, upscale hotels and casinos, cruise ships, and nightclubs. Yet it has none of these, not even a shopping district beyond what can be seen in smaller villages. One thing the city does have—three nasty prisons situated in the middle of town. About half the population lives in slums, while others live in suburban homes, with the nicest of them called villas; a few in the most upscale sections overlooking the city are quite large and very attractive. This is the part of town where the diplomatic missions and the hotels to serve them are located.

There are a few sights to see in Kingston, but not many. Top on the list is Bob Marley's home. He was a musical artist who personified Rastafarianism, reggae music, and the soul of Jamaica. Like Graceland, it is owned by his family and has been turned into a shrine that celebrates the artist.

Port Royal, way across town, was our next stop. It is located on a peninsula that is the site of a fort built by the British in the late 1600s. Lord Admiral Horatio Nelson once commanded it when he was stationed here as a captain before he joined British fleet at the battle of Trafalgar (where the British defeated Napoleon's fleet). Aside from the fort, the airport, and a rundown hotel, there wasn't much to see in Port Royal. (After returning to Port Antonio, I was told that the Royal Jamaica Yacht Club is located there, but we didn't see any signs of it and our driver wasn't aware of it, either.) There are of course government buildings in Kingston, but the streets were blocked around them and we couldn't get close enough to see anything. We did however go to the national art gallery. It is pretty small and features local artists. Some of it was in a primitive style, a lot of sculptures featuring the human black form, some of it very sensual. There was one very memorable watercolor painted in the 1800s of a young black servant that was spectacular, perhaps the finest watercolor I have ever seen. We continued our tour to Trench Town, which our driver told us was named for an open storm sewer that delineates its eastern border (actually we Googled it and found out that it was named after the original Irish land grantee named Lord Trench). It is a dangerous place, and no tourist should be seen taking pictures of the residents for fear of having rocks and bottles hurled at them. Rebecca and Tom wanted to go there to see Bob Marley's boyhood home, which occupies a sort of safe zone for tourists known as the Trench Town Culture Yard. Trench Town is a slum inhabited by hopeless, angry people. We didn't linger. On the way home, we stopped at the other end of the social spectrum to see Usain Bolt's sports bar called Tracks and Records. Bolt's real name is Usain St. Leo Bolt, and his nickname is, what else but, Lightning. Mr. Bolt holds the world sprinting speed record and nine Olympic Gold Medals. Anyway, the bar is a sports bar like any upscale one you would find in the United States, but in Jamaica it is a big deal and source of pride.

March 7   **Customs and Mockingbird Hill Hotel**

Today we didn't have much on the agenda except to write the blog and try to get the internet to work. About 13:00 we walked down to the marina office to see what was up with the sat-phone part we ordered, which turned into an upsetting experience. As it turned out, FedEx claims to offer international service, but from a practical perspective that is a misrepresentation. FedEx delivers a package to the airport, but they do not act as an agent. To get a parcel through customs you have to hire an agent to represent you. So, we had to hire an agent for about $60 to find the part and walk it through customs. (It took about an hour to figure this much out.) Next, we had to determine and prepay the import duty. (The part we ordered was a warranty part that had no retail value per se, and parts being used to repair a ship in transit are not supposed to be subject to a customs duty because they are not technically being imported into the country.) Nevertheless, Jamaica taxes the shipping cost, and applies some sort of other tax on the part itself. The whole thing was a little sketchy. In any case, there were several layers of taxes, fees, and costs. In order for the agent to track down the part, we needed a bill of lading or airline shipping ticket. FedEx is supposed to provide that piece of paper, so we called them and were connected to someone in a US call center. They didn't have the bill of lading, couldn't email it to us, and for some reason wouldn't connect us to their Kingston office. The only way to get the bill of lading was to drive to Kingston, which is a day's travel and $150 in carfare expense. We were told that some people facing this predicament actually took the local customs officer from Port Antonio with them to assist in retrieving their parcel. Since our part was only worth about $100, the whole situation was getting out of hand. Once we had this all figured out and hired an agent in Kingston, three hours had passed. That's when we learned that we couldn't get the part until late Monday afternoon anyway. It turns out that Customs closes at 15:00 on Friday, and of course it is closed Saturday and Sunday. As I looked at my watch to evaluate the possibilities, I realized that it was now happy hour! I guess we will just have to wait until Monday.

For dinner that evening we decided to go by taxi to the Mockingbird Hotel, a 10-room old British resort built in the 1950s. We found it quite interesting. It was perched on the side of the mountain and overlooked the point on the island that separated the Windward Passage from the Caribbean. On one side, we could see the lights of Port Antonio, on the other the moonlit darkness of the vast sea that we would be crossing in the next week.

March 8   **Relaxing in Port**

Early today most of our sail boating friends left for Haiti and the Dominican Republic. As we were waving goodbye, Donavan, the self-proclaimed best fisherman in Jamaica, visited us for a consultation on the adequacy and quality of our fishing gear. I love this sort of thing. A fishing tackle store is to me what a jewelry store is to Rebecca. Every time I go in I always buy a bunch of stuff (thank god Rebecca doesn't do the same thing!). Donavan looked through our tackle and thought we had some very good plugs and equipment. He set up a bunch of our unstrung plugs, and then Tom and I organized the whole batch of equipment into nice, tidy boxes of swivels, hooks, and ties. Later in the day I sharpened knives, worked on our website, and then watched a movie. Rebecca made a delicious Indian dish, chicken vindaloo.

March 9

Port Antonio is a very small place at the base of the Blue Mountains. It has the greatest rainfall on the island (350 inches/year), and it rains almost every day. The little bay is pretty, clean, and the temperature is tropical. Sometimes it is very hot and humid, but most of the time it is quite pleasant. As the humidity builds during the day, clouds form and then drop torrents of rain for a short period of time, clearing the air. The rain comes and goes as clouds pass overhead.

It is often noisy here as cars or pickups with rooftop speakers drive by the road adjacent to the marina, blasting a program of music and advertising, sort of like portable radio stations. It is very annoying. The local bars start around 17:00 blaring an undulating drumbeat with a primitive, sort of erotic, vibe.

March 10   **Waiting for Parts**

We have been waiting all weekend for the part we discovered would be a challenge to retrieve on Friday. I learned this morning it will cost us about $160 when all is said and done. Clearly a ripoff. Well, what is one to do? As soon as our part comes tomorrow, we are out of here and on our way to Santa Marta, Colombia, about 438 miles due south. It looks like the weather will be good.

Chou stopped by today. Who is he? I had never met him before, and he was indeed a strange, squirrelly character. He seemed high on something. He brought a bag of 11 nice, active lobsters (or rather, langoustines since they have no claws) for sale. He was asking just $6 a piece for them, a very attractive deal indeed. I told him I would take them all and pay full price if he cleaned them. He was so excited he did a little jig for us right on the spot! Then he sat down on his bucket and cleaned all the lobsters, which we froze for future use. It's always a little disconcerting to buy seafood off the dock because we know the locals will often fish their waters to extinction in order to make a living.

Tonight, a dinner is planned at Soldier's Hill, a restaurant run by a Vietnam vet to be attended by all the boaters on the dock.

COLUMBIA

March 11–13   **Departing Port Antonio Bound for Colombia**

We planned to get underway today and fortunately our sat-phone replacement part arrived at 09:30. Christina, the administrator of the harbor office, was so kind and helpful in getting our part through customs, and we can't thank her enough. The fees to get this supposedly duty-free part into the country were $156, more than the cost of the part itself. Christina gave us a free day of dockage to make up for our frustration, which was very nice of her. At noon, we departed, as our friends Ismael, Olga, and Paul (the harbormaster) waved us off from on the dock. It was very nice, but sad, to depart from the wonderful people we had met.

The sea state on our way south was as expected: 4 to 5-foot seas running toward the west, in line with the trade winds. Not knowing exactly what we might encounter, we decided to head for Santa Marta on the north coast of Colombia near the Venezuelan border, but retained the option of turning west toward Cartagena or Panama if conditions warranted. Going to Santa Marta was the most aggressive route as it put us directly abeam of the waves, and depending on their size, we might have to heave to and turn westward to put them on our stern. As we progressed southward the wind and waves were in the 24 knot/4 to 7-foot range with periods of both higher and lower conditions. *Argo* rode them very well, but our movement was tedious and tiring. Being bounced around all the time makes me very sleepy at first. Although the seas built as we headed south, things were tolerable and we continued to Santa Marta.

The Caribbean Sea is a cauldron of tormented water. The trade winds blow in from the Atlantic Ocean along the coast of South America. The mountains focus and accelerate the wind at sea level, seas build and blow to the coast of Central America. There they meet solid land and are pushed northward toward the Gulf of Mexico, eventually augmented by the eastward flowing polar air masses leaving the Caribbean via the Gulf Stream. Inside the Caribbean, the water rotates in a clockwise direction, but near the center the currents are random. For a period of time the current will be going in one direction, then suddenly change to another. Wind pushing against the current changes the shape and intensity of the waves, which affects *Argo's* speed as well as her roll and pitch. Wind and wave intensity is also stronger around sunrise and sunset.

Santa Marta is located behind a point that forms a bay, sheltered by the Sierra Nevada de Santa Marta Mountains, which rise sharply several thousand feet above the sea. The trade winds are particularly strong this time of year. They are known as the Christmas trades and reach 20 to 30 knots in the open ocean, but close to the coast the wind is funneled by the mountains down toward the coastline and can reach much higher speeds. The wind was over 50 knots as we approached the coast at 01:00 Friday morning. With big wind comes big waves, and I had been watching the weather in this region for several months, hoping to avoid these conditions. Thirteen-foot seas on a daily basis are not unusual, although they usually subside to an average of 5 feet as the rainy season approaches in April. We hoped spring might come early this year.

As the days passed and we got closer to shore, we became optimistic that we could actually make it to Santa Marta. The hours always pass slowly as we approach the shore. Around 23:00 we were within 3 hours of port, but the wind was building to over 30 knots and the sea started to roll *Argo* in a concerning manner. As the current beneath us changed direction, the rolling ceased for a while, then it changed and the waves built again, which gave me thoughts of changing course. Around midnight winds were in the 40s, and we began to tack against the sea. At 00:30 on the 14th, we were about 5 miles offshore, but the wind was over 50 knots with waves to match. We headed for the lee of a shoal near the entrance to the harbor. It was pitch dark and very hard to read the sea state. We couldn't spot the big rollers or see the direction from which they might come. Tom tried to open the upper part of the pilothouse hatch to look out, but 50 knot winds made it all but impossible to open. It was a dangerous moment. My goal was to cut the waves at a 45-degree angle, but the correct course was hard to determine. The last mile or two into port were tense as the seas moved this big and heavy boat around like a toy, rolling us nearly 40 degrees. That was a little concerning to say the least! Changing course positioned us into the waves and lessened the danger, but slowed our progress to get behind the shoal. By 01:30 we breathed a sigh of relief as we were in calm water behind the shoal and headed into the harbor. The lights of Santa Marta were a welcomed sight.

We made our way to the marina. No one was around, so we tied up to an empty dock and fell into bed. The next morning, we could see that *Argo* was completely covered in thick, gritty salt. Inside, the walls and counters were also covered in a misty-salty coating. She had been through a difficult passage and kept us safe and sound. She is a great boat, and we feel very safe on her.

March 14   **Santa Marta, Colombia**

Santa Marta is a lovely town; clean, interesting, historical, and friendly. It is a famous resort town for Colombians, and is well known because Simon Bolivar died at a hacienda near here in 1830. The marina at which we are staying is part of the worldwide IGY (Island Global Yachting) facilities. They are secure, clean, and well managed, and we are glad to be here.

To enter Colombia by private yacht, one has to hire an agent to deal with clearance formalities. Dino, our agent, was very efficient and reasonably priced. We spent perhaps 2 hours altogether completing formalities; there were no inspections, and they do not seem to care what you have on board as long as you do not bring it ashore. This has been the easiest port clearance we have ever experienced.

Santa Marta is clean, and many parks and modern sculptures decorate the thoroughfares. Along the north part of the bay is a long beach bordered by the Simon Bolivar Park. The park is about 15 blocks long and fronts the city center located between an extension of the park and a second Couples Park. There are many brightly painted colonial style buildings in this part of the city. The parks are clean and neat and occupied by people enjoying the siesta period in the afternoon, or the cooler temperatures of the evening. The main streets are busy with small cars of familiar brands made in Europe, Asia, and America. The sidewalks are narrow and crowded with pedestrians trying to get past each other amid the countless sidewalk shops offering everything from toys to clothing, food and everything else. It is a real cornucopia of sights, sounds, and smells. To the south side of the marina are lovely high-rise apartments and hotels built on the beach. People here love the beach, and no wonder—it is hot as heck here!

Colombians seem to be a mixture of all the races that have occupied this territory over the millenniums: Native Indian, Spanish, African, and Asian. It is very hot and humid here; nevertheless, men wear trousers, often long-sleeve shirts, and sometimes a coat. Rarely shorts (like my old Navy Chief Lingenfelter said: "Women wear pants, and men wear trousers"). Women on the other hand seem to prefer brightly colored and very tight spandex or denim jeans. Whatever they are wearing, it is usually very tight on the top and bottom. The men are handsome; they apparently prefer their women a little plump and pear shaped. Many of the ladies are very beautiful, with jet black hair, almond-shaped faces and eyes, and lovely complexions. There are a large number of native people here, and their appearance is striking. Their skin is a brownish red, and their facial features are just like they came alive from an ancient stone carving. One wonders what their life experience has been. Colombians seem to be a hardworking and very pleasant people who are proud of their country and their culture. I am not sure that we in North America, particularly the United States, have a very accurate image of Colombia or of the depth and beauty of their culture.

March 15–31   **Santa Marta to Cartagena de Indias to Bogotá**

After completing formalities and looking around the town, we arranged for a trip to Cartagena and Bogotá. On Sunday, we hired a private van to take us by road to Cartagena de Indias. The fare was a suspicious $35 each for a 4-hour drive. As it turned out the van wasn't really private, unless you think eight people stuffed in a little Korean box is a private vehicle. Our fellow passengers were foreign travelers like ourselves, and luggage was stuffed everywhere. Anyway, the drive along the coast gave us a chance to see this part of Colombia. The coast from Santa Marta to Panama and beyond to Ecuador is mostly mangrove wetland. There are some beaches, but for the most part it is brackish inlets and swamps. Small, seemingly poor fishing villages dot the coastline except for Barranquilla, a very large city located at the mouth of the Rio Magdalena, the country's largest river. Barranquilla is the third largest port after Cartagena and Santa Marta. The road was in some places a four-lane interstate highway, then, when it entered a town, would converge to two lanes before leaving the town and returning to four lanes, maybe. This part of Colombia is arid. Although the trade winds blow constantly and are heavy with water much of the time, the rain isn't released on the coast at this time of year, rather the clouds float over the coastal mountains, hit the Andes, and drop their payload in Amazonia. In Santa Marta, it hasn't rained for 4 months.

The Andes (called the Sierra Nevada de Santa Marta at this location) in Colombia are divided into three parallel mountain ranges: The Cordillera Oriental (the nominal Andes), the Cordillera Central, and Cordillera Occidental. The tallest range, the Oriental, begins a few miles east of Santa Marta, where a 16,000-foot mountain called Mount Bolivar rises from the sea. The three ranges lie along a southwest path to Ecuador where they merge and turn south and continue down the continent ending at Tierra del Fuego in Chile. As the trade winds strike the Andes at Santa Marta, some of the wind is directed south to the Amazon basin on the south side of the Cordillera Oriental, providing rain and moisture to the Amazon Basin. Bogotá is located on their northern slopes at a level of almost 9,000 feet. On the southern side of these mountains lies the Amazon Valley, which occupies about half of the land mass of Colombia. Some of the air moves inland to the long, verdant valleys between the northern slope of the Andes and the other mountain ranges, forming a rich agricultural region. The Rio Magdalena, Colombia's largest river, flows through the valley between the Central and Oriental Mountains to Barranquilla where it ends in the Caribbean Sea. From the air, these valleys look like California's Central or Sacramento Valleys, although more green and lush. Medellin, Colombia's second largest city, lies at the northeastern end of the Cordillera Central. Cali, the third largest city, is south of Panama and on the interior side of the Cordillera Occidental. We were told that Medellin is the most beautiful city, and that Cali is home to the most beautiful ladies, although we unfortunately cannot verify these opinions as we didn't have time to visit them.

About half of Colombia lies south and west of Panama. The Pacific coast of Colombia is known as the Darien. The southern part of Panama and this Darien region are covered by dense jungles formed on floating plant matter, sort of like peat. The wet part of the Darien will not support roads or structures, but it does provide a home to some of the most remote and primitive Indians on the planet. Part of the Darien is a rich savannah that supports the cattle industry in Colombia. It is also home to the drug cartels and their cocoa fields.

Before the arrival of the Spanish, Colombia and the locality of Cartagena had long been a crossroads of trading activity among the various tribes of the Americas, including the Incas and Aztecs. Native peoples inhabited this region for perhaps 20,000 years, and developed a very sophisticated culture with a complex and vibrant economy involving irrigated agriculture and trading over long distances. Before the arrival of Europeans, Colombia was inhabited by between an estimated 1 million and 2 million people. Like many native peoples, they worshiped the sun as the source of all power, and gold represented the sun. Gold could easily be found in the sands of the Rio Magdalena near Barranquilla. Native peoples invented the lost wax method of making jewelry and fashioned beautiful objects of gold, including gold bells to adorn tree branches at the site of buried family members. From what I could learn, their belief system was very similar to other ancient peoples, and included a belief in an afterlife and the need to send off the deceased man with his principal wife (they were allowed 20), and as many of his belongings as would be necessary to get him started in the afterworld. The corpses of high-ranking people were usually adorned in gold for burial. The museums in Cartagena and Bogotá have wonderful collections of gold art that miraculously survived the Spanish colonial period.

Cartagena de Indias is a port city lying east of Panama and west of Santa Marta. It is a beautiful place. Cartagena was "discovered" by the Spanish in 1506 and became the site of their gold mint. Cartagena was a seaport before the Spanish arrived, but the Spanish expanded and used it as the principal port for the export of gold back to Spain. It was so important that the Spanish built the largest fort in the Americas here, Castillo San Felipe de Barajas, named after the king. Cartagena was the center of Spanish power because it was the point from which gold was minted and shipped to Spain, so of course it had to be protected at all costs. In 1741 the fort was attacked by a large British force under command of Admiral Edward Vernon whose intent was to dislodge the Spanish and capture the nexus of Spanish power in the Americas for England. This war is known as the War of Jenkin's Ear. However, the campaign failed, though the English did manage to take Port Arroyo in Panama, and Veracruz in Mexico. Colombia remained in Spanish hands until Simon Bolivar (a Mason like George Washington) defeated the Spanish and won Colombia independence in 1810.

It is interesting to note that Admiral Edward Vernon's family was the beneficiary of a large land grant in Virginia from the King of England. The Vernons were friends of the Washington family. In fact, Lawrence Washington, George's older half-brother, fought in the Cartagena campaign as a British officer under Vernon. Lawrence Washington subsequently bought some of the Vernon's Virginia holdings and named the estate Mount Vernon. After his death, it devolved first to his wife, and at her death shortly thereafter it fell to George Washington.

Five islands form Cartagena and its harbor. The historic center is on one of the islands and is an intact medieval city that once was home to Sir Francis Drake. It is a UNESCO World Heritage Site. Like other Spanish territories it was the site of an active and vicious Inquisition that extorted wealth from the rich and prosperous in the name of God. Today a public park named for Simon Bolivar and an Inquisition Museum stand on the site where trials, torture, and executions were conducted. Of the other four islands, two are home to beautiful, upscale high-rise apartments and condos as well as a new designer shopping center. The other two islands contain the seaport and the San Filipe fortress. Cartagena is a beautiful, exciting, interesting city that offers some of the best restaurants we have encountered in our travels.

Cartagena, Columbia
March 20, 2014

Walking the streets of Cartagena is a delight. Bougainvillea drape the sides of beautiful, classic buildings; the streets are cobblestone and meander into squares with interesting restaurants and shopping opportunities. Many places have fountains, and the central plaza has a huge Botero sculpture of a reclining nude. The original Spanish fortress wall surrounds the historic center, and is very interesting to walk about.

Occasionally I enjoy a good cigar. I looked all over town, but only found one tobacconist. The proprietor was a chatty, short, plump, red-faced fellow who displayed above the cash register an 8x10 framed photo of himself standing next to Bill Clinton. Under the photo was the caption: "Monica's favorite."

One of the more interesting ancient beliefs that seems to have persisted to this day and can be seen in everyday Colombian life is the idea that fertility in the female can be best predicted by a large bottom, or, in modern parlance, a big booty. Younger women here show as much as possible, wear the tightest clothing possible, and accentuate their derrière in a way that appeals to the primal instincts of man, those same instincts that the church has tried to stamp out in vain for 2,100 years. Colombia also boasts the fifth highest use of plastic surgery in the world. Women here employ all the tools

God gave them, and a few developed by modern technology, to enhance their natural endowments as much as possible.

BOGATA, COLUMBIA

After four delightful days in Cartagena we flew to Bogotá, the capital city. Formerly known by the indigenous peoples as El Dorado, Bogotá lies about 400 miles southeast of Cartagena on the northern slopes of the Andes, 9,000 feet above sea level. The city is home to about 8 million people and is the largest city in Colombia. It is a lovely city with modern high-rises, broad thoroughfares, large parks, and clean streets. We stayed in the nicest part of town and devoted one day to touring its major sights. The major points of interest are in the T zone near our hotel, which is the center of the city's lively restaurant and nightlife. The restaurants are world class, lovely with good service and wonderful food. The Monserrate Sanctuary and former monastery atop one of Bogotá's highest peaks is a spot not to be missed because of the panoramic view of this huge and sprawling city. The historic Spanish center known as La Candelaria is colorful, very interesting, and home to the Botero Museum. Here you can see the delightful paintings and sculptures of Fernando Botero that are sure to bring a smile. A few blocks farther down the hill is the city center and large public square, characteristic of Spanish cities. On the south side is the Catholic cathedral and offices of the archdiocese, across the square is the office of the mayor, and on the other two sides are the National Capital and the Palace of Justice. Behind the capital is the Presidential Palace. The Palace of Justice was rebuilt a few years ago after a fire destroyed it. The fire was set by the minions of Pablo Escobar who were attempting to destroy evidence of his misdeeds prior to his trial.

March 25–April 10   **Panama and the Canal**

We departed Santa Marta at 09:00 with a stiff 25 knot trade wind on our starboard quarter. It was hot and humid, a far cry from the bitter winter still gripping our home in Michigan. We had a 386-mile (2½ day) cruise ahead of us. I felt a little trepidation about this passage as the Caribbean can be quite rough this time of year, particularly at its western end near Colón, Panama. We moved easily out of the harbor's wide entrance, past the mountain island at its mouth, which is brightly lit at night with varying colors, past the ships at anchor, and out onto the sea proper. After an hour or so we settled into our familiar pattern: Tom began to wash the soot off the boat, Rebecca was thinking about food shopping in Panama and provisioning for the next 6 months, and I was checking over the equipment and setting our course. When we leave a port we generally fill our water tanks, but in Santa Marta the dock water isn't potable. If you want drinkable water, you have to order it in 10-gallon jugs and pour it by hand into the ship's tanks. We ordered 40 bottles that were brought to us by day laborers in the morning's already sweltering heat. Our tanks hold 500 gallons of fresh water, enough to last many days if it is carefully used, but the soot in Santa Marta coated the boat with a fine coal dust created by the loading of coal onto ships nearby (ships that take Colombian coal to Jacksonville, Florida), and so Tom began washing the boat. After a little while I noticed that our water supply was diminishing quickly, so I turned on our watermaker. It worked for a while, then quit working. I went below to check things out, but nothing obvious was wrong. Tom and I then went back and started taking the watermaker apart, but we found nothing apparently wrong. Meanwhile, seeing that we didn't have enough water to take showers we reviewed our emergency plan. I called the manufacturer's technician in Fort Lauderdale via sat-phone and reviewed the possibilities, and after 2 or 3 more hours in a hot engine room, still no permanent solution. I did manage to get the unit to work for several hours; that made the difference, and we were able to shower and use our water, but it put quite a scare into us. When we got to Shelter Bay Marina at the south end of the canal, I took another stab at it. This time I removed the low-pressure pump, took it apart to see if the impeller had gone wrong, and then realized that one of eight bolts holding the thing together was loose. That one small, loose Allen bolt allowed air to seep into the chamber and reduce the suction, denying the machine adequate water. **The lesson here is that ocean sailing is as much about keeping all the equipment working as it is about navigation and seamanship.**

People often ask me if I have had any special training that enabled me to diagnose and repair our equipment. The answer is, not really. Men of my age often had cars as boys that required a lot of mechanical work. In the winter, cars often didn't start, which required ether sprayed down the carb, or trying to start it by pushing it in first gear and popping the clutch. My brother and I took a '54 Ford apart in our family's garage. We "bondoed" several rusty cars and did a lot of body work. In the Navy, I was trained as an electronic technician. I repaired radars, sonars, and cryptographic equipment. We also had a twin diesel boat on the Great Lakes. So, all of this experience helped in dealing with the issues that arose on *Argo* and *Odyssey*.

While we were in Cartagena, Tom had a few well-deserved days off. He spoke Spanish and was familiar with Colombia because he had spent part of his childhood here. His father worked for an American company near Cartagena. Colombians love hot weather and the beach, and that's where Tom headed. He met a few locals on the beach, and late in the day as he was leaving a lovely young woman approached and asked on behalf of her sister, who apparently was too bashful to ask herself, for his email address. The next day he met her, and the following day we left Colombia. Shortly after we had gotten underway, Tom received an email. It was a picture of the girl with a business dress on with a short note addressing Tom as "My Dear."

PANAMA

March 26   **Panama Canal**

This morning we are at sea about 200 miles east of Colon, Panama. I am on watch. It is 09:00, and my watch began at 07:00. Everyone else is asleep. The trade winds are pushing us and the sea, which is rolling 3 to 7 feet on our starboard quarter. I love listening to classical music at this time of day; no one is around, and I can turn up the volume as much as I like. The wind is fresh, the sky is a little pink, and the sun is rising. It is great to be alive!

We left Santa Marta yesterday morning after 10 days in Colombia. This is a wonderful country, and we are so glad we came here. It is clean, it offers very interesting tourist experiences, great food, very friendly and accommodating people, and a rich history and culture. People work here; no one loafs. Colombians seem very happy and good natured with an easy sense of humor, yet there is a welcomed interpersonal formality that reflects respect. It is very safe; we felt no insecurity anywhere, and travel was easy to arrange once we were here.

March 27   **Canal Zone**

The cruise to Panama and Shelter Bay was more pleasant than I anticipated with calm seas as we entered Colon Harbor. Scheduling a transit through the Panama Canal is fairly complicated and needs to be made several weeks in advance. For the three of us and the boat, the fees totaled about $3,300. The basic canal fee is $1,500, but an agent is required to complete formalities. That cost $700. The rest is made up of incidental taxes, fees, immigration visas, and so on. Oftentimes the authorities tell you that they are experiencing a shortage of measurers (they send someone out to measure the exact dimensions of the vessel) or some other tradesman. The choices then are either to wait 2 weeks until they can get around to you or pay a $340 overtime charge. There is a bundle of paperwork to complete, and all of the fees have to be wired to the Panamanian National Bank 2 weeks prior to transit. Finally, when you leave your last port of call (for us, that was Santa Marta) you have to email your Zarpe or departure authorization to the agent in Panama. After all the details are in hand, the wheels begin to slowly grind at the canal authority, and the agent calls with a transit date.

We tied up at Shelter Bay at 10:00 on March 27. After checking in at the marina, washing the boat again, fixing the watermaker, cleaning the interior, and trying to use Skype to get ahold of our agent, we headed for the restaurant for a beer on a blazing hot and sultry afternoon. There we met Charlie, a prince of a fellow and very generous guy who tells endless, interesting stories. Charlie is an expat and has lived with his family in Cartagena for many years. He is a lawyer who handles the import/export formalities for large shipping companies. Charlie has traveled all over the region, and when we met him he was in Panama doing work on his sailboat.

Charlie rented a car and invited us for a tour of Colon. By ourselves we would have never gone there, but with such an invitation, off we went. Colon is about a half hour ride from the marina and requires crossing the canal. If a ship is passing through, you may have to wait an hour or more, but on this day, we drove right across. The crossing is made via a single-lane bridge that falls in place when the lock's second gate is closed. Colon, once a pearl of the region, has descended into the darkest oblivion. It is a squalid and dangerous place where the odds of a white person being mugged or worse rise to near certainty after dark. Carrying a weapon for self-protection is commonplace here. The buildings, however, despite their dilapidated condition, cannot hide the architectural beauty of its golden age and the vibrancy that once must have been. Driving around one sees suspicious-looking vagrants and unemployed people milling about, and in contrast you see a large number of private schools with children of all ages dressed neatly in their uniforms, white shirts, and ties for the boys, dresses and bobby socks for the girls. There are also residential areas that seem quite normal and secure. The city fathers are trying to resurrect Colon by making it a cruise ship destination and shopping mecca. We went to its duty-free zone, said to be second in size only to Hong Kong; it's about 10 city blocks square, packed with hundreds of stores. Getting in requires going into a special office at the secure entry gate. Here your passport is screened, and if everything is in order you are granted admission . . . for the price of $9. Once inside, we wandered around for a couple of hours in sweltering heat. It isn't really a very nice place, and despite the heat there was not a single place to buy water or a beer, much less a sandwich. However, all was not lost as I found a very good deal on some Cuban cigars, half the price offered in Cartagena. Nearby Fort San Lorenzo is a popular destination for hikers and sightseers. Both are just a short cab ride from the Shelter Bay Marina and well worth the visit.

Once back at Shelter Bay Marina, we invited our new friends Charlie and Mark to dinner onboard *Argo*. Mark is an anesthesiologist from Seattle who has taken 6 months off to sail with his wife. They had made it from the East Coast to Panama when their boat broke down and was laid up for repairs. Mark's wife abandoned ship and went home to attend to family matters, leaving him to see to the boat while living aboard on the hard with no power in humid 100-degree heat. We thought both Charlie and Mark needed a good dinner, so we invited them over and had a heck of a good time together. Later that evening we learned that Tom had received several other emails from the beautiful girl he met in Santa Marta. The first email was addressed "My Darling" and showed pictures of her in workout gear, shorts, and a tight top. The next email referred to him as "My Love," and showed her in a very small, revealing bathing suit. The emails became hotter and hotter and invited him to return for a visit or bring her to the next port. They continued daily until we left for the Galapagos. Tom told me that Colombian girls ply their charms particularly on Americans in the hope of being taken to the United States, and then bring their extended family along for good company.

The next day, Sunday March 30, we expected two friends, Mark and Dash, to join us onboard for a trip through the canal. Mark is an editor for *Passagemaker*, an important magazine for people who want to learn about owning a boat and cruising the world. Before we bought *Odyssey*, I looked forward to every issue and read it cover to cover. It inspired me to start our own odyssey. So, when Peter, Mark's boss called and asked if they could do an article on our passage through the canal, we thought it would be a lot of fun and readily agreed. With camera and notepad in hand, Mark came aboard early Sunday morning. Later that day Dash came aboard. Dash is an old friend from the 1980s, when he and I attended professional meetings and executive education courses together. We hadn't seen each other in about 25 years, and although still in business, Dash winters at his home in Bocas del Toro, about 100 miles north of Colon.

Our transit through the canal was scheduled for Monday. Before leaving we needed to get four 125-foot lines and 12 fenders (tires wrapped in garbage bags) on board. We hired a line handler (Stanley) to assist with the transit. We were instructed to leave the marina at 13:30, anchor in the harbor, and await a call on VHF channel 12. As we were arriving on station, a call came in and gave us directions to the pilot boat. Around 14:00, a pilot (Ricardo) came aboard, and he was a very pleasant, talkative fellow. Our transit was scheduled for 15:30, but we didn't actually get into the lock until 19:15. In the meantime we held at anchor. The sun had set by the time we entered the Gatun's first of three locks. Upon entering the lock, we were instructed to come alongside and tie up to the steel workboat that preceded us. This required readying lines and positioning fenders between the ships. After some preparation and waiting for the other ship to secure itself to the lock's wall, we came alongside and tied up to it.

New, much larger locks have been constructed and can handle larger ships, but the number of ships that can pass through the canal won't change; smaller ships will not be allowed to use the bigger locks because of water usage constraints. The canal can handle 40 ships per day and each ship now uses 58 million gallons of water during its transit. The new locks will require much more water, which is a potential problem. The canal authority uses the excess flow of the Chagres River to generate electricity, which it sells to the public. In order to operate the new locks, more water from the Chagres will have to be diverted to the locks, which will reduce the river's volume and the amount of electricity that can be generated. Revenue from the sale of electricity will diminish, causing other problems.

Transit charges are also a factor. When the Americans ran the canal, they raised transit fees three times in 75 years. The joke here is that since the Panamanians took over, they have raised prices 75 times in 3 years! The result is that some of the canal's largest customers, such as Maersk Lines and others, have notified the canal authorities that they are rerouting their ships so that they will not use the canal beginning next year because of high fees; apparently, they will send all their ships through the Suez Canal. As it is, Panama is having trouble financing the construction of the new locks. During our transit, we noticed fewer ships waiting for transit despite a stronger economy, and no cruise liners were going through because of the higher fees, now $400,000 per transit. So, the Panamanians seem to be facing serious challenges.

The former Canal Zone, once the jewel of the US Army and a plumb boondoggle of a military assignment, is basically in ruins. The Panamanians have done virtually nothing with it or with the air bases that protected the zone. What they have done is build a beautiful Panama City. They are building a new subway that is due to open this month. Traffic congestion should be reduced considerably. Most of the buildings are condominiums, used by Americans, Russians, and Venezuelans as a refuge from either winter, taxes, tyrants, or all three. The Cleveland Clinic has built a hospital in the midst of it all. Rebecca and I had dinner at the Trump International in the heart of "new town." It is a beautiful building with a Waldorf Astoria Hotel located on the 20th floor and above. We dined at a restaurant on the 15th floor that had a wonderful view of the cityscape. One couldn't help but notice that most of the hundreds of apartments in the buildings around us were vacant; in one 40-story building we counted only two apartments with lights on. Despite it being a Friday night, no cars or people were on the street or dining at the restaurants. Many people say the growth of the city has been financed with laundered drug money; regardless, it is very impressive.

Panama City also has an historic area called Casco Viejo. Originally it had buildings like those found in Cartagena, but the area has fallen into disrepair over the years. Many of the buildings are very lovely, and the community is in the process of redevelopment. We dined in a Habana-style restaurant with our friend Dash and his friend Carolina. Dash also took us to the best restaurant in the city, La Posta, the evening before for a truly lovely dinner in a classic 1940s Panamanian setting. It sure was nice to have a friend that knows the city! When the redevelopment of Casco Viejo is complete, Panama City will have one more jewel in its crown. It will certainly be, if it isn't already, one of the most interesting and vibrant cities in the world.

Several magazines have named Panama as one of the best places to retire, primarily because of the low taxes and availability of domestic help, and we met one couple who have retired here, a forensic tax accountant and his wife. They love it. Personally, I found Panama to be a wonderful place to visit for a week or so, but living here would be problematic due to the extremely hot and humid climate and social challenges. Locations higher up in the mountains provides relief from the heat, but there is a strain of anti-gringoism that pervades Panama. There is a great book, <u>Path Between the Seas</u> by David McCullough, that lays out the fascinating history of Panama and the Canal. Unfortunately, I think too few Panamanians have read it.

Cutting across the narrowest part of the Panamanian Isthmus, from the Caribbean to Pacific blue water, the Canal spans just 45 nm. Transiting ships are raised 85 feet from sea level into the Gatun Lake and back down through twin sets of three locks on either side. Gatun, a man-made body of water created by diverting the Chagres River, is the life source of the Panama Canal and provides the massive amounts of water required to operate the locks.

Each lock requires nearly 27 million gallons of water to go from a lowered to a raised position. Because the sea level of Gatun Lake is higher than that of both the Caribbean Sea and the Pacific Ocean, 54 million gallons spill from the lake into those bodies of water every time the locks are opened and closed. Currently, each lock is 110 feet wide and 1,000 feet long. The Panamanians Have expanded Canal in order to better compete with the Suez Canal in Egypt. The lock widths are a 160 feet, to accommodate larger commercial shipping vessels. The Panama Canal runs full-steam 24/7 and passes more than 40 commercial vessels (20 each way) from ocean to ocean each day, in addition to numerous transient cruisers.

Located on Limon Bay close to the Caribbean entrance of the Canal, Shelter Bay is a small, full-service marina that features floating docks, a pool, bar, restaurant, and a market. There is also a hotel with a handful of rooms. The marina can accommodate yachts up to 70 feet in length and is home to a largely transient population. Marina manager John Halley says the entire marina of occupants turns over every 10 days.

We made our way into Limon Bay by late afternoon to meet our pilot. Panama is the only place in the world where all captains, regardless of their qualifications, are required to hand over control of their vessels to pilots. Panama employs close to 300 pilots, all of whom are Panamanian.

Boats like *Argo* require one pilot, while larger commercial ships often need teams of three. Eventually, our pilot, Ricardo, arrived and made the leap from the pilot boat to *Argo*, briefcase in hand. Becoming a Canal pilot takes about a decade. Every one of them has a master's license and is certified to handle unlimited tonnage. They are also trained to know every nook and nuance of the Canal. Pilots must be able to jump aboard any type of ship and be competent in handling it through the tight quarters of the locks.

"It is a high-stress job, but I carry my little ball here," says Ricardo, pulling a blue stress ball from his shirt pocket and giving it a commanding squeeze. "It is a bit like how far can you go before you scare yourself, but I enjoy [the job]. Doing a boat like this is a treat compared to what we normally pilot."

The Waiting Game

The average cruiser can run from end to end of the Canal in 9 hours if allowed to do it nonstop. However, nonstop transits are the exception for private yachts and transiting the Panama Canal is a test of patience for an anxious yachtsman.

From the very beginning you wait for your transit day, only to wait for your pilot to meet you on the day of transit. You wait for proper weather (fog can make the locks treacherous), for your transit times, and for your turn in the locks. Once inside you wait to tie up, for the doors to close, and for the water to fill or empty, only to repeat the process at each lock, of which there are eight. All of the lock water is moved by gravity via the opening and closing of large underwater culverts. There is no alarm or notification that occurs in the locks to let you know you're being raised or lowered, just a slow rise or fall followed by the sudden realization that the massive concrete walls have somehow disappeared (or reappeared) from either side of the boat.

The waiting is not all bad. In fact, there is no reason to rush the experience of transiting the Canal. We were held in Limon Bay several hours past our scheduled transit time, with the Gatun locks waiting; it had the emotional effect on me reminiscent of the trepidation I felt in junior high school when asking a girl to dance. Our turn in the locks did not take place until after nightfall, consequently *Argo* was anchored in the lake near the Gatun locks for the night. The following morning a new pilot came aboard, and we continued our transit. Being able to witness during the light of day the operation of the Pedro Miguel and Mira Flores locks on the Pacific side is another benefit of spending a night in Gatun Lake.

Gatun Lake is truly a sight to behold and creates an interesting paradox. Intense natural beauty, untouched shores, and crisp, clear, fresh water are punctuated only by the constant stream of metal behemoths passing by. The lake is littered with islands that are actually partially submerged hilltops left over from when the valley was flooded a hundred years ago. The lake provides excellent habitat for large and tasty peacock bass.

Mixed Bag

The country of Panama is an eclectic mix of French, Spanish, and American cultures. Casco Viejo, Panama City's old quarter, is the perfect personification of the country's split identities. The area has undergone a recent urban revival, restoring much of the original Spanish architecture. Panama is a mutt; when you buy something from a vendor even the change from purchases comes in a mix of American dollars and Balboa coins. Open-air salsa clubs blaring Latin-American music directly abut monuments to the original French and Spanish settlers, all in the shadow of downtown Panama City's modern casinos and towering luxury hotels.

The Pacific side is an El Dorado for cruisers. Home to three of the country's finest marinas (Flamenco is widely regarded as the best), the Pacific side is an ideal staging ground. Cruisers can head north up the coast to explore the Yucatan and North America, or wait to head across the Pacific to more ambitious destinations. Conversely, they can head south to Ecuador, Peru, and Chile or head into the Canal and onto the Caribbean. Once reaching the docks of La Playita, *Argo's* port of call on the Pacific side, we began preparing for our journey across the South Pacific toward the Galapagos.

April 6   **Underway for the Galapagos**

We headed out the morning of April 6 for the Galapagos Islands, about 950 miles west of Panama. Our course took us to the Las Perlas Islands about 35 miles off the coast in the Bay of Panama, then out to the open ocean. It was a beautiful, calm day, and we enjoyed a delightful cruise to the islands. Islas Contadora is the main attraction; it is quiet and small but has several lovely boutique hotels and homes located on its beaches. It looks like a great spot for a short vacation and a place where I would like to return.

Later that night we headed out of the Gulf of Panama, past many large ships coming and going to the canal. As we entered the Pacific Ocean proper we encountered moderate ocean swells from the south. For the balance of our 5-day passage the southerly winds on our port bow between 15 and 20 knots, sometimes a little more. The seas were moderate (6–8 feet with a fairly long moment) and pleasant for the most part, except for one day when a weak front came through that was a little uncomfortable.

Four large currents converge in this area of the ocean, and they create a very confused sea. The currents can be fairly narrow, and they have eddies and back currents associated with them, so finding productive ones isn't always easy. Once we found one we might be pushed along at 6 to 8 knots, then lose it and find ourselves fighting a head current slowing us down considerably. Sometimes we might have to travel as much as 40 or 50 miles to get into a suspected current. On the fifth day, we crossed the equator and made landfall at Puerto Ayora on the island of Santa Cruz in the Galapagos.

GALAPAGOS

April 10 to 24   **The Galapagos**

Far out in the Pacific, 500 miles west of Ecuador, the low domed peaks of massive shield volcanoes rise from the depths. They break the surface as the 13 (main) islands of the Galapagos. They are the product of one of the most active geological regions on the earth, a place where the Cocos Plate and the Nazca Plate meet at the Galapagos and Carnegie Ridges. Here the earth's mantle is very thin, allowing huge calderas to form and break the surface as eruptions: in the last 200 years, there have been 60 eruptions. When visiting the islands, you can see massive lava flows, vent tubes, unbelievably intricate and interesting formations of lava as it solidified when it met the ocean and was then, over the centuries, covered in flora such as lichens, moss, or other plants. The islands of Isabela and Santa Cruz bear witness to incredibly violent para-plastic eruptions as boulders and rocks of all sizes litter hundreds of square miles of landscape. Meanwhile the sun beats down with a fierce intensity. There is no fresh water anywhere, only the briny sea fed by several ocean currents that converge here. From the south flows the cold Humboldt Current, bringing nourishment from the Antarctic and the ocean's depths; from the east, the warm Panamanian Current, bringing life from Central America.

Entering the Galapagos Entering the Galapagos Islands on a private yacht requires a cruising permit, a wad of cash, and a fair amount of patience. Ninety-seven percent of the Galapagos Islands are part of the Parque Nacional de Galapagos, a UNICEF World Heritage Site. It is also part of the country of Ecuador. In preparing for our trip to this port we had done a reasonable amount of research and preparation. We were surprised to learn from other boaters in Panama that the bottom of our boat would be inspected for marine growth when we arrive in the Galapagos, so we had the bottom cleaned in Panama and pictures taken of it. We were told stories of boats deemed to have excess marine growth on their hulls that were then subsequently forced to travel 70 miles offshore with a park service diver to clean their hulls at a cost of $500. We were also told that we needed to have *Argo* fumigated and obtain a certificate from a licensed company showing the chemical used. Of course, we complied, although the fumigation company only gave us an official looking paper, charged $100, but never actually fumigated our boat; they said it wasn't necessary. We also read a long list of contraband plants and foods that couldn't be taken to the islands. All of this is understandable when you consider the environmental damage done to the Great Lakes by foreign ships entering without restriction, so we entered ready to comply with any demand.

About 20 miles offshore of the Galapagos we were surprised to be hailed by name by the park service on VHF channel 16. They must have monitored our AIS signal that broadcasts our name, course, speed, and other identification information. The official didn't speak much English, but Tom spoke Spanish and between the three of us we managed to find out that he was instructing us to go to the wrong port. This was a little disconcerting, but after being persistent, we were authorized to follow the correct heading and course and make our way into Puerto Ayora. Our first sight of the Galapagos Group was of Santa Cruz Island. Just as Darwin noted in 1835, the island was shrouded in clouds. It was a moment of deep personal contemplation to think that not only had we made a 1,000-mile open ocean passage safely and found this little dot in the middle of the ocean, but that we were now here observing the same sights and hearing the same sounds that the great explorers had experienced in the historical past. As we came closer, we could make out the arid, rocky, lava-laced shoreline.

We nervously groped our way toward Puerto Ayora as our charts were not very detailed. Eventually we saw the harbor and pointed *Argo* toward other ships at anchor. It is a crowded harbor with no breakwater. There were two or three small freighters offloading onto barges, as there are no docks at Puerto Ayora. There were about 10 sailboats and catamarans at anchor. We were the largest yacht for most of the time we were there. The other 20 or so boats were tour boats waiting for this week's plane load of tourists to arrive from Guayaquil. Swells rolled in directly off the ocean. Boats at anchor constantly pitched up and down and rolled from side to side despite being very close to each other. As we gingerly picked our way between the boats and their fore and aft anchor lines, we found an empty mooring ball and tied to it. This in itself was quite a feat in that we had to launch the tender while holding our place in the rolling sea, then tie a heavy mooring line to a moving, heavy anchor buoy and *Argo's* deck 10 feet above the waterline. It took about an hour to get it all resolved. Later we deployed a stern anchor to hold us into the swell, put out our passive paravane stabilizers, and dropped our forward anchor in case the mooring ball failed (often mooring balls fail because they are not properly maintained). A few moments after we were secure, we called our agent and he arranged for the commencement of entry formalities.

To stay in the Galapagos, one needs a cruising permit that can only be obtained through the Capitania de Puerto at a port of entry. There are effectively two ports of entry into the Galapagos: Puerto Ayora on Santa Cruz Island, and San Cristobal on San Cristobal Island. The length of stay is at the discretion of the port captain, but cannot exceed 21 days without a visa. If a visa is desired, one must apply 3 months in advance of the visit. To get a cruising permit, the port captain together with a National Parks official, a police officer, an immigration officer, a health inspector, and a diver all visit to inspect the boat. Since hardly any officials speak English, we hired an agent to help us through the formalities. All the officials came to our boat shortly after we anchored in Puerto Ayora and completed all their inspections in about 2 hours. While on board they looked through all the compartments, took pictures of our black water tank and our soap dispensers, read our trash policy, looked around the engine room, checked out our refrigerator, and, as a special request, the port captain asked if we would take his picture while he stood next to our helm and wooden wheel. He said he never saw a pilothouse like ours nor had he seen a wooden helm. So, we were happy to comply. Meanwhile a diver came to the boat and inspected our hull. After all the official business was conducted, pictures taken, and departing pleasantries exchanged, the bill was presented: $2,183 for a 21-day permit. If we wanted to travel to other islands via our boat, we would need a guide and a ranger. This would cost about $1,500 per day, including permits. Later, in talking with other boaters, we found out that one of the boats had no black water tank and dumped sewage directly overboard (frankly, I didn't know any boat was built or allowed to do that). They showed the officials a fresh water tank and he took pictures of that, and that seemed to satisfy them. More importantly, when we went ashore we found that the city dumped their sewage directly into the bay. So much for all the pollution consideration.

While all the officials were on board we received a call on our VHF. A 52-foot Oyster sailboat from the USA was calling. They had left Costa Rica 8 days before with four adults and two children aboard. They motored all the way to the Galapagos (instead of sailing) and arrived with hardly any food or water left and only a few gallons of fuel. They were desperate and afraid. We heard them call Ricardo, our agent, for help in getting a cruising permit, but he told them he was too busy to help them. Unfortunately, they were technically not allowed ashore until they had a permit and cleared customs. Apparently, they saw the inspection party come aboard *Argo* and our American flag off the stern and decided to call us to see if we could help them get the inspection party to relent and come to their boat. Of course, we asked Ricardo, and he agreed. Later they brought a bottle of Johnnie Jameson over as a token of their gratitude. Really nice and completely unnecessary, particularly in light of the absence of any water or nourishment on their boat! In talking with them later, we found out that these Californians had planned to cross the Pacific just as we were doing, but I think they realized that they were not properly prepared or had insufficient experience to continue on such an ambitious journey. A few days later they pulled up their anchor and headed back to Costa Rica.

Puerto Ayora

Puerto Ayora is the tourist capital of the Galapagos. The little town has about 3,000 permanent residents, a substantial commercial area, many restaurants and shops, and the Darwin Center. We anchored *Argo* in Puerto Ayora for about 3 weeks, and toured several other islands by plane during our visit staying in local hotels. We were especially excited because our daughter, Kathryn, was flying in for a week to tour the islands with us.

In Puerto Ayora the harbor was always rolling with ocean swells, and *Argo* was in a constant state of motion. Often the swells were large, and *Argo* rolled significantly to our chagrin. Kathryn had to take Dramamine just to tolerate sitting in the salon.

To get off the boat and into town we hailed a water taxi on VHF 14 and asked for a pickup. The fare was 60 cents per person each way. The taxi dropped us at a municipal dock especially constructed for the purpose. Sometimes customers had to step over a sea lion or two that were resting on the gangway. Sea lions could be found lounging on a park bench on the upper walkway completely oblivious to passersby. A short walk past the skateboard park at the end of the dock brought us to Main Street, which was very nicely constructed of brick with wide sidewalks and newly planted trees to shade the weary walkers. The heat at midday was really intense, perhaps 100 degrees with equivalent humidity. It was almost unbearable, which I am sure is why siestas are popular. Most businesses open from 9 a.m. to noon, then close and reopen at 3 p.m. and remain open until 8 or 9 p.m. Many of the restaurants were quite acceptable, and we enjoyed them frequently. Food shopping was fun; we went to the farmers' market on two Saturdays and enjoyed the bounty of the highlands amidst all the sights, smells, and cultural delights of a country market. At the waterfront, we bought an 18-pound yellow fin tuna for $2 a pound, a pretty good deal considering Monahan's Fish Market in Ann Arbor wants about $40 a pound. The local mercado (grocery store) offered the usual packaged goods, but it also had a very good bakery whose products we enjoyed on several occasions. On Good Friday, we went into town for an ice cream cone and unexpectedly witnessed the Easter Passion Festival. Hundreds of people reenacted The Way of the Cross, complete with Jesus dragging the cross along the route with costumed Roman soldiers and statues of several apostles carried aloft on the shoulders of devout believers.

One evening we met our tour agent, and she invited us to Casa del Mar restaurant for a freshly caught tuna and wahoo dinner (someone also brought a little goat meat) with friends and the Uruguayans who caught them that day. The fish was perhaps the best we ever had, and the two Australians we met were very interesting people who piqued our interest in the Kimberley area of their country.

Back on *Argo*, we noticed that the harbor was a little cloudy because of all the algae in the water. It caused our watermaker filters to frequently clog. We had to make drinking water from harbor water because they do not offer any services for yachts in Puerto Ayora. If we left the harbor for the open ocean to make water or empty our black water tanks we would need a permit. (All the boats dump black water in the harbor.) Since a watermaker filter only lasts a couple of hours, we were running through our supply very quickly. I was wondering if this would end our trip, or at least alter it significantly because you can't cross the Pacific Ocean without a functioning watermaker. So, as we had a long trip ahead of us, I thought we better see if we could buy some 5-micron seawater filters. Our agent Ricardo Arenas directed us to Bodega Blanco, a boating supply store about 10 blocks from the taxi dock. Rebecca and I decided to walk, and even though it was only 9 a.m. it was already so hot that I was drenched with sweat by the time we got there. Everyone spoke Spanish, so trying to find what we wanted was a little difficult until we talked to the owner, who spoke perfect English. He inquired about us and we about him; he grew up in L.A. and his mother graduated from U of M as an English major! It is a small world. He found the filters we needed, and we bought a huge supply to assuage our concerns.

Touring

Kathryn, our daughter, arrived and brought with her a few parts for *Argo* that we wanted, like a 10-pound low-pressure pump for the watermaker.

She enjoyed a day of rest from her 18-hour flight from NYC, and then we started our tour of the islands. The first place we went was to the Charles Darwin Center on the outskirts of Puerto Ayora. The institute raises various species of tortoises for reintroduction on the appropriate islands. Many islands have distinct species of tortoises, and after a little while you can distinguish them by their shells. *Galapagos* means "saddle" in Spanish. It was the original Spanish discoverers who thought some of the tortoise shells looked like saddles, and indeed some do. When Darwin arrived in 1835 there were an estimated 400,000 tortoises roaming about. By the early 1980s there were only 3,000 left. At the Darwin Center, they have a hatchery and raise the little ones until they can fend for themselves. Historically they had no natural enemies aside from man, but as humans released dogs, cats, pigs, and goats into the wild, these feral animals have eaten either the little tortoises directly or consumed their forage. So, the idea is to raise tortoises in captivity until they are large enough to protect themselves from these predators. Officials have been conducting a program to eradicate non-native species for some time and with some success. The Institute also has a number of large enclosures in which they keep adult tortoises of various types for breeding. Watching these huge, cumbersome animals is really something to see, particularly when they are eating or mating. The Institute also has both marine iguanas and land iguanas, the latter of which are large and very colorful.

The next day we hopped a plane to the group's largest island, Isabela. Isabela is only partially available to visitors; most of it is reserved as a wildlife sanctuary. The history of the Galapagos is one of near abandonment. Sailors, in particular whalers, used it as a food source and respite from the ocean, but since it had little or no water available, it was never significantly populated. Ecuador annexed it in 1832, and the HMS *Beagle* along with Darwin visited there in 1835. During WWII, the United States used it as a military base. After the war, the Ecuadorians used the remains of the military base as a prison. It was here that the **Wall of Tears**, a huge stone wall, was built from the rocks thrown out by the volcano thousands of years ago. The wall has a sort of hideous beauty; stone by stone the hopeless prisoners piled one upon another after carrying them from distant places in searing heat. Surely many of them died, but living here would have been truly hell on earth. The prison was closed in the late 1960s.

The next attraction on Isabela is the marine iguanas. They look like octopi when they swim, are pitch black, and match the color of the lava rocks on which they cling. They have webbed feet and long claws; they spend their time going in the water to eat algae growing on the rocks, then back to shore to warm up, then back for more food, et cetera.

Next was a hike along the shore and a climb into one of the many lava vents or tubes through which lava flowed from underground to the ocean. They were very interesting. The largest one we entered was big enough to accommodate a two-lane highway. Along the way, we stopped at a vista observation deck. After climbing up a couple of hundred stairs to the top of a vent/hill, we could look over the vista of a volcanic island, which was simply beautiful. Farther along the road we stopped at the Isabela Tortoise breeding center, just like the one we saw at the Charles Darwin Center.

Our hotel was located in Puerto Villamil, a shabby little town with dirt streets. Every one of the 110,000 tourists each year that come to the Galapagos will at some point probably find their way here. The village caters to tourists and has a few very small hotels and several restaurants. The one restaurant we tried was horrible. Fortunately, our hotel served very good food, particularly the ceviche, which was actually the best I ever had. Kathryn was full of energy and being from NYC wanted to go out our first evening on Isabela: so down the beach we walked toward the place she heard was the best night spot in town. Later we learned her recommendation came from the tour guide, and later yet we learned that his boss owned the place. Anyway, he was probably right and it turned out to be lot of fun. It was a surf side bar complete with a sand volleyball court and, most interesting of all, a tightrope on which young beer drinkers tried their skills as wannabe Wallendas. We watched them through the evening as they practiced their skills while we consumed the local favorite, Coco-Loco!

The next day was packed with interesting experiences. We were picked up early at the hotel and taken to the dock, then aboard a speedboat for an hour's ride to an area I can only describe as mind-blowing. It was truly otherworldly—formed by lava flows frozen in the most interesting and bizarre configurations both above and below water. Getting into the place required real local knowledge and skill; first we had to pass over the very large 10-foot sea swells rolling in from the ocean, and then maneuver between rock formations that broke the swells into surf, then around and through the maze of lava formations, all the time avoiding rocky outcroppings that could have easily broken the propellers. We landed and offloaded on a cliff that was 5 or 6 feet above the waterline. Once we had climbed up the rocks onto a flat surface we could really appreciate why we were brought here. The pitch-black lava formed arches and bridges in an endless maze that was interwoven with the brilliant blue water of the ocean, creating small lagoons that sea turtles and sharks frequent during their mating season. It was fascinating to watch the sea turtles effortlessly glide, almost fly, through the water. Blue-footed boobies were everywhere. When we first saw two of them standing together above a nesting site (a flat, black rock surface encircled by white bird poop), they just stood there and looked at us despite the fact that we were only a few feet from them. Like all the animals we encountered in the Galapagos, they are not afraid of human beings. The boobies are a beautiful bird; words can't really describe them. Their heads are covered in small, blue-brown-white feathers, their bodies are brown and white, yellow-rimmed eyes, blue-gray beak, and of course the most distinguishing feature of all, powder-blue webbed feet and legs. They are just spectacular, and when they go fishing, they form flocks and dive like arrows into the water after their prey.

After exploring the lava field, we went snorkeling. Here we got to see the underwater world: many tropical reef fish as one might expect, and just an arm's length away sea turtles (huge 4 x 3 feet turtles) feeding on the algae growing on the rocks, penguins 10 feet away, sea lions playing and dashing adroitly through the water, marine iguanas, frigate birds, boobies, and whitetip and blacktip reef sharks tending to their young ones in a cave. We were a little cautious around those animals! Later as we headed back to the little town and our hotel, Kathryn dove with 12-foot manta rays in the open ocean; wow, what an experience!

The next day we visited another lava field. It looked like nothing I had ever seen on earth before. The lava was formed into twisted figures about 3 feet

88

high and partially covered in white lichen. It looked like a field of strange outer space beings. Amidst all the little stone "men" were marine iguanas.

That afternoon we flew back to Santa Cruz. We could see the rims of partially submerged, extinct volcanoes rising out of the ocean as well as a vista of the entire western part of the island. After we landed we drove to the highlands for lunch at a coffee farm. The owners were the extended family of our tour operator. Apparently, Ecuador never knew quite what to do with the Galapagos until UNICEF made it a World Heritage Site. Nothing much can be grown here commercially or mined. It is so hot that agriculture cannot be sustained on a commercial basis, there is little soil, and little water. Many people have tried to establish homesteads here and failed. The government used it for a prison colony for a time, but even that failed. During the 1970s Ecuador granted 200 acres to any citizen willing to make a homestead here. That's how our friends got hold of this farmland, but they couldn't clear it all or maintain it, so they gave 100 acres back to the government. Now, in light of tourism and the fact that 97 percent of the land is part of the Parque Nacional, land here is very expensive and almost impossible for an outsider to acquire. Immigration to these islands is no longer permitted.

On the way to the farm we stopped by a lava tube buried deep in the hillside. It was at least 30 feet in diameter, much like a subway tunnel, but one that extended about 3,000 feet or more. Later we returned to the farm and walked about to observe the tortoises living in their natural environment. There were many large old males and many smaller females walking laboriously about. It was the mating season. As we walked the paths in the lush jungle forest we could hear the grunting of the male in the act of mating. We were told that it takes about 4 hours to complete their mission. Meanwhile the beast grunts and extends his head several feet out of his shell. The 500-pound male somehow climbs on top of the female who weighs in at a scant 100 pounds. She seems to just sit and wait for the event to end. Meanwhile, several other females nearby wait on standby. Apparently, these animals live up to approximately 200 years. We were told that females can hold the sperm of several males simultaneously for up to 5 years and release it into her eggs when conditions are right. Interestingly, they walk as far as 20 miles or more over rocky and inhospitable terrain to the beach to lay their eggs in the sand (like the sea turtles). It must be a primordial impulse; at any rate, it is an incredible feat. After leaving the tortoises we drove back to Puerto Ayora, but along the way we stopped to see two very large sunken calderas and associated lava vents. These geological features exist at an altitude of 650 meters and support an unusual forest of trees peculiar to the Galapagos. Unlike most other places on the island, Spanish moss hangs on the tree branches, creating a most unusual effect.

After returning to *Argo*, we needed to decide on a spot for dinner. Kathryn had heard from NYC friends who had recently traveled here that a place called The Deli had the best fish and chips anywhere this side of London. So, we tried it out together with our friends Javier and Jill, two lovely people that owned the tour company. Kathryn's friends were absolutely correct; these were the planet's greatest fish and chips!

The next day we set out for North Seymour Island and the land of the frigate birds. Once again, we had to make the 50-mile car trip across Santa Cruz to the island of Baltra, then by boat to North Seymour Island. We made the trip in a bus along with about 40 other people, but because we had a private guide we were comfortably ushered along. From the boat dock, we went by dinghy to an old cabin cruiser anchored offshore for the hour or so trip to North Seymour Island. Inside was the captain in full dress whites with epaulets, and a heavyset, friendly cook in the galley making lunch for the 20 or so passengers. On the menu: sautéed yellow fin tuna, and it was very good. The trip was a lot of fun.

North Seymour Island is a mile square, flat slab of arid rock lying about 25 feet above sea level. It is volcanic in origin. The island's fauna seemed desiccated as it hadn't rained in 5 months, but the rainy season was just around the corner. All the grass, sparse as it was, was brown and dried up; prickly pear cactus trees, also unique to the island, punctuated the rocky landscape. Here and there were dwarf, gray-bark, spindly trees that at the time had no foliage. In the branches of the trees were nests, some of which held hungry chicks. Neither the nests nor the chicks were small. These were frigate birds, and it was mating season. Love was in the air literally as red-pouched male frigate birds sailed overhead looking for females and a suitable place to inflate their mating equipment. As we walked along the path we saw several land iguanas with their oddly beautiful orangey-green-gold-tan coloration. They are much larger than their marine cousins.

The male frigates have a flaming red sack on their throat, which they inflate to attract the females. Our walk through the strange pigmy forest was fascinating as we looked for a male frigate in full mating display. We were able to get within a few feet of several of these birds and get some wonderful pictures. The birds themselves are much larger than a pheasant, but smaller than a turkey, and their red display is about half the size of a football. It is really something to see. We spent about 2 hours there, and it was one of the most interesting animal adventures we have experienced.

On the way, back to the boat we stopped at a beach that turtles use to dig their nests. It was a broad expanse of beautiful white coral sand that rose broadly and steeply to 100 or more yards above the waterline. It was there we found the large concave bowls dug by the turtles for their nests. Over the ridge at the crest of the beach we came upon a brackish pond. There we could see a flamingo. We watched the beautiful bird feed on little shrimp, its long neck moving about to allow the angled black beak to sift through the mud on the pond's bottom. Suddenly the magnificent bird started to run, its stick-like legs and knees awkwardly gaining speed. Then it extended its wings and began to take off, its fabulous pink plumage accented by the black feathers under its wings that makes its pink body unbelievably brilliant. Then the awkwardness was transformed into graceful, effortless flight. On the beach were two lava gulls, part of the only remaining 200 known to exist. They too were magnificent: they look like a sea gull, but dark gray and black to match the color of lava. These animals are simply a spectacular sight to behold.

Our Final Few Days in the Galapagos

We returned to *Argo* late in the day on Friday. Kathryn was scheduled to go home on Sunday, so we had a day for her to rest and roam around Puerto Ayora. Saturday morning, we all went to the farmers' Mercado, which was a lot of fun. It was hot even early in the morning. Kathryn wanted to order some Ecuadorian pastries like the ones she had on Isabela—she's a foodie! We spent a couple of hours at the internet store, about the only place you can get online in Puerto Ayora, then had lunch and then dinner on the boat. We had a lovely visit and were, of course, sad to see her go as always.

After Kathryn departed it was time for us to organize for our departure from the Galapagos, arrange for fueling, and obtain departure permits. Each island in the Galapagos has a port captain. To enter or leave a port, the captain where you are currently must contact the port captain at the next port and apply for a Zarpe or clearance permission form. In the Galapagos, this requires an agent who arranges for the Zarpe and our fuel needs. This cost $7.81 plus an agent's fee. The fuel docks were located 32 miles north on the Island of Baltra. To buy fuel we had to tell a government official the amount of fuel we wanted, and pay for the fuel in cash in advance at a special office (or in our case we bought it through a fuel agent in the United States who arranged everything, otherwise we would use our own local fuel agent). The fuel price is set each Thursday morning and holds for 1 week.

Wednesday morning before departing for Baltra, we took a water taxi into Port Ayora to finish up our internet chores and pick up more fresh provisions. We met our agent Ricardo Arenas, who gave us our Zarpe permitting us to move the boat to Baltra. Meanwhile Tom took down our sun shades that cover the outer decks and prepared *Argo* for sea. When I came back, we hauled in our flopper-stoppers (the passive stabilizing system that is intended to help keep the boat stable in a rolling anchorage). When we finished all our preparations and cleaned the lines that had been in the water for 10 days, we called a water taxi to help us raise our stern anchor and untie from the mooring ball. Once completed, we raised the anchor and began to make our way between the densely packed boats at anchor and out to open water and Baltra. It was a beautiful day.

Once out of the harbor, the vistas from *Argo* were simply fabulous. Santa Cruz Island is a volcanic island, as are all 18 islands of the Galapagos. The top of the volcano is shrouded in clouds, and the mountainside gradually descends at 5 or 10 degrees for the 10 or 15 miles it takes to get to the sea. The upper part of the mountain is lush and green, and the mist from the clouds is the only source of water on the island. The flora changes in type and density every few hundred meters until it gradually becomes arid near the sea. The coast is made up of lava rock for the most part, sometimes formed in cliffs, and sometimes in lava flows that end in the sea, punctuated here and there by coral sand beaches that are the destinations of nesting sea turtles and land tortoises during the egg laying season. Off the coast are rock formations; these are the tops of volcanoes that once were above sea level during the ice ages, but now are partially submerged so that only the uneroded part of their cone remains in view. Along the way we saw sea turtles rising for air, and tuna jumping in schools. Galapagos sea lions dove and played along the way. Frigate birds, some males with their red mating pouch visible although deflated, rode the air pressure wave above our boat and hung there for hours. Occasionally a blue-footed booby (everyone loves boobies) would come along, sometimes landing on our railings for a rest. This was maddening for Tom, since the birds often made a mess, and he is devoted to keeping *Argo* in Bristol condition.

Cruising around the Galapagos is somewhat dangerous as the charts are very sketchy and either don't show hazards at all, or fail to show them at the right location. For example, the channel between two islands as drawn on the chart was shown as wide open, yet upon looking at the reality of it, one could plainly see that it was obstructed by a rocky outcropping from the island. In another case, the chart showed a clear and navigable passage and I set our chart plotter and autopilot accordingly. After a couple of hours, we could tell that we were headed into an unmarked ancient volcano top several acres in size! I was told by a local boat captain with whom I consulted before departing Baltra that the charts used until the 1990s were created by Captain Fitzroy of the HMS *Beagle* (the ship that brought Darwin to the Galapagos in 1835) and the current charts aren't any better! About 17:30 we arrived in Baltra and anchored for the night.

At 08:00 the next morning we were called to the dock, but because our agent hadn't arrived yet, they couldn't start pumping fuel. It was a Thursday morning, so this created special problems because our agent had to pay for our fuel before we could load it, and the payment office opens in Puerto Ayora at 08:00, but that is an hour's drive from Baltra. Once the agent arrived, he had to bring the port captain and the head police officer aboard to inspect our yacht and fill out the same paperwork that we completed in Puerto Ayora. This port captain is the one who grants the exit Zarpe, clearing us out of the Galapagos and to the Marquesas. Rebecca and I had to laugh as the uniformed port captain, complete with gold-striped epaulettes, carefully read with arms extended in the most officious manner the Zarpe from Puerto Ayora. He must have read a document like that a thousand times before, yet here he was meticulously examining every period and colon! We concluded that if you are going to be a government official, you have to be able to read the most mundane form as though it were unique and complicated and that its meaning can only be understood in its full complexity by an anointed one.

We needed to buy as much fuel as possible since we planned to leave Baltra directly for the Marquesas, 3,000 miles away. But an expensive problem developed—we discovered that our fuel tank measuring system was very inaccurate; we had sight gauges on each fuel tank, but they were not accurately calibrated and only provided an estimate of the fuel onboard. Basically, the two main tanks had an extra 100 gallons each that didn't show up on the sight gauges. I ordered 1,325 gallons, but as it turned out we could only take on 1,125 gallons, so we paid for 200 gallons that we couldn't put aboard and lost over $1,000 at the fuel price of $5.25/gallon. I have never experienced a fueling procedure like the one in the Galapagos; in addition to being arcane, inefficient from a buyer's perspective, and inconvenient, it seems, like many things here, designed to relieve gringos of as much money as possible. So, at noon we sucked it up and shoved off for the Isle Marquesas. God help us (please)!

Galapagos to the Marquesas

The following section begins each day with the 12-noon entry into our ship's log. The engine rpms were always 1245, so the variance in speed and fuel consumption was due entirely to wind and currents. It is customary to describe the wind direction as the direction from which it emanates, whereas wave direction is described as the flow direction of the waves. For example, an east wind world emanate from the Americas on this voyage and would be called an Easterly, whereas the waves generated would move toward Asia and would be described as westerly seas.

3100 MILES AT SEA

April 24   Departing the Galapagos – Day 1 – Thursday 0°28s/90°26w

We managed to get underway from the fuel dock at 12:00. In leaving Galapagonian waters, I was very cautious in giving a wide berth to hazards, and I transited the waters mostly during the day so I could see as much as possible and avoid unmarked rocks and hazards. Late in the day as we were passing the last reef at a distance I thought would surely be safe, I noticed that the depth sounder was reading 16 feet, then 45 feet, then 85 feet, then

16 feet again. Could it be a reef? Rocks or mountaintops just under us? Had I missed something?

I swung *Argo* directly south and tried to put some distance between us and the island, although we were already 6 or more miles offshore. Then I turned on our special, very sophisticated directional sonar, and, low and behold, there it was. I stepped outside to confirm what the sonar showed; we were enveloped in a living biomass of phosphorescent plankton thicker and denser than anything I had ever seen before. It had emerged from the depths at sunset and was about 100 or more feet thick, so thick in fact that it fooled our sonar into thinking it was a solid mass! Outside, the ocean was all aglow as *Argo* peeled back the water and made its way toward the Marquesas.

The most difficult aspect of crossing the Pacific was knowing that for 17 days we were truly alone; we were out of range for rescue or medical assistance. The beauty and excitement of the cruise and the adventures on land and water did make it worth the risk. My memories are priceless!

-Rebecca

That evening, Rebecca made a lovely apple bread with walnut-brown sugar crust that evening. It was her best yet. She loves to bake, and we are her lucky recipients. Dinner that night was sliced sautéed chicken breasts on a green tossed salad. Dessert: sautéed bananas with rum on soy ice cream. Excellent!

April 25   **At Sea – Day 2 – Friday 2°09s/92°41w**

Noon Position	Course	Speed	G/Hr	WS	Dir	Bar	Wave Dir	Height	Mom
2°09.320 S	242°	7.7 kts	5.9	9.3	E	1016	N	5-9	7 sec.
92°301.41W									

Our route to Nuku Hiva in the Marquesas is 3,168 miles from Baltra. Our goal was to find the South Equatorial Current (SEC) and ride it all the way there. That current could increase our speed by as much as 1 knot and save a considerable amount of fuel, if I can find it. I thought we could locate the current by heading southwest on a course of 240 degrees True until we reached 3 degrees 37 minutes south of the equator and 95 degrees west of the International Date Line (which is roughly midway between the Meridian and the International Date Line in the western Pacific). We selected this precise course because it takes advantage of favorable currents along the way and avoids those that are adverse. The equator is by definition located at 0 degrees, and the Galapagos are 45 minutes south. Since each degree of latitude is 60 nautical miles and each minute 1 nautical mile, the Galapagos are therefore 45 nm south of the equator. Our goal was to be 217 miles south of the equator and then turn west on a course of about 266 degrees T at which point we should be in the SEC. At 7 knots, it should take us about 17 days to make the trip; at 8 knots, it would take about 15 days.

Our first day in the open ocean was very pleasant, and we all agreed that if the remainder of the trip would be like this, we would be lucky and content. The sky was clear, the breeze delightful, and the sea rolled from our port bow gently under our keel. The swells were large, perhaps 8 to 10 feet, but they were widely spaced and *Argo* rose and fell in a pleasant manner. We were in a very favorable current, making over 8 knots and burning less than 6 gallons per hour of fuel; sweet!

Rebecca made a very good Indian curried shrimp and rice dish for dinner with fresh peas from the Galapagos, presented with vegan biscuits and honey. Dessert was fresh Galapagonian pineapple, which is sweet and delicious.

April 26   **At Sea – Day 3 – Saturday 3°53s/95°13w**

Noon Position	Course	Speed	G/Hr	WS	Dir	Bar	Wave Dir	Height	Mom
3° 53.271S	216°	6.8 kts	6.5	28	S	1016	N	6-10	7 sec.
95° 09.353W									

Today was entirely different. A low front was moving south of us, and the wind gusted up to 30 knots. The sea boiled as 8 to 10-foot swells in a short moment slammed into us. The radar showed storms all around us. We had to adjust our course so as to handle the sea state because Argo was sliding sideways off the side of the swells at a serious angle. Everyone was getting nauseated. Bouncing around in a constant state of motion is no fun, and we were also a bit concerned because we didn't know how long this would last, if it would get worse, and how much extra fuel we might consume. I read one account of a yacht that made this passage having to put up with this sort of sea condition for most of the trip. The thought of that was very depressing. As the day progressed and the wind rose, we continued to adjust our heading to accommodate the sea and our speed slowed considerably. It was very unpleasant. We didn't eat much as the rolling of the boat precluded galley activities, and all anyone wanted to do was stay put and try to sleep through it. Late in the day we saw a clearing ahead. The radar showed that the storms had passed. Shortly after sundown the seas subsided to a much more tolerable state, and we breathed a sigh of relief.

April 27   **At Sea – Day 4 – Sunday 5°18s/97°27w**

Noon Position	Course	Speed	G/Hr	WS	Dir	Bar	Wave Dir	Height	Mom
3⁰ 5 17.887 S 97⁰ 25.030 W	265⁰	7.7 kts	5.9	12	ESE	1015	NW	3-7	8 sec.

We awoke to a relatively pleasant day. Swells of 7 to 8 feet approached from our beam to port quarter. Winds had subsided. We still had not found the current we were seeking, and proceeded southwest. Many people never find a good current. I downloaded a fresh set of weather and current charts off the sat-phone, and they confirmed our course and heading. We were making about 6.5 knots and using 6 gph of fuel. A Japanese freighter crossed our course about 10 miles ahead of us, and we saw a whale spout. About a dozen flying fish and squid litter our decks each day. One wonders how they manage to get up on the boat deck, which is 15 feet above the waterline – must be jumping off the top of the waves. Rebecca made a lovely tuna, okra, and grits dinner. It was tasty!

April 28   At Sea – Day 5 – Monday 5°34s/100°15w

Noon Position	Course	Speed	G/Hr	WS	Dir	Bar	Wave Dir	Height	Mom
5° 33. 942 S	265°	7.5 kts	6.0	16	ESE	1015	NW	5-8	6 sec.
100° 15.337 W									

As we continued on our southwestern course, we finally began to see our speed increase, indicating that we had found a favorable current and that our predictions about the location of the current were correct. Our speed increased to 8 knots or above, and we glided over the swells, which were still in the 8-foot range. Later in the afternoon the seas became larger, perhaps in the 10-foot range. It is very hard to estimate the size of the swells, but when they continuously range above the tops of our salon windows they have to be big. To me, they are frightening: huge, menacing, mindless, cold, dangerous, desolate, full of creatures with teeth that are hungry. This is no place for human beings. Am I afraid? Of course, you would have to be a fool not to be afraid. But, we have planned well, and overcoming the fear and trying to manage the risk are part of the adventure. Also, an important part is understanding how to live with the natural world: for example; when the sun rises, or sets, the sea gets very angry out here. The swells grow larger and closer together. After sunset, they lay down somewhat. Later in the evening, the dew point falls and the clouds release their water vapor as rain. Storms dot the radar screen, and near them the wind rises. Overnight the sea builds, and by morning the storms are mostly gone, but the high seas remain. By evening it sometimes calms down, and then it starts all over again. Another interesting thing to me is that the swells change all the time. You can hit a very unpleasant area for 10 or 15 minutes or even less, and then for some inexplicable reason (at least to me) the sea takes on a different character. The same is true of currents.

On Monday afternoon, the seas were high, and I became concerned about our fuel bladder becoming unstable. It had done very well in larger seas, but it was beginning to track around and our lines were not as taut as they had formerly been. We had it lashed down pretty well, but still I thought it would be best to get the fuel into our tanks and off the deck, particularly if things deteriorated overnight. We hooked up our Jabsco 20 gallon/minute 120 V pump to the bladder and the other end into our port fuel tank. In 15 minutes, we had transferred 300 gallons, and we put the rest into the starboard tank. *Argo* was rolling all over the place, and in the process, I pulled a back muscle. I limped around for a while helping Tom get the final fuel onboard, then he took over and cleaned things up and stowed the equipment. With the fuel bladder and its 3,500-pound load below decks, *Argo* rode the waves better.

That evening Rebecca took my watch and recommended that I stay in bed with a heating pad and Tylenol. That was fine with me. I have learned through experience that the best place to be in bad weather is below decks, in bed, assuming someone competent is at the helm.

Night watch on calm seas can be the ultimate meditation experience. I had many hours of quiet and darkness surrounding the pilothouse radar screens. Those were the times I felt so fortunate to be on a great adventure with Randy.

-Rebecca

For dinner Rebecca made seared tuna with sautéed potatoes and corn. We had ice cream and berries for dessert.

April 29   **At Sea – Day 6 – Tuesday 5°49s/103°23w**

Noon Position	Course	Speed	G/Hr	WS	Dir	Bar	Wave Dir	Height	Mom
5⁰ 49. 453 S	265⁰	6.8 kts	8.0	17	ESE	1015	NW	5-9	6 sec.
103⁰ 22.641 W									

I spent all day in bed watching vacuous TV serials and reading a very interesting book, *The Idea Factory*. My back was getting better, and *Argo* was making steady progress. We passed the 1,000-mile milestone (from the Galapagos). Tom and Rebecca stood all the watches for the day. I must say that lying in bed is an excellent way to pass the time; honestly, watching these big waves approaching the boat is not pleasant. While lying in bed you don't think about it or know what is going on. I prefer that, as long as someone is watching. Regarding our watches: we always have someone at the helm. We don't want to bump into anybody out here! So far, we have seen only one freighter; no sailboats. There is nothing and nobody out here. That is a surprise to us; we thought we would encounter at least a few sailboats on the way. Our watch involves an hourly engine room check in which we look over the engine for oil leaks, look at alternator belts, check the shaft and its drip rate, and look over the hydraulic system for water cooling and leaks. We periodically check the rudder and autopilot pumps, as well as the stabilizer fin drives, too. Of course, we check fuel pressures and the fuel level in all tanks. Hourly checks help to assure that if something starts to go wrong we might be able to address it before it becomes an emergency or puts the boat in jeopardy

April 30   **At Sea – Day 7 – Wednesday 6°05s/105°26w**

Noon Position	Course	Speed	G/Hr	WS	Dir	Bar	Wave Dir	Height	Mom
6° 04.617 S	265°	6.8 kts	6.8	17.7	ESE	1016	N	5-8	5 sec.
106° 25.637 W									

It was a relatively pleasant day with light clouds, sunshine, and blue skies. Seas were moderate, but nothing like the beautiful, loping swells off the coast of Baja that we had pictured in our minds as characteristic of the Pacific. There is nothing nice or loping about these waves, which are large, short period swells. On top of the swells are wind waves of a foot or two. The good news is that they are on our port quarter. Winds are constantly in the mid-teens, and the temperature is in the mid-80s all the time.

My back has been getting better, but I was surprised when Rebecca came into our room early in the morning to ask me to get up right away. During his hourly engine room check, Tom had discovered that our hydraulic seawater pump wasn't working. The water flow indicator had stopped. If that situation was allowed to persist, our hydraulic oil would overheat and the system would shut down. This was potentially serious. Without hydraulics we have no stabilizers, and in these seas, that is very dangerous, so I rushed to the engine room. Tom had already cleared storage containers away from the seawater pump and was getting ready to shut off the water to the sea strainer. If we had taken in a squid or jellyfish, it could have clogged the through-hull intake or strainer. I went to the bridge and moved *Argo* perpendicular to the swells so as to reduce the need for stabilizers and then turned off the hydraulic pumps. Tom examined the sea strainer. Nothing. He then took the cover off the pump and examined the impeller: it was good, too. That was a problem; no identifiable problem was a problem. At any rate, he put it all back together and we turned things on. It worked! We don't know what was wrong, maybe a squid or something got sucked into the through-hull opening and then fell out when we shut things down. It was disturbing. In fact, I am feeling the need to do an engine room check again right now!

May 1   **At Sea – Day 8 – Thursday 6°20s/109°28**

Noon Position	Course	Speed	G/Hr	WS	Dir	Bar	Wave Dir	Height	Mom
6° 17.773 S 109° 28.783 W	273°	8.1 kts	5.8	13.9	ESE	1017	NW	7-9	6 sec.

At 12:00 we completed 7 days underway and made 1,300 miles since Baltra. Rebecca is thawing filet mignons for a mini-celebration of our halfway point, which we will probably reach tomorrow. We set our clocks back 1 hour, so we are now –7 hours from GMT, which is the same as Denver or Phoenix. Tom just announced that he found a squid on our fly bridge, about 15 feet above the waterline. That one was a true champion; the fly bridge is a long way up and an indication of how big these waves are. Rebecca is doing her yoga with Priscilla (on DVD) this morning.

We continued on our course of 266 degrees T as we have been doing for several days. *Argo* plugs away, clipping along at 8 nautical miles an hour. For the last 18 hours, we have been in the South Equatorial Current, which flows east to west at a rate of about 1 knot. For us it is a free ride; we are making 8 knots and using only 5.6 gallons per hour of our precious fuel. This is exactly what I had hoped for. We still have wind in the mid-teens blowing at 140 degrees relative, and swells in the 7 to 8-foot range.

Tonight's dinner: fried chicken breasts, spinach, and couscous with nuts and raisins. Dessert? Of course: ice cream (vegan ice cream) and cherries.

May 2   **At Sea – Day 9 – Friday 6°36s/112°39w**

Noon Position	Course	Speed	G/Hr	WS	Dir	Bar	Wave Dir	Height	Mom
6° 35.558 S 112° 39.059 W	266°	7.9 kts	5.5	15.9	ESE	1017	NW	3-6	7 sec.

Today we reached the halfway point, 1,550 miles at sea. We have about 7 or 8 days to go to reach Nuku Hiva. Rebecca cooked up the filet mignons, and we had a delicious dinner, sans red wine, though: no alcohol while underway. We are all looking forward to a brewskie in Nuku Hiva! Everything has been going well. We thought the shaft drip was too slow or nonexistent, so we loosened the collar a bit and readjusted it a couple of times. It was fun. It gave us something different to do.

I was standing outside trying to cool off from being in the engine room when it dawned on me that we hadn't seen a thing since leaving the Galapagos: no airplanes, boats, porpoises . . . nada. We are so far away from anything I don't know if a plane could rescue us. The sea is full of life, though; flying fish and squid litter the decks every morning. Albatross fly about, sometimes convening on a school of fish off in the distance. The waves are so steep at times, a life raft would surely flip over. Well, better to concentrate on something else. Maybe I'll watch another episode of *Breaking Bad.*

May 3   **At Sea – Day 10 – Saturday 6°51s/115°44w**

Noon Position	Course	Speed	G/Hr	WS	Dir	Bar	Wave Dir	Height	Mom
6° 50.873 S 115° 44.036 W	254°	7.8 kts	5.6	12.1	E	1018	NW	4-7	7 sec.

Rebecca's a champ. I don't know what I would do without her. Yesterday she took the late shift, that is, she stayed up till midnight when Tom relieved her, and then was up this morning at 06:50 to relieve Tom. She doesn't sleep well, so despite the fact it was my turn, she got up and let me sleep in. I don't usually have trouble sleeping. Anyway, now she is doing laundry, will take some private time, and then start lunch. She is always on the move! She had some reservations about going on this trip; I think she felt anxious about it, and for good reason I might add. Like climbing a mountain, you have to be crazy to do this. It took a lot of guts for her to come, and she is doing very well. Like a friend of ours says about these adventures: "It's sort of like fun, but different." Her fears are justified, but we are well prepared; others have done it, and so will we.

When we left the Galapagos, we were still having trouble with the watermaker. The low-pressure alarm goes off again. I considered aborting the trip, but thought we could venture out a day or two and see if we could get the thing to work. Same old problem that I thought I fixed by tightening the bolt on the pump (which did help for quite a while). The seawater filter is housed in a clear Lucite container that threads onto a top connected to the machine. It was only partially filling with water. I suspected a vacuum leak. This time I taped the threads on the top of the canister with plumbers' tape. Since then we have used it almost every day with no problems. Maybe I got it this time.

The night sky is something to behold. Of course, there is no light whatsoever except the stars, and last night for the first time on this cruise, a moon. I looked out and almost couldn't believe my eyes as the silvery light reflected off the waves. The moon hung in the crystal-clear, black night sky, surrounded by billions of stars. Seeing the Southern Cross is something of a benchmark in sailing for a Great Lakes fellow like me. It is a wondrous sight to behold.

Rebecca's feast tonight: crab cakes with corn bread, pan-fries, and broccoli.

May 4   **At Sea – Day 11 – Sunday 7°07s/115°54w**

Noon Position	Course	Speed	G/Hr	WS	Dir	Bar	Wave Dir	Height	Mom
7° 06.603 S	266°	7.6 kts	5.3	14	E	1018	NW	3-6	7 sec.
118° 54.082 W									

A beautiful day with 5 to 7-foot swells in our far port quarter. Wind blowing 13 knots on our stern. We checked the fuel and mileage for yesterday: 179 miles using 130 gallons of fuel, 0.8 gpm, just as I have planned all those months ago in Michigan. We should be in Nuku Hiva next Sunday. We did some yoga today, read a little, wrote in the log, and watched some *Breaking Bad.*

Dinner tonight: spaghetti and vegan meatballs, corn, and peaches.

May 5   **At Sea – Day 12 – Monday 7°21s/121°59w**

Noon Position	Course	Speed	G/Hr	WS	Dir	Bar	Wave Dir	Height	Mom
7° 21.913 S	266°	7.5 kts	5.5	12	ESE	1018	NW	2-6	7 sec.
121° 59.201 W									

Rebecca says that we have consumed almost all our fresh stores with only apples, potatoes, onions, and a few other things left. We have plenty of canned and frozen food, so we won't starve. In fact, we probably have enough stored food to last a month or more.

The ocean is very pleasant this morning; following seas of about 2 or 3 feet. It is now 87 degrees with light winds. We are well into our routine. We fill in the ship's log every hour and do an engine room inspection. Rebecca and I take the 18:00 to 24:00 and 07:00 to 12:00 watch. Tom takes the 00:00 to 07:00 and fills in from 12:00 to 18:00 as it seems comfortable. At 12:00 we measure the distance traveled over the last 24 hours and measure the fuel onboard and our rate of consumption. We use the generators for cooking, making water, laundry, and for A/C at night. We usually try to combine a few of these functions and only use our small 13.5-kilowatt generator so as to conserve fuel. We wind up running it about 10 hours a day. It consumes about 1 gallon an hour. On a 20-day trip (give or take a few days), it adds up. At this point it looks like we will have 800 gallons or so to spare when we drop anchor in about 6 days.

At this point, and I surely hope I am not jinxing us, *Argo* has performed marvelously. She is comfortable, quiet, economical, and roomy enough so everyone has some personal space and quiet time. We also have air-conditioning for those muggy nights! She is a perfect boat for our purposes. As I sit in the pilothouse, all I can hear is the low drone of our John Deere engine turning the screw at 1,245 rpm. The waves make muffled sounds as *Argo* pushes them aside; that's it. She moves relentlessly onward about 180 miles per day.

This evening the seas have subsided to their lowest level on this cruise. I estimate that we have 2 to 3-foot ocean swells separated by about 8 seconds and almost no wind waves. The sun is bright and beginning to set. It is 85 degrees with a 12-knot following breeze.

Dinner: sautéed sea scallops, okra, rice with edamame, and cashews in coconut milk. Excellent.

May 6   **At Sea – Day 13 – Tuesday 7°37s/125°03w**

Noon Position	Course	Speed	G/Hr	WS	Dir	Bar	Wave Dir	Height	Mom
7° 37.152 S 125°03.570 W	266°	8.1 kts	5.2	8	ESE	1018	NNW	2-4	12 sec.

Last night was the most beautiful night imaginable. It was truly sublime; it was the picture in the mind's eye that we pursue in our dreams. The sea had settled down to the point that we had hardly any motion on the boat. The wind was refreshingly cool, blowing gently from the astern. When the sun set and the moon dominated the sky, its silvery glow was so bright it illuminated the periphery of the sky in a blue-black glow, almost like a mini-sun shining. The clouds were silhouetted with the moon's metallic light. In the deep space overhead, there were so many sparkling stars in addition to the Milky Way that the blackness of the canopy seemed even deeper. The Southern Cross to our south reminded us that we are cruising in unaccustomed waters, yet the Big Dipper on the horizon to our north reminded us of home far away.

This morning the seas were calm, and life's good! 900 miles to go. We've been doing about 8 knots all day. The sea life over the last couple of days seems to have diminished. We are now over the abyssal plain, which is the name for this area of the ocean. It is almost 3 miles deep in spots, and the amount of plankton seen at night is much smaller than we saw earlier. We do not have any squid coming on deck, and the number of birds is way down. For a couple of nights, we had birds land on our cockpit and spend the night, much to Tom's annoyance, but they are gone now.

Lunch today was the fancy meal: Rebecca ventured into a new place today, a Syrian dish of some sort.

May 7   **At Sea – Day 14 – Wednesday 7°50 S/127°42 W**

Noon Position	Course	Speed	G/Hr	WS	Dir	Bar	Wave Dir	Height	Mom
7° 52.516 S	266°	7.6 kts	5.2	6.5	ESE	1020	E	1-3	10 sec.
128° 09.537 W									

The sun just came up, Tom's off to bed, Rebecca's sleeping in, and I am witness to the wonder of it all. The sky is cast in pink, the puffy clouds floating in the blue sky are touched with pink, and the ocean too has a pink reflection. It is magical. The sea is calm, only a gentle small swell to move

Argo rhythmically. The wind is only 5 knots, the temperature is 83. The current here is a little more confused than we have had so far, and likely to remain so for the duration of our voyage.

Nothing much going on, just moving at about 7.5 knots toward the Marquesas now 700 miles away. The engine hums along, the sound of waves breaking on *Argo's* bow, and the Brahms' *Hungarian Dances* to start things off this morning. We are making about 180 miles per day and using about 150 gallons of fuel. Last night we saw lights in the distance; it was a fishing trawler with its nets deployed. It moved across our bow over the next couple of hours and then disappeared over the horizon. I hailed them on the VHF, but no response, which isn't all that unusual where fishing trawlers are concerned. Seeing it was a bit of a surprise; at first, I thought it was a star. We haven't seen anything since day four, 11 days ago.

Dinner last evening: lobster stuffed ravioli with broccoli, fresh bread, and for dessert a banana chocolate mousse. Wonderful and rich.

May 8   **At Sea – Day 15 – Thursday 8°05 S/130°39 W**

Noon Position	Course	Speed	G/Hr	WS	Dir	Bar	Wave Dir	Height	Mom
8° 07.250 S 131°02.211W	266°	7.7 kts	5.4	9.9	E	1020	W	1-4	10 sec.

Same-o, same-o. Now we are 530 miles away; about 2 ½ days to go. Watermaker is giving us problems again, this time a different and, as yet, an undiagnosed problem. When Tom rises at noon, we'll go look into it. The sky is blue, a high-pressure system continues to dominate, and the sea is all but flat. The ocean is beautifully blue. No marine life or phytoplankton to speak of.

Sort of like an aquatic desert. The night sky was really cool: clouds had moved in and obscured the moon except for a hole someplace ahead of us. The sea was illuminated with a giant silvery spotlight.

May 9   **At Sea – Day 16 – Friday 8°23 S/134°18 W**

Noon Position	Course	Speed	G/Hr	WS	Dir	Bar	Wave Dir	Height	Mom
8° 23.860 S 134° 29.351W	264°	8 kts	5.9	9.9	E	1018	W	3-6	7 sec.

We caught a good current and ran about 8 knots or more overnight. 350 miles, 1 ½ days to go. We have enjoyed 12 days of high pressure, virtually perfect weather. However, it's a little gray this morning: heavy cumulus clouds with some altocumulus mixed in. A weak low must be passing south of us. The winds picked up to 16 knots for a while, and the wind waves picked up too. By 10:00 it cleared pretty much, and things are settling down again. The altocumulus are still ahead of us, so there must be an upper level disturbance somewhere around.

May 10   **At Sea – Day 17 – Saturday 8°32 S/136°09 W**

Noon Position	Course	Speed	G/Hr	WS	Dir	Bar	Wave Dir	Height	Mom
8° 38.656 S 137° 28.850 W	267°	7.3 kts	8	15	ESE	1016	NW	3-6	6 sec.

RPM's are now 1302.

Bad stuff seems to always happen at night. At 02:00 Tom called from the pilothouse; the water-maker failed, and the stabilizer alarm was sounding. The seas had been picking up, and our ride was indeed rougher. Losing the stabilizers would be a big if not dangerous problem. I shut the unit off and tried to restart it, thinking that might get an unknown gremlin out of the works. That didn't work. Tom and I went to the crew's quarters and removed the lower bunk so that we could access the stabilizer unit. The locking pin was locked in place, which it shouldn't have been. A problem with the hydraulic system was one that I dreaded since I have the least knowledge and experience with this equipment. We got the manuals out and looked over all the hydraulic system components as best we could. Nothing

113

was leaking, and everything looked OK. Finally, I called the ABT tech in Ft. Lauderdale, Steve Owens. Ft. Lauderdale was 4 hours behind us, and by this time it was 08:00 there. Lucky for us Steve answered the phone. We spent quite a bit of $1.50 a minute phone time troubleshooting the unit. His diagnosis—a bad locking pin assembly. We would need about a half a dozen parts, which will be transported here by Gus and Lyle, our next guests. In the meantime, we can get along on one stabilizer fin. We could have gotten the fin working by removing the locking pin assembly, but this requires an extremely large Allen wrench that I don't have onboard.

The rest of the night was pretty nerve-racking. The waves were bigger than usual, but *Argo* rode them well. Tom and I started working on the watermaker again, and although we replaced the low-pressure pump with the new one Kathryn brought us in the Galapagos, it didn't fix the problem. We remain very worried. We are all looking forward to getting into port and out of harm's way. Only 100 miles to go.

LANDFALL AT THE MARQUESAS ISLANDS

May 11   **At Sea – Day 18 – Sunday 8°56 S/139°05 W**

08:00 Position	Course	Speed	G/Hr	WS	Dir	Bar	Wave Dir	Height	Mom
8° 56.679 S	252⁰	8.5 kts	11.2	21.8	ESE	1020	NW	5-8	6 sec.
139°57.197 W									

07:00 was the start of my watch. I was excited to get up and see landfall at Nuku Hiva. The pictures of it show a fabulously beautiful, exotic place. Unfortunately, I was called early to the bridge because the seas had become dangerously large. Apparently, the low-pressure system that had been forming over the last day or two had intensified. We were only 9 miles from port, but were experiencing huge and nasty seas. The waves were somewhere north of 15 feet, and they were stacked in very short intervals, maybe 6 seconds. *Argo* was tossed around like a toy; furniture was on the move, things were sliding as she rolled sideways in the storm. With only one stabilizer working, we were all concerned. I turned *Argo* so as to approach the waves at a 45-degree angle.

We kept that course for about 10 minutes. Winds hit 40 knots. Then it began to subside a little. We were 90 degrees off our course and had moved a couple of miles off our rum line to port, but that distance allowed us to turn stern to, and with the lessening of conditions, we made port within the hour and our voyage was safely over.

Nuku Hiva is a dormant, immense volcano that rises thousands of feet almost straight up out of the ocean. Its cliffs are reminiscent of El Capitan in Yosemite, but they are hundreds of times larger. Nuku Hiva is one of the most awe-inspiring geological sights on the planet. The harbor of Taiohae where we are anchored is situated in the cone of the ancient volcano. The sides of the mountain rise steeply all around us except for a slice of about 20 degrees, which is the entrance from the sea. The walls are nearly vertical, and covered in tropical plants and lush greenery. The ocean is cerulean blue and clear. The air is warm, the winds calm, and we have reached a paradise, safely.

We traveled 3,168 miles, burned 2,800 gallons of fuel, and averaged 7.76 knots. Believe it or not, it all went mostly as planned. Now we are in Taiohae at anchor. It is a little village of 2,100 people. There are a couple of little Tiki restaurants, a bank, of course, grocery store, a church, and a few government offices. The bay, which is pretty large, is positioned to allow the ocean swell directly in, so *Argo* rocks and rolls constantly. We will take an island tour while we are here, and spend a few days doing maintenance and poking around before moving along to the next island, Ua Pou.

The Islands and Their History

The Marquesas Archipelago consists of 12 islands lying in the middle of the Pacific Ocean approximately 3,500 miles west of Peru and 3,500 miles southeast of Hawaii. The Marquesas are volcanic islands formed approximately 3 million years ago of basalt and tuff rather than black lava. Each island is different in appearance, yet they are all strikingly beautiful with very tall peaks that rise almost 4,000 feet into the clouds. On the south side of the islands, the passing clouds are caught by the mountain peaks where they disgorge their rain and provide moisture to lush, green, tropical jungles accented with brilliantly colored flowers. On the north side, the islands are generally arid during the dry season.

For millions of years the islands were uninhabited. Human beings arrived sometime between 500 and 300 BC. These adventurous people were probably from Taiwan or the Philippines. They made use of the outrigger canoe that was invented during that time, which made open ocean sailing possible. The islands offered little to support human habitation other than sea birds, fish, rats, breadfruit, and coconuts. There were no large mammals or reptiles. Archeologists have found the remains of dogs, chickens, and pigs of Asian origin, so at some point the aboriginal discoverers must have brought these animals with them to the Marquesas. I have often wondered how ancient people found islands out in the middle of the ocean. It is like finding a needle in a haystack. One of our guides told us that pigs carried aboard ships can smell the scent of land from far out at sea. After a long voyage, they become very agitated when they smell land (as will dogs). If the pig is released into the ocean it will swim toward land. On the other hand, if a dog is thrown into the water it will return to the ship. It is theorized that the original discoverers brought these animals with them on their boats or rafts. Today, Marquesians venerate the pig because of its role in discovering the islands (and they invite them for dinner on special occasions). In language and culture, the Marquesan people are closely related to Hawaiians.

The original Marquesians lived in hunter-gatherer societies. Families owned the rights to land, but individuals who were not part of a landed family were disenfranchised and subject to harsh living conditions. Each island had at least one tribe, and often more. Like other hunter-gatherer societies around the world, each tribe claimed a territory and young men proved their manhood by making war on their neighbors. Losing a battle could very well result in an invitation to dinner: cannibalism was practiced here well into the 20th century. Infanticide was also practiced as a means to control the population. We were told that today incest and rape are the most common serious criminal offenses; during our visit three men were in the tiny jail in Taiohae for these crimes. About a third of the men are thought to be homosexual or effeminate, but are not discriminated against. These men in the ancient days did the cooking and household chores when the women were in the "red zone" and thought to be unclean. Today it is common to see transvestites almost everywhere you go and are readily apparent to the casual observer. They love to party, and the term *gay* is said to have originated here by GIs during WWII.

Many archeological sites can easily be seen all over the islands. Paepaes (pie-pies) are raised stone platforms on which a grass and wood hut was built, and are common. Most have a pit in place to ferment pu-poi (breadfruit). In some places, they are grouped into villages with a ceremonial stage, marriage rock, and other platforms built around a central plaza about the size of a football field. The marriage rock was a large, flat stone about the size of a king-size bed on which the nuptial ceremony was performed and the marriage consummated for all to witness. Apparently, this sparked a rather erotic celebration that went on for days, and was one of the first aspects of their culture that the missionaries sought to eliminate. On Nuku Hiva the ancient village we visited had a large, deep pit used for keeping prisoners. Prisoners usually found their way to the BBQ!

Likewise, the funeral ritual had a special twist to it; ancients believed that the brain was home to the soul and that the spirit of an ancestor would continue to assist the family when consulted during times of crisis. Archeologists have found the heads from many generations of ancestors buried in paepaes. When a person died, the head was severed, the eyes and brains eaten, and the skull placed under a rock in the family's paepae. The body was eaten, the skin used for drum heads and other purposes, the bones carved into ornaments and fishhooks. Grandma apparently helped with fishing too!

The islands were discovered by the Spanish in 1595. Like other aboriginal societies around the world, the Marquesan population was devastated by European diseases. When Commodore Perry arrived in 1813, he estimated the population at 80,000 people, but by 1920 the population had fallen to about 2,300. At that time, the government offered land to any male willing to marry a Marquesan woman and start a family and farm. Today, there are no native pure Marquesians left, but the evidence of the racial mixture from the sailors of whaling ships taking up the offer of land and a family is evident everywhere. There are now about 8,000 people living in the Marquesas.

The islands are named for the parts of a house, metaphorically, all islanders living under one roof; *Hiva* means roof, *Nuku*, as in Nuku Hiva, means roof beam, *Poa* as in Ua Poa means standing pole, *Oa* as in Hiva Oa means lateral timber, etc.

The Islands Today

The weather here is lovely: there is a constant trade wind breeze between 15 and 20 knots, freshening the 85-degree air. Most days are sunny, with an occasional rainy day. Tsunamis are a concern, as Chilean earthquakes give rise to tidal waves that can sweep through the small coastal villages, destroying houses and buildings. The islands are full of wild chickens and roosters, goats, and horses. The roosters crow all the time. They have very beautiful and varied colored plumage. It is a lot of fun to watch them strut about crowing and demonstrating their prowess. Dogs occasionally make a game of chasing the chicks about (perhaps for a snack if they can catch them), which sends the mother hen into a frenzy. People are heavyset; they like fruit and foods that make them fat. Diabetes is surely the number one public health concern. They speak French and drive crew-cab pickup trucks, mostly Toyotas, but some Fords. They are by-and-large Roman Catholic and are family and community oriented. If they don't work for the government, most islanders make a living selling carvings of wood or stone to the tourist stores in Tahiti, or by selling agricultural products like copra (coconut prepared for oil extraction) and other fruit. Unlike Jamaicans, Marquesians bring their children to the beach for a swim frequently. Children are schooled in the village until eighth grade, then they are sent to Tahiti (600 miles south) for the later grades. Many never return, and this is one reason why the Marquesas have such a low population. Men race outrigger canoes in the harbor every afternoon. The outriggers have a very thin beam, are about 20 feet long, and are made of fiberglass. There is a tiny compartment in the middle of the craft for the paddler to sit, much like a kayak. The outrigger pontoon is rather small at about 4 feet long, 1-foot wide, and deployed about 4 feet off to one side of the canoe on two curved rails. Some boats are designed for as many as six crew. They are the fastest human-propelled boats I have ever seen, in addition to being graceful and stable.

Our Experiences

We visited five of the six inhabited islands: Nuku Hiva, Ua Pou, Tahuata, Hiva Oa, and Fatu Hiva.

At **Nuku Hiva** we anchored in the bay near the village of Taiohae. This is the largest town in the Marquesas with a population of 2,300. The bay is formed by the crater of an ancient volcano with the sides of the volcano rising above the sea and enclosing the bay. It is spectacular. The walls of the volcano are covered in lush jungle, and the sun's light changes the color and texture of the mountain every hour. The bay is a turquoise blue, clean and deep. When we arrived, there were about 20 sailboats in the harbor. The bay is open to the ocean, so the ocean's swell rolled in and necessitated a stern anchor to hold *Argo's* bow into the swell. After 17 days at sea and a very rough few hours getting into the harbor, we were anxious to go ashore.

After lowering the tender and securing *Argo*, we went ashore. There we found a dinghy dock of sorts. It was a stainless-steel ladder attached to a quay wall about which 10 or 15 tenders were clustered. The lower part of the ladder's rail was unprotected, puncturing several rubber dinghies that got trapped under it during low tides during the week we were in Taiohae. It was challenging to get ashore. On shore we found our agent, an American named Kevin, who set us up and got us oriented.

Argo needed a fair amount of cleaning and maintenance after our long passage, and we needed several days to walk around and stretch our legs. Taiohae had several little restaurants, one of which was pretty good. It offered several dishes, including pizza that wasn't too bad. They also offered peach Melba with homemade ice cream that I particularly liked. We shopped for food and souvenirs. The most memorable thing we did on Nuku Hiva was to take a daylong tour around the beautiful island. Our tour guide was Phillip, a crusty English curmudgeon who arrived here 16 years ago and never left. Not many things were agreeable to Phillip, but he conducted an interesting tour and was very well informed about local customs and history.

Nuku Hiva is certainly one of the most beautiful places on the planet. The island has two volcanoes, one forming the bay and a larger one forming the high mountains and central plain about 1,000 feet above sea level. It also has a number of interesting villages, including Taipivai, the largest archeological site in the Marquesas that has a hundred or so paepaes and ceremonial plazas, pu-poi pits, and pits to store human prisoners. We found it exceedingly interesting. It was partially overgrown with huge banyan trees, but was restored a few years ago. Herman Melville lived in Tohua Teiviohou and wrote a novel here in 1843. Nuku Hiva has several beautiful bays, lovely beaches, lush tropical jungles, and soaring peaks that have been eroded by wind and rain into fascinating sculptures. We shared the tour with Tom and Karen of Scottsdale, Arizona. They are sailing these waters in a steel-hulled sailing vessel. We enjoyed their company very much.

After 6 days in Nuku Hiva we bade her farewell and hoisted our anchor for **Ua Pou.** It was a bumpy 28-mile passage against both wind and wave. After about an hour at sea we could see the island at a distance; it was breathtaking. It is an emerald green mountain island with 12 huge spires of basalt rising thousands of feet into the clouds. Ua Pou dominates both the sea and one's imagination. It looks like a Jurassic gothic cathedral with spires all about, but of such an immense scale that it boggles and fascinates the mind. We put in at Hakahau, a little bay and village of the same name on the northwest coast. The bay was at the foot of the spires and provided a fabulous vista for the week.

The harbor is tiny and had about 15 boats at anchor when we visited. We didn't think there was any place for us. It has a seawall, but it's short and doesn't stop the swell from circling its way in. We looked about for a place to anchor but had to settle for a spot between two sailboats that were spaced about 50 yards apart. We split the distance and anchored both fore and aft. We were very close to these other boats, that is the way it is done here as the harbors are often very small. Lucky for everyone but, our stern anchor worked like a charm. For the next 2 days, the wind blew and it was cloudy with rain, but we met several other sailors who were interesting, adventurous people who shared their stories and experiences.

The second evening in port we dined at the pension high on a hill above the little village. The pension was built in the Polynesian style and is quite lovely as it is partially open and exposed to the wonderful breeze. Owners Jerome and Elisa met in France. Elisa, a Marquesan, worked as a hairdresser for celebrities while a student at Le Cordon Bleu school of cuisine. Jerome was a commando in the French armed forces. They met in Paris, married, and returned to Ua Pou to take over her mother's pension and build the business. Elisa cooked up a delicious meal of sea bass (200+ pound fish caught in 1,500 feet), yellow fin tuna prepared as ceviche in coconut milk, curried goat, scalloped breadfruit, rice, and topped off with French wine. For dessert, a lovely cake of mango and two other fruits. After dinner, we arranged for a tour of the island with Jerome.

Ua Pou's main town is Hakahau, and it is a nice, clean little village that is home to about 1,500 people. The streets are paved, the homes are nicely kept bungalows, open to the breeze and surrounded by lush, flowering gardens. The town has several little restaurants (that open when the cruise ship *Aranui III* comes in each month), four little grocery stores like those we used to have before supermarkets. The grocery stores have staples and processed food, some frozen meat, beer, wine, and some fresh pastries. They do not offer much in the way of fruits and vegetables because people grow them at home. In the center of the town is an historic paepae that was formerly the home of the chief that founded Hakahau many hundreds of years ago. The paepae is now used as the stage for outdoor dances and other entertainment. The little cruise ship that came into the harbor during our visit afforded us the opportunity to see a Polynesian dance show that they put on for the tourists onboard. All the craftsmen come to town on this day and offer local goods to the few tourists who are there. In the evening, the town put on a BBQ and staged a band on the dock. It was fun, but they do not offer any beverages, only BBQ meats and rice.

The island's beauty is almost beyond description. Most of the island is owned by family clans, and there are very few roads. In the morning, we drove east to a little village that was the site of the original European landing. Considering the cannibalistic nature of the inhabitants, one can only imagine the nature of their reception! Then we ventured to an overlook to see a spectacular vista of the ocean and the island's rugged shoreline from high up the mountainside. Later we drove to a beach where we walked through a path sheltered by an arch of rosewood trees. In the afternoon, we doubled back on the road and went southwest past the little airstrip to the town of Hakahetau and had déjeuner at a little two-table restaurant run by Perrot, a retired French Navy quartermaster. Perrot was a very jolly man and a wonderful chef. Our menu began with a lovely French sauternes accompanied by smoked yellow fin tuna on brioche with crème fraîche, barracuda in a Chinese wrap (like a spring roll), wahoo sautéed in lemon butter, and rice over sautéed peppers. Dessert was chocolate mousse. It was both delightful and delicious. After lunch, we visited the Tetahuna archeological site and the bay at which you could see at least eight of the 12 peaks in a setting, which was unbelievable. The road back to Hakahau provided wonderful ocean vistas as well as an overview of the little town and bay.

The next morning, we bade goodbye and hoisted our anchor for the island of Tahuata, near Hiva Oa. It had rained heavily overnight and was a little windy in the bay, but we set out anyway. After about 2 hours we had had enough; huge seas on the nose. We decided that discretion was the better part of valor and headed back to Hakahau. The government dock was empty, so we tied up there. As soon as we were secure, every person in town came down to the dock to look us over. One gentleman in particular was very helpful and brought us fruit to add to our stores. Jerome dropped down and gave us a car to use and invited us to dinner, which was very kind. The car gave us a chance to see a little more of the island and to buy some heavier items at the grocery.

The following day an American doctor and his companion (Brian and Kim) came to the dock and said that someone had told him that I knew a lot about diesel engines and he wanted my advice. He had run his engine out of fuel because he had forgotten to switch to a tank that had fuel in it. He had been working on it for 2 days but couldn't get the engine started, and his sailboat was anchored in a terrible place that was exposed to the large sea swell. We wondered how anyone managed to live on it considering how it was tossing about. Trying to work in the boat's tiny engine room must have been horrible. Anyway, we volunteered to use our tender to haul his boat, *Albatross*, out of the swell to a quieter place. He went back to his boat and rigged a yoke that could be attached to our tender. Once we were in place he then raised his anchor and I started to pull with our tender. The sea swell was so large that it overwhelmed our tender's ability to pull his much larger boat. The wind pushed his boat around, and my tender just sort of dug in at first, and then turned sideways to *Albatross*. I thought we would have to abandon the project, but gradually *Albatross* began to move and we pulled it clear of the swell. The next problem was to stop it before it ran into *Argo*. The old saw, "No good deed goes unpunished," ran through my mind. Brian dropped the anchor and we tugged on *Albatross* to stop, and it did. The following day he got a mechanic onboard, and by the afternoon he and Kim were on their way.

The next evening, we were evicted from the government dock when the Navy Customs boat came into the harbor. We had to get underway and decided to make a night passage to Tahuata. The passage was 65 miles, and at 5 knots we would be there at sunrise, so we set off hoping that the seas had calmed down. Although the seas were better, it turned out to be a rough passage anyway with head seas and winds.

At sunrise, we made **Tahuata** and beautiful Virgin Bay. Tahuata is the baby sister of Hiva Oa. Its main claim to fame is a trio of beautiful anchorages with beaches on the southwest coast. We anchored there overnight to enjoy the scenery. It was like a page out of *Robinson Crusoe*; a long, beautiful, white sand beach lined with coconut palms and crystal-clear turquoise water. Rebecca and Tom couldn't resist a swim and snorkeling with the tropical fish.

Next stop: **Hiva Oa**, 7 ½ miles away. This is the second largest island in the archipelago and one of two ports of entry. Paul Gauguin is buried here as is singer Jacques Brel. The harbor is the worst we have yet encountered. It is very small. The little village of Atuona is a 1 ½ mile walk uphill. There is a taxi sometimes, but it is atrociously expensive. The harbor has no facilities other than a fuel dock. The dinghy dock consists of steps carved in rocks or cement steps with exposed rebar (to puncture the tender) and no place to tie. It was dangerous and damaging to our tender. The harbor is so crowded that boats must often anchor outside the ineffectual sea wall. The outer bay is very turbulent, and the swell rolls right into the harbor. *Argo* rolled around more at anchor than she does at sea! When this harbor is full, you must anchor in the outer bay if conditions permit. To compound matters, some of the sailors seem very inexperienced, adding to the hazards involved. One wonders at how a port that is so necessary to sailors crossing the Pacific could have such poor services. One can only conclude that the local people have no interest in serving the basic needs of the sailors who call here. Today there are about 30 boats in the harbor; half of the boats are from European countries, the rest from the United States or Canada. There are no boats from South America, India, China, or most of the rest of the world. One afternoon a small 36-foot sailboat came into the harbor with three bedraggled young sailors aboard. They had just made landfall after 36 days at sea!

The little town of Atuona is much like the other villages we visited: it has a population of about 1,200. It has a couple of stores, a bank, post office, gendarmerie, two restaurants, a school, and a Catholic church. Tomorrow (Thursday) everything is closed because it is a religious feast day, and then Friday a marathon is being run, so almost everything is closed. This leaves Saturday (some businesses are open half a day) and Sunday (everything is closed). The harbor is situated in the sunken cone of an ancient volcano. From here you can see four other volcanoes. It is very beautiful. On the lush hillsides are perched lovely homes looking out on the bay and the ocean. Our friends Gus and Lyle joined us here. They brought 50 pounds of parts and supplies for *Argo* with them. Included were stabilizer parts needed for the repair of the port stabilizer. Within an hour of their arrival, Gus was in shorts and working at full speed along with Tom and me. We were on the phone with the manufacturer's technicians for about an hour ($2.50/minute), but finally we got things working.

The next day we visited Atuona and its grocery store and watched the marathon runners. We visited the grave of Paul Gauguin and French singer Jacques Brel high on the hill overlooking the bay and the test of the town of Atuona. Gauguin's grave was interesting. Aside from it being a famous place, visiting artists and admirers place little pieces of art on top of the tomb, some of which are macabre and strange; skulls and bizarre death ornamentation. One evening the four of us decided to go to the Pearl Hotel for dinner. It is a very nice hotel with a reasonable good restaurant. Gus and I decided on a Manhattan to start the evening off. The server and bartender didn't know what that was, so I offered to go behind the bar and make one. After pouring the various ingredients into a shaker, they all seemed to know what it was—a Monaton! After a lovely final evening in Hiva Oa, the next morning we weighed anchor for Fatu Hiva 45 miles away.

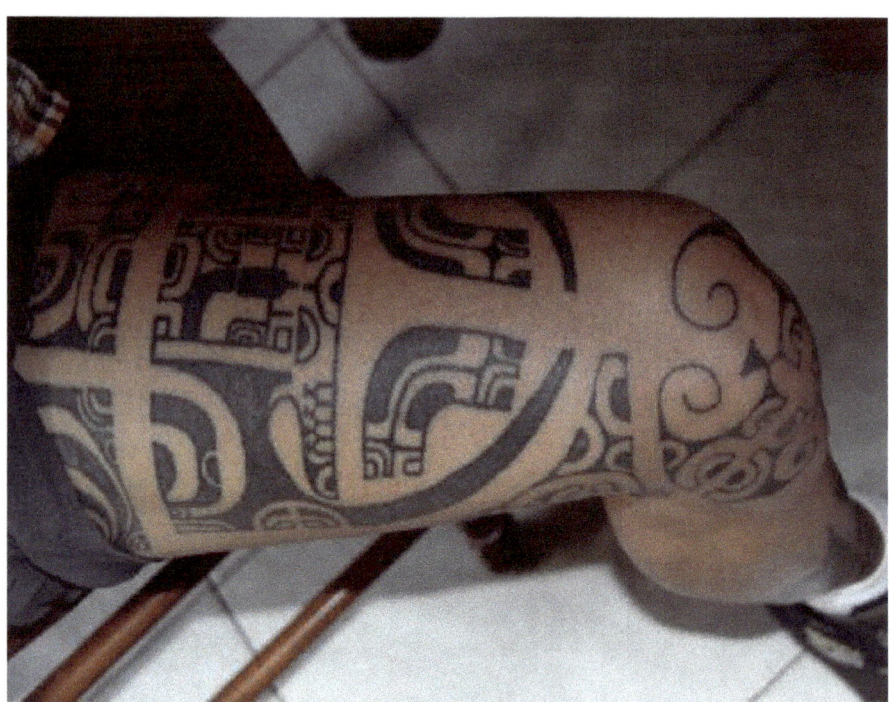

Our cruise to **Fata Hiva** was tough; we were headed directly into the teeth of the dog, so to speak. Although it was only 45 miles, it was a slog with waves in the 10-foot range on the nose and winds up to 35 mph. Gus and Lyle were turning green. Rebecca, Tom, and I were in less than peak condition, but *Argo* pushed along, plowing through the waves at around 7 knots. This was the first test of our recently repaired stabilizers, which thankfully were now working fine. Once we got behind the lee of the island, things calmed down and within an hour we found the little bay of Hana Vave and its fantastic cliffs and sculptured mountains. The harbor was very deep, and we laid out 450 feet of chain on 110 feet below. We also deployed our flopper stoppers to dampen the roll. The main concern for us in this harbor was the very high winds that blew down from the mountains; 45 knots were not uncommon, and the wind blew constantly. I worried that the wind could cause us to drag our anchor and pull us off the sand shelf. If that happened we would be in much deeper water. As it turned out, our anchor held well and we didn't move an inch over our 3-day visit.

The bay was bordered on three sides by huge cliffs that were covered in coconut palms on one side, a narrow rocky beach opening to a valley in the middle, and massive, high, wrinkled cliff on the third side. Behind the sea cliffs were even higher ridges of the inside cliffs of an extinct volcano. The mountainsides were perhaps 3,000 feet straight up! Above the little village were four or five tremendous rock formations; one looked like a carrot with its leaves pulled off but the stem intact, the second was a dead ringer for the largest penis I have ever seen, and one had a top that from a distance looked like a bust of George Washington. The scene was unbelievable.

We dropped the tender and went exploring in the little village. It was lovely and very isolated. There were about 300 people living here in a sort of paradise. The only way in or out of Fatu Hiva is by boat. The village lies within a valley formed by very steep and beautiful mountain cliffs. It was Sunday, and things were pretty quiet, although Gus approached one woman sitting on the stoop of her bungalow and inquired as to where there might be a restaurant. Luckily, she spoke a little English. There aren't any restaurants here in the sense they exist in a city, but people do cook for others in their homes. The lady called her friend who was known to make pizzas. The pizza maker asked if we had French Polynesian francs, what kind of pizza we wanted, how many of us there were, et cetera, and then said she would make a pizza for us. We were directed down the road, past the chief's home, around and across the bridge over the stream, and then back to that house painted blue with a corrugated steel roof . . . over there. It was a very lush, green, verdant area. When we arrived, there was a little sign out front advertising "Pizza to Go" in French. We sat in her utility room while she made our pizza in the kitchen. Pigs were oinking in the backyard, roosters cock-a-doodled, dogs barked, and all was right with the world on Fatu Hiva. She put a tropical fish-colored oil cloth on the table, and her husband brought out four plastic porch chairs. We had wonderful, fresh, homemade lemonade to drink. It was served in a previously used large Coke bottle. We all enjoyed it.

That afternoon a couple we had met in Panama came cruising into the harbor on their lovely yawl named *Amelit III*. Kaj and his friend Eva are from Sweden. We entertained them on *Argo* in Panama, and now they returned the favor with an invitation for drinks. It was a welcomed change from our normal routine. Kaj showed us a video he had taken of his experience of being arrested in Venezuela. It seems he was cruising up a river and hit a power line. An entire village lost its power. He was arrested in short order and briefly put in jail. The story was very interesting and too long for this journal, but the result was that the authorities spoke only Spanish and demanded $800,000 in damages. He wound up settling for $5,000! Pretty darn good negotiating, I'd say.

We returned to *Argo* and grilled a beautiful yellow fin tuna that we bought from a fisherman that morning for 10 francs. It was delicious. The next morning, we pulled the anchor for the Fakarava Atoll in the Tuamotu Archipelago 540 miles to the south.

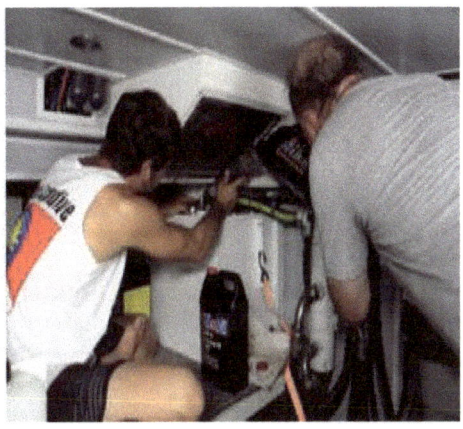

Boating in the Marquesas

Fueling: There are only two ports at which to take on fuel: Hiva Oa and Nuku Hiva. It is necessary to make a reservation for the time and the amount of fuel needed. In Nuku Hiva they were very low on fuel when we arrived and would only permit 200 liters of fuel per yacht until the supply tanker arrived a week later. If you intend to sail to the Marquesas, I would recommend using a fuel agent. When checking into the country, a tax-free fueling certificate can be obtained for cruising yachts. We had enough to put off fueling for a couple of weeks, so we elected to take on fuel via a tanker truck in Hiva Oa. This required a stern tie, which meant backing *Argo* to the dock after deploying the bow anchor, holding her into the swell until stern lines could secure her from moving side to side, and then tightening the whole thing up. In our case there were two other yachts tied to the pier, so sidewise motion was a danger. Rebecca went ashore first, Tom manned the stern and threw lines to Rebecca, and I maneuvered *Argo*. A fuel truck showed up in short order, and we passed the hose via our tender to our stern and began filling our tanks. It took about an hour to load 2,000 gallons, and then we were full of fuel again. The price was about $1/gallon higher than in the United States.

Food and Other Supplies: Each island has several small grocery stores that carry the basics. There is a limited selection of frozen veggies, only baguettes in the morning, small amounts of fruits and onions, carrots, and potatoes. People here grow their own fruit and cultivate their own vegetables, so these items are not available in stores. In Nuku Hiva there was a fresh vegetable market that had tomatoes, lettuce, and cucumbers as well as breadfruit and almost everything else we wanted. Nuku Hiva is unusual in this regard because it is a large island that has a large fertile plain in the center where the volcanic crater once existed, and it is at a high enough altitude, gets enough rain, and has moderate temperatures that make the cultivation of vegetables possible. Beer is about $3 a bottle. Things are expensive.

Boat Supplies: There are no boat supplies in the Marquesas. There are hardware sections in some stores, but if a boater doesn't have it aboard, he is unlikely to find it here.

Communication: The internet is very slow, limited, and costs about $7 an hour. Local phone service is available, as is AT&T roaming. Via AT&T you can text, snap-chat, and pick up data at a high price. Tom uses iMessage via the internet to keep costs down.

Stern Anchors: There are no marinas, and all the anchorages that we saw or knew of are exposed at least partially to the ocean swell, which means the boat is in constant motion and tends to roll from side to side unless it can be held into the waves. This is something that we had never read about and has proven to be quite annoying and energy depleting. The harbors are very small, and at this time of year are crowded with sailboats making the passage across the Pacific. About 300 boats a year make this passage. We are the only motor yacht we have seen so far and the largest yacht that we have seen in any harbor, save for a 120-foot magnificent ocean racing sloop. In order to anchor in one of these tiny harbors you must be able to control the boat's swing. We use a 65-pound Fortress anchor, which seems perfect for *Argo*. We deploy the forward anchor first, then lay out enough scope to set it properly, then lay out an extra 100 to 200 feet and back to the desired place at which time we deploy the stern anchor. Then we lay out enough line to hopefully get it set, and then move forward by reeling in the bow anchor until the stern is set. Then we move farther forward to tighten the stern line. Sounds simple, doesn't it? It has taken us a considerable amount of time to learn to do this without scratching everything up and wearing ourselves out.

Most boaters deploy their stern anchor with their tender, and we do too on occasion. First you load the anchor in the tender, haul it out to the desired location with enough line, and then throw it overboard. Hopefully no one has line wrapped around a leg or foot and the tender isn't damaged by the anchor flukes. If the anchor sets, you won't have to pull it up and do it all over again. In my experience, stern anchors only work well in shallow water. In Nuku Hiva, we tried several times to set the stern anchor in 45 feet of water. We may not have had enough scope out or the bottom was too hard, but in any case, the anchor came loose over time and wrapped around our main anchor chain. To untangle things, we had to haul up the main anchor and deploy Rebecca and Tom in the dinghy, spend the better part of an hour unwrapping heavy lines and chain from our tender, while it bounced around on a 5-foot swell.

An aluminum Fortress anchor seems like a good choice for the stern anchor application. It is relatively light, can be disassembled for easy stowage, and can be rigged with a trip line so that you can pull it up from the crown rather than the stem. It took us quite a while to figure this out and get this system to work well.

Watermaker: We have also experienced a learning curve with this all-important machine. The water here has a lot of algae and marine life in it, and in the harbors, there is a lot of sand that gets churned up. Our 5-micron filter gets clogged very quickly. The main thing I have learned is to have patience, make water in calm seas (although cavitation issues in rough seas creates problems on our boat), and have a lot of filters on board. We also added a small amount of bleach to our water tanks to make sure nasty microbes weren't reproducing.

Formalities of Checking In: We joined Pacific Puddle Jumpers, which made things very easy because they organized local agents to take care of us and they arranged to have the bond waived for our yacht and crew. The government extends a 90-day visa with a simple application; 90 days was enough time for us. We found complying with all the formalities quite easy. Boaters normally have to post a $1,500 per person bond with a bank or show a ticket for a return flight home, but this too can be easily dealt with without posting the bond. Customs is concerned with how much booze is aboard and they count the bottles (and cigars), but there is no duty imposed on ship's stores. All-in-all it was a simple, pleasant experience.

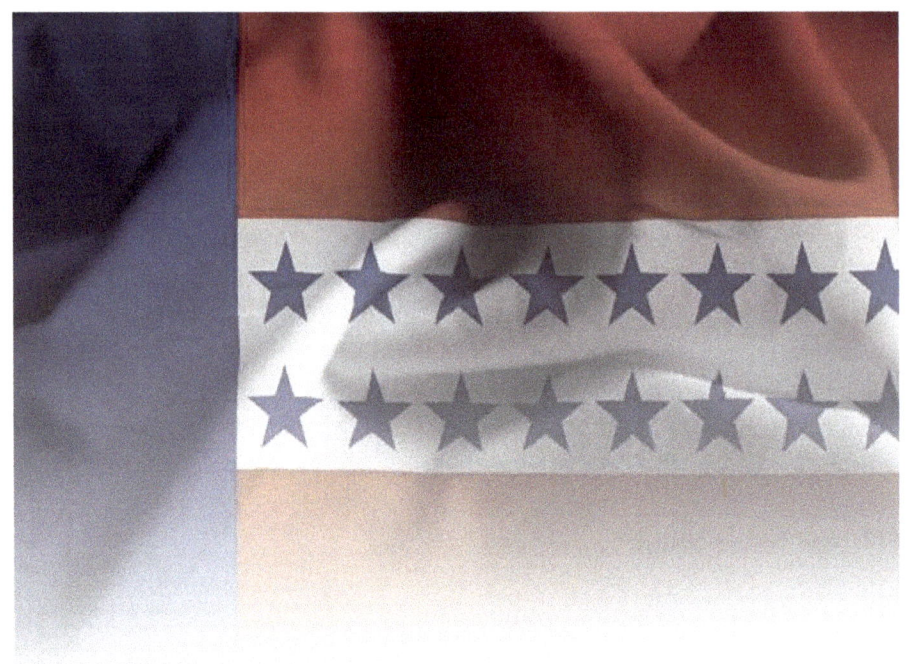

TUAMOTUS

June 3–June 28   **The Tuamotus**

The Tuamotus is an archipelago made up of 77 atolls. Each atoll is composed of a circle of motus or islets made of coral sand and rock perched on the rim of an ancient volcano and enclosing a lagoon. The motus are barren except for coconuts and breadfruit trees, and have a maximum elevation of about 10 feet above the sea. The only source of fresh water on these islets is rainwater. There are no fruits or vegetables on these atolls, nor are there any indigenous animals. There is almost no known history to these islands, but it is thought that human beings first came here from the Marquesas in 1000 AD. The motus enclose a lagoon, the largest of which is about 20 miles in diameter. The atolls are very beautiful and contain a wealth of sea life that is relatively easy to access and are some of the best dive sites in the world. In cruising near the Tuamotus, one is struck by the contrasting color of the deep blue indigo ocean, the light sand of the motu shoreline, the green of the coconut palms, the aqua of the lagoons, and the white of the clouds sailing across the light blue sky.

Passage to the Tuamotus

We left the beautiful anchorage at Fatu Hiva at 10:30 and headed for Fakarava 540 miles southeast, one of the more popular and larger atolls in the archipelago. The seas were calm for the first couple of hours, then we passed outside the shelter of Fatu Hiva and the swells built and built until we were in high, combing seas of 10 to 15 feet. Waves of this size are really large and quite intimidating. *Argo* did nicely, but Lyle was green and seasick and spent most of the next 2 days and nights on the couch in the salon trying to remain as quiet as possible. The rest of us had varying degrees of mal de mar, but all in all we were in decent shape. After 15 hours of somewhat miserable conditions, I began to consider alternatives to lessen our discomfort. After a group discussion, we decided to alter to a less strenuous course and go to the little atoll named Ahe. Just then the hydraulic alarm sounded, indicating an overheating situation. This is a critical problem for *Argo* as she needs her stabilizers to maintain her posture, otherwise she would roll uncontrollably in these seas. It was pitch dark, and the swells were huge, but we needed to shut down the hydraulics and the stabilizers. Gus and Rebecca stood by the doors to the pilothouse trying to see the exact direction of the waves so that I could be sure to point her into them and avoid rolling violently from side to side as much as possible. Tom, who was now awake, rushed to the engine room to look at the impeller on the hydraulic cooling pump. We had changed it in Panama, so he knew exactly what to do. In an amazingly short period of time he had it replaced and we resumed our course in comfort and confidence. After things were repaired, he brought the defective impeller up to the pilothouse and I could see that it seemed to have overheated; strange for something that should be pumping water. (Later we concluded that cavitation caused the pump to air lock and burn out the impeller. When we had *Argo* hauled in New Zealand we had scoop strainers installed so as to force water into the pump. That did the trick and solved the problem.) On our new course to Ahe the angle to the swells improved and things got a little better. After a couple of hours Lyle started to come around and everyone seemed to perk up as the waves were still huge, but their moment lengthened, allowing *Argo* to ride up and down rather than roll sideways off them.

On the third day, we began to feel better and almost enjoy the cruise when the hydraulic alarm sounded again (36 hours later). This was an unwelcomed surprise. Once again, we had a potentially serious problem on our hands. Thankfully it was daylight and the waves were somewhat better for dealing with this problem. I turned *Argo* into the waves again, and Tom and Gus flew to the engine room. Tom checked out the strainer and then the impeller. The strainer was clear, but all the blades of the impeller had been sheared off. We looked for an obvious reason for this unusual part failure, but nothing seemed apparent. We replaced the impeller and things returned to normal, for a while. We talked about the problem and concluded that the seawater strainer had begun to rust. It looked as though small bits of it could have broken loose and made their way into the impeller, shearing off the rubber blades, although this was unlikely. (Later, after consultation with experts, we learned that Globe Impellers can weaken over time. The impellers, although recently purchased, were probably defective, leading to their failure. No more Globe Impellers for us!) By 06:30 we were close to Ahe and looking forward to anchoring in a calm harbor.

Ahe Atoll

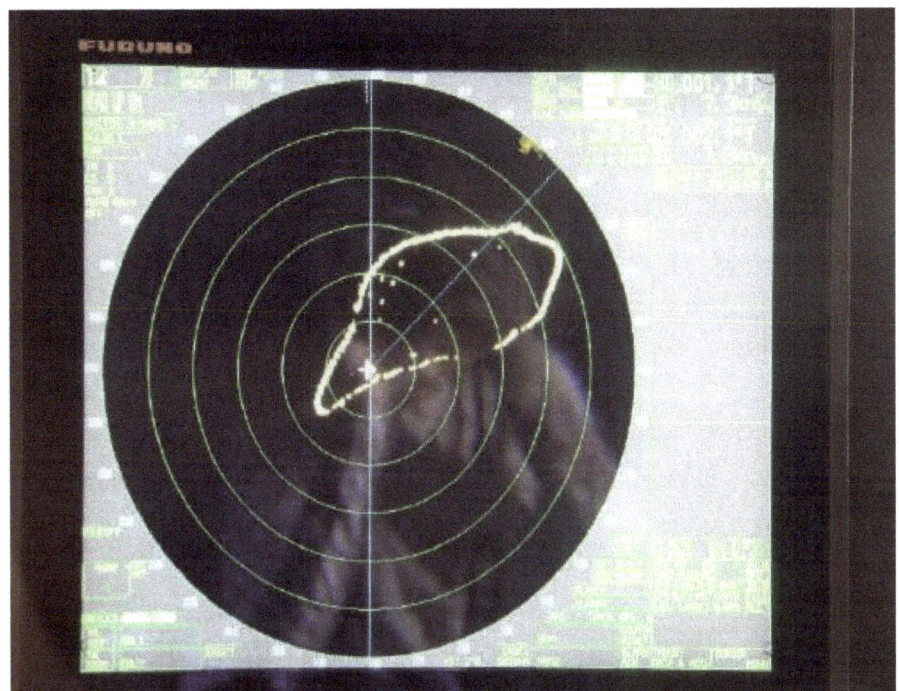

Getting into atolls can be difficult, and most have only one entry pass or channel. In the case of Ahe, its entry pass was very narrow (maybe 50 feet), very shallow (13 feet), surrounded by coral shelves, subject to very swift currents at tidal changes (9 knots), and requiring mid-channel turns. The ocean near Ahe is over 18,000 feet deep and rises almost straight up to the motus or islands. The little islands that make up the atoll are like beads on a necklace. Once inside the atoll the lagoon is comparatively shallow, crystal clear, and a beautiful turquoise. The motus are white sand islands covered in coconut palms. Some of the motus have houses on them, and the lagoon near them is dotted with buoys that are attached to oyster beds that are used to cultivate the famous Tahitian black pearls. The Ahe lagoon is about 16 miles long by 8 miles wide. At one end is a little village with a government dock at which we moored. It was the first time since leaving Shelter Bay Marina in Panama that Argo was in a calm anchorage.

Robert R. Tisch

As Fatu Hiva's Bay of Virgins disappeared over the horizon, we began an arduous voyage to the Tuamotus. After three pounding days at sea, the sight of land on the horizon was most welcomed. As we neared the island, we spotted the narrow channel through the reef into the lagoon. As waves crashed over the rocks, methodically our Captain, Randy guided Argo slowly and safely into the calm, majestic lagoon with the help of his capable first mate Rebecca. Once inside the sunken caldera we found the refuge of calm seas and picturesque white sandy beaches abutting the turquoise water.

It was a thrilling experience!

-Gus and Lyle Gialamas

See YouTube Video Standing Out From Pass Tareoa, Tuomotus

144

The village was home to a couple hundred people. They started showing up at the dock when we arrived: kids in swimsuits or underwear, adults riding three-wheeled bikes, men interested in boats, the local gendarme, and several transvestites. The village had two streets and an intersection. The homes were small bungalows on paved streets surrounded by tropical plants and flowers, and each had a rainwater collection system for drinking water. There was a Catholic church and a Mormon temple of sorts and the only restaurant was a hamburger stand that for $13 provided fries, a burger, and a drink (the voracious flies were complimentary!

The first day in port we rested and took a swim off our swim platform. Tom dove *Argo's* bottom to see if anything was clogging the water intake for the hydraulic cooling pump or the watermaker. His report: all was in apple pie order! Our conclusion is that the problems with the watermaker and the cooling pump are the result of cavitation caused by turbulent seas. This causes air to be sucked into the pumps, lessening their effectiveness. The proposed solution is to install scoop strainers to the hull at our next haul out, which would force water into the intakes when we are underway and lessen or eliminate the problem.

The second day we took an 8-mile excursion across the lagoon to the lovely Pension Chez Raita for lunch. When we arrived, Raita was standing on the white sand beach, ukulele in hand, singing Polynesian songs that she recorded in her youth (CDs anyone?). The scene was picture postcard perfect.

Lunch was served after a refreshment of fresh lemonade and fried banana chips. Raita and her husband, Willy, told us about their life on Ahe and their travels. They come to the United States each year to visit relatives and for shopping and skiing; she shops, he skis. Lunch began with an appetizer of thinly sliced pearl oysters marinated in garlic, oil, and lime served on an oyster shell. These shells are rather flat and about 8 inches in diameter, not like the typical New England variety. The entree was fresh white fish sautéed in breadcrumbs and coconut, accompanied with breadfruit, green beans, and a nice white Bordeaux. Dessert was a fabulous yellow cake with a vanilla cream center and chocolate glaze frosting. Rebecca doesn't eat much, but she did eat that!

The next day, Sunday, we had hoped to move up the lagoon to anchor at Chez Raita, but unfortunately a squall line came through and it rained torrentially all day. We tried playing cards, but soon migrated to watching movies. The next day, Monday, the sky cleared and we got underway at 06:30 for Rangiroa 75 miles to the south. We tried fishing, but only succeeded in losing a couple of lures and catching the fattest skipjack we ever saw. It was a pleasant cruise, if not productive, and we arrived in Rangiroa about 18:00.

Rangiroa

Prior to entering a harbor, we study the navigation charts carefully, obtain tide information, and talk with others who have been there—sailors if possible. Prior to coming to Rangiroa we learned that the 125-foot French customs military boat hit a reef nearby and sank. This was very unsettling. Our charts showed the path to Rangiroa as a rhumb line course through the very narrow Tiputa Pass, which required several turns in a narrow channel to avoid reefs. We approached the pass at 18:00 hours. The sun was setting, it was getting dark rapidly, and in order to make a safe passage we needed light to see the banks of the channel. Time was of the essence. From the pilot-house, we could see a channel between two motus with white water and high surf rolling in from the ocean to the mouth of the channel. The chart showed the channel to be surrounded by reefs and subject to strong currents. Because the surf was high I judged that the current was outflowing, which was favorable to our entry because it would aid our steering if it wasn't too strong (more water flowing past the rudder makes the rudder answer up faster, causing the yacht to turn more responsively). We proceeded nervously, judging that we still had enough light to see the banks of the channel. *Argo's* bow began to lurch from port to starboard as the swells pushed her from one side to the other. She was pitching up and down about 8 feet as the waves rolled under her. I didn't fight from the helm, but let her move in a natural manner. As we moved forward, the side-to-side movement increased, but we seemed to have steerageway, so I maintained about 7 knots speed and hoped that we would stay online without exerting additional force, which might result in a lot of unproductive maneuvering. Slowly we moved forward, and finally we began to leave the swell zone, mindful of the waves crashing on the reef to either side. As the waves subsided, our speed fell off rapidly; we had entered the narrow zone where the outgoing current is confined and focused. As our speed dropped I increased our rpm so as to maintain steerageway. The current was so strong that 2,100 rpm (which would normally move us at 10 knots) was now propelling us at just under 4 ½ knots. This was another tense moment. We had the wing engine and thrusters ready to use if we lost headway, but after a very long 2 minutes we began to gain speed against the apparent 6-knot current. Tom was on the bow pulpit looking for coral heads. When our speed reached 6 knots I began to ease back on the power so that we could make a 45-degree turn to port and not overrun the turn and slide into the next reef. *Argo* didn't turn easily because of the current, and I couldn't be sure of the accuracy of our charts in such a confined space, but in due course we made the turn, and we were past the reef and safely inside the atoll. By then it was pitch dark. We could see the mast lights of several boats at anchor, and we began to look for a suitable place to drop our anchor. Not all sailboats turn on their masthead lights, so I turned on our night vision to try and see them in the dark.

Special skills are required when anchoring in an atoll or near coral formations. The seafloor can be spotted with coral heads and rock piles. If you anchor near any of these obstructions, the anchor chain can become entangled or wrapped around them as the boat turns in the wind. If a swell forms and rolls under the boat, it can raise the forecastle and potentially damage the boat if the chain holds it firm and makes it impossible for the yacht to answer the sea state. In the case of Rangiroa there is a 20-mile fetch across the atoll, so large waves were possible under certain wind conditions. The recommended way of dealing with this problem is to lay out extra scope, buoyed by a float so as to isolate the boat from a chain that is caught on a coral head.

We used our sonar to identify an area without coral heads and wound up anchoring in 75 feet of water. We laid out 450 feet of chain and then enjoyed one of Rebecca's masterpieces of galley fare: a wonderful dinner of scallops, risotto, and bok choy with a lovely white Bordeaux followed by rum bananas and ice cream for dessert.

The Rangiroa Atoll is about 75 miles in circumference and encloses the second largest lagoon in the world. It has the largest village in the Tuamotus and is also one of the world's top dive sites. Many divers from around the world come here, particularly Japanese divers, to experience the coral reefs at the two passes, Tiputa and Avatoru. (The Japanese divers are the ones with large and exotic underwater cameras and multiple electronic gadgets attached to their arms and dive suits.) These reefs are large, in good condition, and home to an amazing variety of sea life, including tuna, sharks, and dolphins. Inside of Tiputa Pass is a large lagoon reef that we circled on our way into the atoll. It is situated in quiet water and perfect for beginner divers. The locals call it The Aquarium, and for good reason; it is full of colorful fish of many species, including lemon sharks, barracudas, and moray eels. Gus, Lyle, Rebecca, and I took our initial scuba qualification dives here shortly after we arrived.

The Tuamotus are coral motus or islets and have no native edible plants other than coconut and breadfruit. Fruits and vegetables are scarce. Onboard we have stored fruit found in other parts of French Polynesia, including a grapefruit-like fruit called a pamplemousse. This fruit is about two or three times the size of a grapefruit, but sweeter. It's delicious. There are a few restaurants here that offer wonderful fresh fish and New Zealand lamb and beef. The one thing I have particularly enjoyed is tuna ceviche salad prepared in coconut milk. It is heavenly.

The beaches are coral rock and sand, not really suitable for swimming. They are lined with coconut palms. The water is crystal clear with the color ranging from turquoise to indigo to cerulean blue. Absolutely gorgeous. Besides tourism, the Tuamotus are home to the black pearl industry. We toured a pearl farm located just west of us that has over 2 million oysters under cultivation. During our visit, they operated on oysters and showed us how a blank seed (obtained from mussels raised in the Mississippi River) is inserted in the appendix of an oyster and how they graft another piece of an appendix from a sacrificial oyster to start the process of culturing a pearl. It was very interesting, and of course they had a showroom with plenty of inventory.

Tom's objective since beginning this voyage has been to become a Master Scuba Diver, and to that end he has been diving almost every day. One of his dives was on the outside reef at Tiputa Pass where a number of dolphins are known to come in from the sea every afternoon. During an afternoon dive, one of them approached Tom, rolled onto its back and closed its eyes while he stroked its stomach. The dolphin stayed with him for a couple of minutes until an older dolphin, perhaps its mother, urged it back to the pack and they all swam out to sea together. While Rebecca and I were diving the reef earlier in the day, we saw several dolphins, including one mother with baby, which was thrilling. That experience made us feel as though we were part of the whole panoply of sea life. While we were hovering in the current at a depth of about 75 feet and enjoying the dolphins, below us at 125 feet or so was a very large school of several hundred fish, perhaps Maori perch or bream. There we saw several beautiful, spectacular, silver darts in the sea; whitetip and blacktip sharks cruising outside the school of fish and occasionally darting through them. When a shark did so, the whole school scattered like sparrows on the wind. As we drifted along and past this area of the reef, I must admit to looking behind and over my shoulder to see if any sharks were following; an unavoidable consequence of being part of the *Jaws* generation.

The nearest motu to our anchorage has a very nice hotel located on it, the Kia Ora, which features Polynesian style huts and bungalows with thatched roofs, some built over the turquoise blue lagoon, others in a village configuration. It is a Polynesian paradise for sure and just the sort of place that is featured in everyone's dreams of the South Pacific. Our friends, Gus and Lyle, treated us to 3 days in one of these splendid over-the-water bungalows at the end of their visit on *Argo*. It was just what we needed after a long voyage, and a very generous gift, indeed! We were particularly grateful to be at the Kia Ora as it had been about 10 weeks since we had been in a first-class restaurant with a bar. After 3 days at Kia Ora, we bade a fond farewell to our good friends and returned home to *Argo*. When we arrived back aboard *Argo* she was shinier than new. Tom had taken this 3-day respite at anchor as an opportunity to wax and clean her after months of sea time. She looked beautiful. At this point, after 5 months underway she is the only motor yacht we have seen in the South Pacific.

We stood out from Rangiroa at 07:30 Sunday morning June 22 bound for Tikehau, a small atoll about 20 miles west of Rangiroa. We made Tiputa Pass at slack tide and enjoyed a glorious passage to Tikehau. The sky was clear, the weather calm, and the day was perhaps the best of our cruise so far. A few minutes out of the pass we were joined by a pod of the largest dolphins we have ever seen. They swam toward *Argo* and jumped high in the air as if to celebrate finding us and to announce their presence. Several of them were perhaps 8 or 9 feet long and 300 or 400 pounds. They were fabulous animals and a joy to see!

Tikehau

Tikehau is a small atoll like Ahe, but known as a great dive spot. Its most famous dive site is inside the lagoon and is a manta ray "cleaning station" where mantas come to have resident fish clean them of parasites.

We made Passe Tuheiava at slack tide, and the passage through it was straightforward and uneventful. We turned south in the lagoon, went about 6 miles to the main village Tuherahera, which is home to a couple of pensions, a luxury hotel similar to Kia Ora, and a dive shop. We called the dive shop and arranged two dives at the pass for the following morning.

At 08:30 sharp the next morning (Monday) Fanny and her dive boat crew arrived. Fanny was a lovely 20-something French national who was full of energy and enthusiasm as well as an expert diver. She took Tom and me first to the reef inside the lagoon to see if any manta rays were in for a cleaning; unfortunately, they were not. Then we went outside the pass for two dives, one on each side of the channel. The water was 83 degrees with a brilliant blue sky overhead, no wind, and a sea as calm as a millpond. We donned our scuba tanks and fell back off the aluminum boat into the sea. Suddenly we were practically weightless and enjoying the illusion of flying over the coral reef. As we descended to 93 feet we could see large schools of fish, including bigeye tuna, Maori perch, jacks, snappers, barracuda, thousands of tropical fish of every imaginable color and configuration, a large whitetip shark, and a huge emerald green and blue, domed-head Napoleon fish that surely weighed in at 100 pounds and just casually floated past, looking at us curiously. It was glorious. We arrived back at *Argo* at 14:00 and enjoyed a lunch on the back deck. Rebecca had stayed aboard and accomplished most of the items on her list: doing six loads of

laundry, baking a couple dozen cookies, cleaning the shower, and miscellaneous other tasks. She is a doer!

On Tuesday, a squall line moved through and brought with it wind and rain, so we stayed onboard. On Wednesday cabin fever got the best of us and we took the tender to town despite the squalls. Tuherahera covers most of a small motu. It looked to be home to about 1,000 people. The roads are nicely paved, and the homes are a sort of bungalow ranch style and placed on about a half-acre of land. Some have glass windows, while others are just open to the breeze. Many are surrounded by beautiful tropical flowering plants. There are two Catholic churches with large buildings for social events. Everyone seems to have a car, truck, or motorbike, which seemed surprising to us given that the motu couldn't be more than 2 miles long and a few hundred yards wide. Anyway, everyone has a vehicle. Fanny, our dive instructor, told me that since there is no gasoline station on the motu, people ship their gasoline in from Tahiti in drums. They need a truck to carry the barrels from the dock to their boats. There are a couple of small restaurants, but they keep irregular hours so no one knows when they are open unless they call the proprietor on the phone (if it is working). The village has a tiny grocery, but it has no fresh vegetables or fruit. I don't know what people eat here, but I do know that seafood gets a little boring after a couple of weeks. There are no shops or stores for any other products. I suppose people go to Papeete by plane if they need something, which is 170 miles due. Maybe they order by phone or on the very slow internet and have it shipped via the weekly supply ship that comes. Roosters strut about and crow all the time, and large-eared dogs are everywhere. Vacationers from Europe are the most frequent visitors. There are no bars or other forms of entertainment, but there are a couple of pensions that cater to the tourists. So, it isn't much of a place for a single person; honeymooners, on the other hand, flock here. The motu has three things going for it: beautiful pink coral beaches, magnificent sunsets, and lovely dive sites. If you are looking for a place to vacation that's away from it all, and I mean all, Tikehau is it!

On Thursday, another squall line was passing through. In the Tikehau Atoll, waves have a fetch of about 10 miles, so they can build to a muscular size in 30-plus knot winds. Winds reached 30 mph on Thursday, and the waves at this end of the atoll reached about 4 feet. *Argo* pitched and pulled, but her anchor held firm. Our dinghy rode the surf behind *Argo* and rose above our transom on the waves, which is saying something.

Friday was our lucky day. The sun rose and presented us with a beautiful day; gone was the wind and rain. Fanny, the charming and pretty French dive instructor, came by around 09:00 with a dive boat full of tourists. She picked us up from *Argo* and took us to two wonderful dive spots. The first one was a coral head in the lagoon that manta rays frequent to have parasites removed by remoras and other fish. Rebecca and I fell off the boat into an amazing primordial scene: huge manta rays with wings 8 or 10 feet across were floating above us over the reef. The top side is black, and the underside is white. They have wide-set eyes placed on the end of protruding limbs on either side of their mouths, and below the limbs and eyes are articulating flaps that they use to cover their mouths or guide food inside. In this case they guided juvenile fish of a species common on the reef into their huge, gaping mouths, and the little fish went about their business of cleaning their mouths, eyes, and gills. The little fish formed a ball of dense black living organisms within the manta ray. The manta moved slowly through the water so as not to dislodge the little critters. Under the great fish were remoras, members of the shark family that have a sucker apparatus on the tops of their heads. They were cleaning the mantas' undersides. Rebecca and I gazed transfixed at the scene we were privileged to witness and wondered: for how many millions of years has this been going on?

Our second dive was on Buoy Reef, just outside of the pass. The water here is crystal clear and full of sea life, certainly among the best dive spots in the world. This was Rebecca's first dive here. On today's dive, we saw a whitetip shark, which was intimidating and attention getting as it swam close enough to give us a good look before abruptly turning and heading away (thank God). We also saw a manta ray on this reef, which was quite lovely. Two dangerous animals also got our attention. First was a rockfish, which was hiding in a hole on the reef. They are very difficult to see as they hide deep in a crevasse and are so well camouflaged that you can't tell them from a rock. They sport deadly spines to keep unwelcomed visitors at bay, and they have a tongue that looks like a little fish to attract dinner guests to their table. The other animal we saw was a moray eel; always a little disturbing (I suppose because it is hard to relate to them and they have teeth)!

After the dive, we returned to *Argo* and prepared to stand out for Papeete, Tahiti, 167 miles to the south. It was a beautiful day for a cruise: bright sunshine, a cloudless sky, a following 8-knot winds, and 3-foot sea. We don't get enough days like this! We started to raise the anchor, but the chain had apparently gotten caught on a coral head. We worked on it for 10 or 15 minutes, and I thought Tom might have to make a dive on the anchor, but by maneuvering the boat around and pulling as hard as seemed prudent, it eventually came loose and we were underway. On the way, out we deployed our fishing lines in the hopes of catching something in the pass. Shortly after we cleared the pass and turned on our course, King Neptune offered up a beautiful mahi-mahi.

The passage to Papeete is an overnight run. Rebecca and I take the evening watch from 18:00 to 00:00. Tom takes the night watch from 00:00 to 07:00. I take the 07:00 to 12:00, and Tom and I take turns as it suits us on the afternoon watch. We all enjoy the night sky at sea, which is unlike anything to be seen on land, and the night sky in the South Pacific is positively spellbinding. Out here the unobstructed vista, clear atmosphere, and lack of light pollution allow us to see things we would never otherwise see, such as the whole Milky Way down the middle of the sky with the relatively less occupied parts of the universe on either side. The stars themselves are dazzling, brilliant, and so clear as to light the heavens like an outdoor Christmas tree on a frosty winter's evening. We always look for the beautiful Southern Cross. Often, we see falling stars and satellites passing over. At Fatu Hiva, Gus and I saw the International Space Station fly by at tremendous speed. Last night Rebecca and I laid on the forecastle and gazed aloft at the trillions of tiny and not so tiny bodies shining down on us. We saw several meteors entering our atmosphere, two in particular will stay in my mind's eye: one was huge, like a comet that flashed across the sky with a tail and then disappeared, the other a streak that ended in a tiny red ball. Of course, for the whole of human history up to recently people often looked at the night sky in wonderment and awe. Since the invention of electricity and television, no one looks anymore, and besides, it can hardly be seen given the light pollution. As *Argo* plies the water she rolls back the sea, and atop the white foam are tiny star-like sparkles of phosphorescent plankton spreading out around us. It is nights like this when I am so glad we made the decision to undertake cruising on *Argo*.

This morning, Saturday, we are at sea about 35 miles out of Tahiti. The sea is calm, and it isn't much of a day for sail boaters as the wind is only 5 knots. All our doors are open, and a lovely breeze is blowing through the boat. I have two lines out, but the ocean is very deep here, and because I do not see any birds I doubt there is anything to catch in these parts. We will make Papeete in a few hours, and I can see the great mountains of Tahiti from here.

We will tie up at Marina Tiana, a focal point this time of year for sailors making the passage across the Pacific. If the internet has sufficient bandwidth in Papeete, I hope to upload some new photos of the Galapagos, the Marquesas, and the Tuamotus.

THE SOCIETY ISLANDS

June 29–   **The Society Islands of Tahiti, Moorea, Huahine, Raiatea,**
August 6   **Tahaa, and Bora Bora**

The September issue of *Passagemaker* has been published and includes a feature article and pictures of our passage through the Panama Canal. We are very complimented that *Passagemaker* syndicates our newsletter, *The Argonaut*, and publishes it on their website (http://www.passage-maker.com/category/destinations/cruiser-blogs/the-argonaut/).

 Rebecca and I have been accepted as members of the Ocean Cruising Club, which isn't an honor of any sort except that applicants have to log a lot of miles on the high seas. It's just fun to be part of a group of people who have made long open ocean passages. Members often display their burgees in port so we can identify them and learn of their adventures. So far, we have traveled 10,500 miles on this Pacific trip.

Tahiti: We enjoyed a lovely 22-hour cruise down to Papeete from Tikehau. The sea was calm, we cruised before a light 5-knot breeze, and the sky was blue and clear. It couldn't have been more beautiful, perfect for deploying our fishing gear, and Father Neptune gave us two mahi-mahis and one huge skipjack for our effort. The skipjacks are a type of tuna, and in these waters, they grow to 25 or 30 pounds. It was a picturesque passage in every way.

Geography: Tahiti is located in the middle of the Pacific Ocean about 3,300 miles due south of Hawaii and 2,000 miles northeast of New Zealand. It is an island formed about 2 million years ago by ancient volcanoes. Tahiti is made up of two mountains joined by an isthmus to form Tahiti Nui and Tahiti Iti. Mt. Orohena is the highest peak at about 7,000 feet above sea level, but it begins its ascent over 11,000 feet below the sea's surface on the ocean floor. Its peaks are often surrounded by clouds, and its rugged mountaintops encircle what used to be the volcano's crater. Mt. Orohena is composed of basaltic rock, which is soft and has eroded over the centuries into spires and carved edges that delight the eye and the imagination. Its mountaintops yield to valleys that are covered by jungle vegetation of every description. Papeete sprawls around the northwest edge of the island and flows down the lava slopes. As we approached the island, we could see lovely homes perched precariously on the hillsides, and the town itself nestled inside the lagoon at the harbor. The island is surrounded by a coral reef. Large rollers meet the coral with thunderous roars and white surf. The coral ring is easily seen as a pale blue circle of water around the island punctuated by rocks that pierce the surface and then submerge on the inside of the lagoon to form a dark blue navigable waterway between the island and the reef. Every so often there is an opening that permits passage over the reef and into the lagoon.

Arriving at Papeete: Papeete was a welcomed sight for us because we hadn't been to a town bigger than a few thousand people for several months. We were looking forward to provisioning and other benefits of civilization. We entered the lagoon at Passe de Taapuna, about 7 miles south of Papeete. The pass was a little tricky as it is shallow, subject to the effects of the surf, and requires several turns in the shallow area, but we negotiated it with only a slightly elevated pulse. We proceeded north up the lagoon's channel to Marina Tiana, the largest marina in French Polynesia and home to several hundred boats. We stern tied to the so-called super yacht wharf and within a few hours we had rented a car, dined at the restaurant on the pier, and began shopping.

Shortly after we arrived, Rebecca arranged a tour of the island by car; other than in Papeete there is essentially one road around the island. The island is very steep, so most of the homes and gardens are located near the lagoon that surrounds the island. It is very lush and verdant, providing a high standard of living for Tahitians. At the southeast end of Tahiti Nui is an isthmus that joins the bigger portion of the island to the smaller Tahiti Iti. We drove up the side of the mountain on Tahiti Iti to see the view of the isthmus and its surrounding lagoon. This was one of the most beautiful geographic sights I have ever seen. Tahiti is also a world-renowned surfing location.

Shopping in Papeete was relatively easy. French is the national language, but English is taught in school and most people are happy to converse in English. A half mile walk from the marina was a shopping center stocked with virtually everything on our provisioning list. *Argo* was in need of some oil filters and a couple of extra impellers, and this proved a bit of an adventure to find a heavy equipment parts supplier on the wharf at Papeete. Driving in alleys and around ships being broken apart for scrap was interesting, and the supplier we found was staffed by knowledgeable and friendly people who were very excited and interested to learn of our adventure.

The downtown area of Papeete is not particularly memorable from an architectural point of view. Most of its buildings are of a 1960s vintage that surround a busy, working harbor, but to us it was a welcome respite of civilization after several months in places with few people. Papeete is the capital of French Polynesia, which is a protectorate of France. The French support the country by paying for most of the cost of government (teachers' salaries, the gendarmeries, customs and immigration services, and many other government functions totaling $18 billion), yet there is an active, if ill-advised political movement to separate from France. Without French subsidies, the Confederation of French Polynesia would not enjoy its relatively high standard of living, so I cannot imagine that the majority of Polynesians would be willing to give up French support. Economic activity here peaked in the 1990s, with cheap airfares appealing to tourists and black pearls fetching a very high premium. Today, however, the Chinese are selling black pearls cheaper than they can be produced here, and the tourist industry has not recovered from the Great Recession; tourist revenue is below 1997 values. Papeete is home to the CFP government and offices of the French government. Students over the age of 15 from all the seven archipelagoes that make up the CFP come here for high school. There are universities and a sophisticated medical center here. Papeete is the main distribution center for all the islands.

The money here is the CFP franc. Its conversion value varies from day to day; on some days, we received as little as $1 equals 0.83 francs less a commission of 1 percent plus a fixed charge of $17.50. Only some bank offices convert dollars, and their hours of operation are hard to predict due to holidays, the equivalent of a siesta in the afternoon, and local factors. Banks will only convert $500 at a time, netting us considerably less when all is said and done. Prices are generally higher than we pay in the United States, particularly for food and restaurants. These factors have us relying on our credit cards. The CFP government waives its tax on fuel and parts purchased by transient yachts, making things more affordable for yachters. We purchased fuel here for $4.53 a gallon (which I didn't think was too bad); a hamburger with fries, on the other hand, cost about $20 (which I thought was pretty expensive).

Local Customs: Our guide told us that people in Polynesia do not find it necessary to get married in order to live together or raise a family. Instead they move in with each other and maintain separate financial dealings and ownership of property. Women maintain their own name and are free to leave the man or vice versa without legal squabbling. Sometimes they marry in the church, but often this is done later in life. I assumed wrongly that people were free to be promiscuous, but she told me that if her partner went wandering, that would be the end of their relationship. If there is a breakup, the children go with whom they wish, and there are often children from many liaisons living under one roof. So, what's new?

One thing that is apparent here is that life is slower paced. The climate is so agreeable and the temperature is never cold, so the cost of housing and clothing is much lower than in the Northern Hemisphere. A lot of fruits and vegetables are grown in family gardens, and fish is cheap and plentiful. People don't seem to be in much of a hurry, cars are available and expensive, but with only 10 miles of road cars are not the status symbol that they are elsewhere. Many people live on an island their entire life and are buried with their ancestors on the family homestead. There is a rich

163

connection to the ancient past. Land ownership here can be tricky because much of the land is subject to tribal-family claims (requiring perhaps tens if not hundreds of people to approve the sale of their rights), while at the same time the same piece of land may be subject to ownership under subsequent colonial and church claims. The legal system, particularly where property ownership is concerned, favors those who look Polynesian.

Europeans here are primarily from France, and from what I can gather, are people who have opted out of the rat race. Many own small businesses, shops, or restaurants.

Heiva: French Polynesians celebrate the Festival of Life or Heiva every July. All the islands that we visited had something going on, such as outrigger canoe races, coconut husking competitions, cookouts, and above all dance and singing competitions. Canoe clubs are popular and easy for us to identify with as an athletic event, but the dance groups are something entirely different. The biggest Heiva is held at Papeete, where dance and choral groups from all over the hundreds of Polynesian islands come to perform and compete.

See YouTube Video Heiva at Papeete, Tahiti

Dance groups are formed as a social club in many villages or islands such as the Huahine Island group that we saw perform one evening. Dance groups have a membership of perhaps 150 people with about 20 of them being orchestra members and the rest being dancers. They practice for 6 or 8 months before the Heiva begins each summer, readying themselves for the competition. The orchestra is predominantly a percussion orchestra comprised of several different-sized drums, a ukulele chorus, and other unusual instruments. The performance begins when the orchestra creates a primitive, pulsating, loud, rhythmic sound that will soon send the dancers into an erotic frenzy. At other times during the performance they sound like a Kabuki orchestra, making it all the more exotic. A narrative in the Tahitian language is given by what appears to be a chief or shaman who relates a mythical story of how the islands were formed by Maui or Pele or some other god or goddess, or perhaps the story of a great battle between tribes in ancient times; the dancers then interpret the story in dance. When the narrative is over, the dancers swing into action.

The dance is viewed by the audience in an arena setting, so that they can appreciate the choreography and precise movements of this tribe of people. The dancers are dressed in costumes made of grass, leaves, and flowers. They are quite beautiful and very colorful. The females move their hips with amazing rapidity that is clearly intended to be erotic, while the men move their thighs in a way that reminds me somehow of spawning or reproduction in the animal world. In any case, it is a spectacle to behold. The dance lasts about an hour and closes when the males and females pair off, all the while shaking and quivering as they and the audience reach a point of ecstasy as the drumbeat intensifies. It seems to evoke ancient tribal customs, sometimes savage, sometimes erotic. If you allow yourself to get caught up in it, you can almost smell a missionary roasting on the spit!

The Credit Card Debacle: We have had a devil of a time with our VISA cards. We carried two of them from different banks as insurance against having one cancelled, but as fate would have it they were both canceled in the course of our travels because of fraud issues at participating stores. After literally hours and hours of phone time, repeatedly answering the same security questions over and over and talking with all levels of incompetence, having the phone blank out after talking to the third tier in their hierarchy and having to start all over at the bottom rung again, we sweated out having new cards sent to Marina Tiana. In the course of trying to track them and find out if they made it here, we discovered that the lame brain in the Bank of America's VISA office sent it to "Tamiti." Of course, there is no such place. To make matters worse, the UPS form doesn't have enough lines on the computerized address label to accommodate addresses in Tahiti, so this increased our anxiety. As the days ticked off, we finally got a tracking number and learned that the cards actually got to Papeete. UPS uses a private vender here. The phone system here is adding two digits to all phone numbers, so once we found the right number, we contacted them and arranged to drive over to their offices and pick up our cards since they had no idea of the final address to which they should have been delivered. All's well that ends well, I suppose, but our AT&T bill was over $1,400 largely due to calls to the credit card companies!

New Friends: One of the greatest pleasures of traveling on a yacht is meeting new and interesting people. In the Tiana Marina, we met several couples we really enjoyed. One was Don and Laurie aboard *True Blue*: he was a prominent plastic surgeon and she an interior designer. Don told me that last year they sold everything: the house in Sausalito, the helicopter, the motorcycle, the cars . . . everything, and bought their Oyster 66 and began their odyssey. They're having a wonderful time and dealing with a few bumps here and there, like their captain and his girlfriend (the cook) getting into a terrible row leading to their departure and the emergency hiring of a replacement captain, and don't forget the failed generator that took 3 weeks to get parts for.

Johnny and Veronica and their three kids moored next to us on *Walkabout*, a Nordhavn 62; they have been spending the 3 summer months when the kids are out of school sailing as far as possible. Every year they leave their yacht in the last port they reach for 9 months until next season. They have traveled up the west coast to Alaska, then across the Aleutian Islands and down to Japan, then to Korea, Shanghai, Vietnam, and other places, including Borneo, where they sailed up a river and saw orangutans, pigmy elephants, and other exotic creatures.

Julie and Mike: My sister Julie and brother-in-law Mike flew to Papeete for a 2-week visit. They are sharing all the experiences that I am describing, particularly the Heiau Dance festivals and snorkeling.

Moorea: After almost 2 weeks in Papeete we shoved off for Moorea, a gorgeous island just 12 miles away. Our passage was a little rough, as wind speeds reached around 25 knots and seas were in the 6-foot range. Julie gets seasick easily, and this little jaunt was no exception. She is a good sport and after getting sick she just came back up on deck for more.

The passage across the reef into Cook's Bay was easy. We anchored in 60 feet of water near boats that we had seen in other anchorages. Cook's Bay is one of the most beautiful places I have ever been. Like other Polynesian ports of call, the bay is the remnant of an ancient volcano with the eroded sides of the crater forming the peaks of the mountains. Like Tahiti, Moorea is surrounded by a coral reef that is teeming with all types of colorful tropical fish. It wasn't long before we arranged for a scuba dive on the reef, the big attraction of which was the sighting of a huge 9-foot lemon shark. Unfortunately, it was a rainy day but underwater that didn't make any difference except that it was rather low light and a little chilly after two dives.

The next day we toured the island with our charming Polynesian guide, Paulina, and saw the vista from Belvedere, went to the local distillery, saw the ruins of her ancestors, and had lunch at Snack Mahana. The place occupied a beautiful waterfront location and served up gourmet fare known far and wide, including its featured dish, *Poisson Cru au lait de coco Tahiti*, a raw tuna salad in coconut milk that was simply delicious. It is made with slices of raw blue or yellow fin tuna marinated in coconut milk and lime and served with cucumber slices and onion.

Of course, no tour would be complete without a little shopping, and Moorea had some very nice artisan shops that Julie and Mike took advantage of, including the black pearl jeweler.

That afternoon Julie, Mike, and I took the tender on a snorkeling expedition. This proved interesting in that we saw quite a few sting rays and managed to get stuck in shallow water in the labyrinth of the coral reef, but otherwise all was fine and it was a lot of fun.

Huahine: We decided to do a night cruise to Huahine so that Julie and Mike could see the ocean and sky at night. It was almost 100 miles from Moorea to Huahine, and it was a lovely evening for a cruise. We left Moorea at 17:00 and by the time we transited the pass into the open ocean the sun had nearly set. The cruise was everything I had hoped it would be for them: the sky was pitch black and the stars twinkled in the firmament with a brilliance of clarity and in numbers that bewitch the mind. The Milky Way appears as a cloud of stardust extending from one horizon to the other. The waves peeling back from *Argo's* bow revealed stars in the water—starlight-like bursts from the plankton rising from thousands of feet below.

We made Huahine the following morning and put in at the little village of Fare, and fair it was. We anchored in 90 feet of water and laid out 450 feet of chain; it's a good thing I ordered 650 feet of chain on this boat! Tom secured *Argo* and gave her a bath after our cruise. Everyone else but me went ashore for shopping and reconnoitering while I laid low with a very bad cold. That evening I managed to join the family for a really great happy hour and dinner at the beachfront restaurant, which we later found out is known to boaters far and wide. After dinner, we went to the local Heiva, which was very provincial compared to the more professional performances in Papeete. We stayed overnight, and the next day we cruised down the lagoon to another anchorage that was not only a visual knockout, but had some of the most beautiful coral formations we had seen. The troupe went snorkeling, while I nursed my cold. After they returned and dined on one of Rebecca's fabulous meals, we took the dinghy through a passage to another bay that connected to the other side of the islands. There we found a little tavern. We enjoyed a libation in a very rural and authentic setting, and it gave Mike a chance to pick up the bill as I forgot my wallet.

Raiatea and Tahaa: The next morning we hoisted the anchor and departed for Raiatea, a couple of hours away. It was a beautiful day, but the fish weren't at all interested in what we had to offer. We moored at the town dock at Uturoa and dined at the little French restaurant on the dock. We were all anxious to get to Bora Bora because of all we had heard about it. That evening Harry Smith, an Australian that we met in Jamaica and who had made the crossing during the same time period that we had, came by for a visit. He offered us some advice on Tahaa, the next island, and reported a phenomenal coral garden there. He also helped me plan our 2016 trip down the coast of Australia to Tasmania. The next morning, we left Raiatea and moved over to Tahaa, which was only a few miles away. After we anchored in a secluded bay, we launched the tender and spent 2 days floating in the fabulous wonder of its coral garden. It was located in a channel between two motus with the seawater from the outer reef flowing through rather briskly to keep things fresh for all sorts of fish, corals, and other creatures. We anchored our tender at one end of the channel and walked up the motu to the headwater about ¼ mile away, and then floated down the channel to our boat, all the while watching the fabulous aquatic scenery as we slowly passed by. Among the hundreds of brightly colored tropical fish swimming about their business, oblivious to us, were two particularly interesting creatures that I hadn't seen before. One was a sea anemone that was a beautiful red with sticky tan tentacles and beautiful little fish weaving in and out. The other were maxima clams or small giant clams with curved edges that have beautifully blue, red, or brown lips. It was so fabulous, words fail to describe it.

Bora Bora: We reluctantly left Tahaa but looked forward to coming into Bora Bora, which is a seminal experience for a captain; it's like coming into New York or San Francisco harbors. The pass channel is wide and easily navigated, but the bay is full of coral heads and reefs. As we entered we saw the beautiful rollers breaking on the reef on both sides, the reef awash with turquoise water, and the deep blue lagoon inside the reef. Dominating the whole scene is a huge megalith of a receding mountain named Mt. Otemanu that was once a mighty volcano. The caldera beneath the volcano has cooled, and the mountain has eroded and collapsed over the centuries; it sinks about a centimeter a year into the sea. Eventually it will be like the Tuamotus, that is, a ring of motus surrounding a lagoon.

We expected a bustling island with lots to do and see, but in reality, it is a small and quiet place with only a few restaurants. Most of the activity here is at the famous hotels and resorts scattered about the motus that surround the island. The room prices are an unbelievable $2,000 to $3,000 per night. A friend of ours went to a cheap $1,200 place where they got the third night free. We have been told that the resorts are all full, yet you don't see many tourists about as they are locked away behind the gates of their resort.

Julie and Mike had a few more days with us so we planned an island tour that proved to be fantastic. We were picked up by a four-wheel drive, open-back Range Rover pickup truck with bench seats in the bed. I must say I wasn't very enthusiastic at first, but in a few minutes, I was having a lot of fun. This thing climbed 50-degree slopes: it was fantastic. We climbed all over the mountain including a place where the Americans had placed gun mounts during the Second World War. We examined the guns, which had a legend marked with the name of the manufacturer and the date of manufacture, 1907. I asked our guide about this, and he told me that they were taken from ships that were sunk at Pearl Harbor on December 7. Later they were removed from the sunken ships and brought here as defensive weapons. They were probably part of the weaponry on the battleship *Texas* or some other old ship that wasn't salvaged after the attack. The guns looked like they were cut from the ship's deck plate, moved here, and then cemented into position on the top of the hill, deck plate and all.

One of the interesting things we found on the tour, aside from the fabulous views from the mountain peaks, was the fact that people bury their dead next to their homes. As we drove up the mountainside we could see that almost all the homes had small, roofed tombs in the yard near the homes with colorful plastic flowers to memorialize their ancestors who were buried there.

Life on the Dock: During the last few days, Tom, handsome and youthful as he is, has been the object of attention from at least two young women who have found themselves stranded on the dock in Bora Bora. It seems they were crewing on sailboats that are crossing the Pacific. Usually these women offer to cook, clean, and perhaps stand watch in exchange for free passage across the ocean. As you can imagine, people often get annoyed with one another while being in close quarters over such a long-time period, so it isn't unusual to see people leave a boat and look for other arrangements. Sometimes they fall in love, dare I say? In the two cases this week, the captains had put it to them bluntly. The ladies took great offense, and in their righteous indignation immediately left their boats, penniless and without an apparent means of support. We fed one hungry young woman (a 30-year-old Chilean on her way to New Zealand for a job) a healthy meal, and both found temporary accommodations on other sailboats until some stability in their lives could be arranged. After a brief period of time during which strangers rallied to extend a helping hand, both have now moved on to new arrangements and the dock has returned to the its normal tranquil and bucolic state.

One of the sailors holed up in Bora Bora waiting on the weather reported that one of the men associated with the hassle with the ladies left port without the permission of the gendarmes and without a clearance to the next port. At his next port of call, he could face a stiff fine, perhaps as much as $10,000, or be required to retrace his steps back to the last port and obtain a clearance there, or both. He is now 800 miles out at sea, in seas of 14 feet and winds over 30 knots, having lost his mainsail and his engine.

Getting Underway: After Julie and Mike left, we planned to get underway for American Samoa. We found out from our fuel agent that American Samoa requires a customs agent for motor yachts (but not sailboats) to enter. The agent's fee is $500, plus a bunch of other government fees, so we decided to skip the islands and their hospitality. Instead we decided to move along to independent Samoa about 100 miles further west, which as far as I know is more reasonable. The passage is 1,200 miles, and it will take about 6 days. The weather will be less than ideal, but we are looking forward to the trip. In the course of preparing *Argo* for this journey, we discovered a few problems.

Mechanical Problems: In preparing for any long voyage we check the yacht thoroughly. This time Tom found the unwelcomed presence of hydraulic fluid in our bilge, which is not a good sign.

As you know the hydraulic system has been a repeated source of difficulties. We began to hunt around for the source of the leak and found that the actuator on our port stabilizer had begun to seep oil, but it was a small and slow leak, not enough to cause us to lose 2 gallons of oil. Up forward however, we found two more leaks at the manifolds of the windless and thruster. Apparently two seals had failed, and oil under 3,400 pounds of pressure was spraying everywhere. It was a mess and a very big concern.

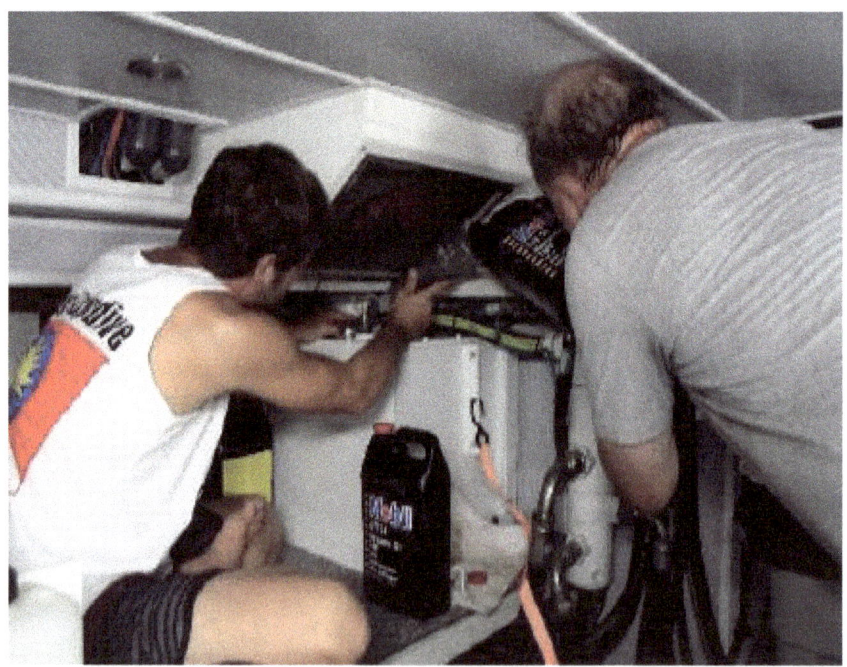

Lucky for us we bought *Argo* from Nordhavn, which subcontracts the hydraulic system from American Bow Thruster. Once we notified them, parts were with FedEx within 24 hours and a technician in New Zealand was organized to come here. Despite the disappointment and concern over the failures, we are grateful for the fast and wonderful service we are getting from Nordhavn and ABT. However, it will delay us by almost 10 days.

Meeting Garrick Yrondi: We are staying at the Mai Kai Marina in Bora Bora. Here we are Med-moored or stern tied to a dock that is attached to the outside terrace of the restaurant. The main business of the marina is the restaurant and a small hotel that's part of the little complex. The restaurant is quite good and is run by Teiva and his wife Jessica (she is a Californian). Teiva is not only the chef, but also runs the marina and everything else. He is a very energetic, happy Polynesian who has been extremely helpful to us.

In the restaurant are hung several interesting paintings that I was immediately attracted to. Rebecca says they "speak to us." They are humorous, bright, and colorful pieces of modern art. I asked Teiva to introduce us to the artist, Garrick Yrondi. He is the fourth generation of his family to be artists and sculptors, and is widely known. Garrick came by the marina and invited us to his Tuscan-style villa, a sprawling compound built on the hillside overlooking the sapphire blue bay and Mt. Otemanu. On the living room terrace is a life-size sculpture in bronze of a gorgeous, nude young woman sculpted by Garrick's father. As we were looking at this beautiful woman, Garrick told us it was his mother. After he told us, I was a little embarrassed to continue looking at her, but she was so beautiful!

We had lunch at his home, and he showed us his studio and collection of pottery, sculpture, and paintings. Our lunch was Poisson Cru accompanied by a fine bottle of Kistler Chardonnay that we brought along for the occasion. At lunch, we discovered that we were both born on the same day, which made for a lovely coincidence and a lot of fun. We bought one of his paintings, and it reminds us of the wonderful time we spent in Bora Bora. The most interesting subject of our conversation revolves around his vision of the world and how he has developed his style of painting and sculpture to express it. He sees the Polynesians as people with a wonderful spontaneity unfiltered by the psychological defenses necessary in a more complex society. He sees them as people possessing an innocence of an earlier time. He loves the light here in Bora Bora, a light that is warm, but changing and pure. His paintings reflect the dominance of the sea and its creatures, but also the beauty of the flora as it meets the sea, all expressed with his intrinsic good humor and optimism.

Next Stop: We will be in Bora Bora until at least August 6. In the meantime, the nasty weather to our west will abate and we will hopefully be on our way soon. Next stop, Apia, Samoa, after 1,200 miles of open ocean to the west.

August 5   **Fixing Argo on Bora Bora**

We began the day by stopping by the gendarmerie to check out of French Polynesia and obtain our Zarpe or clearance form. The gendarmes were very courteous, and within a few minutes we had filled out their forms and were on our way. We needed the Zarpe to enter the next port, Apia, Samoa.

We picked up Stu Parker (the mechanic from the hydraulics company) on the ferry dock at 09:00. Stu was an affable Kiwi, and after the 10-minute cruise in our tender across the harbor, he set to work on the stabilizer. Fixing the problem proved more difficult than expected as the bearing on the actuator collar had seized up, which was probably the reason for the actuator seal failure. After applying a crowbar, hammer, bearing puller, and a lot of elbow grease, he got the actuator assembly apart. Stu suspected that the cause of the failure was probably the lack of grease on the bearing, which should have been applied when it was manufactured. Altogether it took about 2 hours, and then he turned his attention to repairing the seals on the manifold up forward. Meanwhile, Rebecca and I walked the mile or so to Panda d'Or, a Chinese restaurant with takeout like nowhere else we have ever been.

From the street, Panda d'Or looked like a conventional Chinese restaurant, but around the side in the alley was an industrial roll-up door that, when opened, revealed a stainless-steel counter and a hive of activity inside. People were in motion everywhere. Lying about on the alley pavement cooling themselves were a few dogs, a type of pit bull common to all the islands. We found them a little intimidating. At the counter were perhaps a half dozen people standing around waiting for their food orders, all dressed in shorts, flip-flops, and T-shirts. In their hands were large bowls used to bring home the stir-fry for their family's lunch. We stepped forward to place our order with the frantically busy owner who was fully and simultaneously engaged in taking orders, collecting money, and delivering meals to the waiting and hungry customers. He kindly handed us an English language menu from under the counter. We quickly gave him our order, and he turned to the refrigerator with glass doors beside him, selected our portion of fish, chicken, or tofu from within, put each in a small stainless-steel bowl, and slid them across a worktable behind him to a waiting chef. So far, so good. The surprise is the wok and chef. I have never seen anything like it; the chef flipped a lever under the stove-type apparatus that ignited a large blowtorch that blasted forth from a metal collar designed to perfectly fit the wok. It sounded like a rocket engine at launch. It produced a huge blue-white flame and a tremendous amount of heat. With his large spoon, the chef flicked a few ounces of several magic Chinese gastronomic solutions into the wok, then at the right moment he dumped our waiting bowls into the bubbling cauldron and within seconds he had made our meal. At the same time, a couple of other chefs were working at the row of woks. Suddenly, somewhere along the line, a flame erupted from a wok and—voila! Another meal was ready.

We walked back to the boat with our treasures, passing little bungalows, some well-kept, others lazily shabby, and many with little backyard shrines atop the tombs of buried ancestors, perhaps recently, or maybe long ago. Cars whizzed by on the narrow road that ran along the lagoon. Unfortunately, you cannot see the water for all the buildings that are crammed along the shoreline. When we finally got back on the boat we laid out a nice lunch. When we finished, Stu wrapped up the repairs and inspected the entire system. By then the time had come for him to return to the ferry dock and catch his plane back to Papeete and later Auckland. That evening we invited Garrick Yrondi (the artist) to a farewell dinner. He is a lovely man, and we both thoroughly enjoyed his company. Rebecca made a wonderful meal, and I grilled filet mignons. Garrick brought a fantastic bottle of Bordeaux. It was a productive day and a memorable evening.

August 6   Departing Bora Bora for Samoa – Day 1 – Wednesday

A front had moved in, and it was raining cats and dogs. Untying from the Mai Kai dock was quite an ordeal. *Argo* was tied to the dock at the stern with three lines. There were no lines to the dock on the port side, as we were moored at the end of the dock. The bow was initially held in place by the anchor, which was set 300 feet off the port bow in 65 feet of water. The anchor and chain are not enough to keep her stationary, so bow and beam lines were attached to concrete moorings placed on the harbor's floor. Teiva, the very helpful and energetic marina owner, scurried about in his tender/mini-tug to hand off lines and push *Argo* to the desired location for final tie-up. (We didn't need his help as a tug because we have thrusters.) Altogether we had nine lines and an anchor chain to hold us in place. Undoing all this was quite a job, given that there was a boat tied next to us on the starboard side, it was raining heavily, and the wind was pushing us to starboard. Once free of the lines, we needed to recover our chain and anchor, which took about 10 minutes. Meanwhile, other boats at anchor were close enough to swing into us, so Teiva pushed them about in his mini-tug until we could get free. We then proceeded a couple of miles to the fuel dock.

Fueling the boat in the driving rain was miserable. Tom had caught my cold; however, he wouldn't hear of me taking over for him on the deck. Wet and miserable though we were, we accomplished refueling and left Bora Bora at 16:00 after taking on 5,700 liters of diesel fuel in preparation for our passage to Samoa. Fuel prices were fairly reasonable at $4.43/gallon, so we decided to use our bladder and take on an extra 500 gallons. Our trip to Samoa was 1,200 miles, and with the fuel taken on here in Bora Bora, we should have enough to get us to New Zealand. The weather forecast called for pleasant conditions, although the sea state in this area over the last 2 weeks had been in the 11 to 12-foot range with winds up to 50 knots in places. We learned of a sailboat at Suwarrow Island that dragged its anchor during the high winds, went onto the reef, and sank during the storm. As we left, it was pouring rain as it only can in the tropics. One of the young waitresses at Mai Kai Restaurant had told us that if you leave the island in the rain, it means Bora Bora is sad. What a poetic thought to end our visit here.

August 7   **At Sea – Day 2 – Thursday**

Exercise is difficult on a boat, particularly when we are underway and the boat's motion makes me feel a little fatigued. I like yoga, but it is difficult to perform on a moving boat, however it does put extra stress on core muscles!

- Rebecca

It is a pleasant day, light winds, a fair sky, and low seas in the range of 6 feet on the port quarter. We always feel a little seasick on the first day out, followed by a day or two of fatigue. By the third day we are usually into the routine of watch standing and feeling normal again.

Argo is making about 7.5 knots, which adds up to 185 miles or so a day. On this trip, she is burning a little less than a gallon per mile. There is no consistent ocean current to help move us along, so it will take more effort than on our last long passage. We observed no other ships or sea life.

What do we do all day when we are at sea? We stand watch, which means watching *Argo's* mechanical operations by visiting the engine room every hour, then returning to the pilothouse and watching the radar and other instruments and filling out the ship's log. Sometimes I work on the computer writing the blog or editing pictures, reading, or watching videos. Sometimes I plan our next cruise or study charts and timetables to plan future passages. Rebecca likes to bake or prepare meals. She does laundry about every other day, and reads or does CE for her medical professional certification. Sometimes we take a nap, or exercise if it isn't too hot. We like to watch extended series like *The Tudors, Breaking Bad,* or *Dexter*; and I have read more important and interesting books than I have since college. Somehow the time flies!

August 8   **At Sea – Day 3 – Friday**

The sea state is low with loping swells in the 6-foot range, very light winds, and a clear sky. Overnight squalls formed in line aft of *Argo* and slowly spread over us. The direction of the swells is a little confused, caused perhaps by the large fronts both north and south of us. In any case, it is a pleasant cruise. We haven't seen any sea life—no whales or dolphins.

Maybe the noise of our engine scares them away, but we saw plenty of whales up close when we traveled on *Odyssey*. A few albatrosses are flying about, but not many. There are no flying fish or squid on deck as in past passages, and no ships or boats, either. It seems to be a lonely ocean!

For eight months, we cut each other's hair. Randy's was occasionally a bit shorter on one side than the other, but he didn't seem to mind.

- Rebecca

August 9   **At Sea – Day 4 – Saturday**

Not much has changed from yesterday except that the seas may have come down a little. It is clear and beautiful.

We emptied the bladder tank into our main engine room tanks, which seems to have improved our posture on the sea and the speed we are able to make. Since taking that 3,500 pounds of weight off the stern, we have been making over 8 knots at 6.8 gallons per hour. The night sky this evening is nearly like daylight, with a full moon pouring its beautiful silvery beams on the black ocean.

Although this weather is perfect for a motor yacht, it won't be welcomed by our friends with sailboats who headed out for Samoa or Tonga this week from Bora Bora; the wind is so light they will have to motor, which makes them less stable than if they were under sail. When full, the sails hold them to the waves, which keeps them from bouncing around, although they would be hove to an angle. In this weather, they will have to motor so they will be bouncing around in the swells and traveling at a much lower speed than to which they are accustomed. We hope to see quite a few of our sailor friends in Samoa.

I think we will put out the fishing gear tomorrow and see what Poseidon has for us!

August 10   **At Sea – Day 5 – Sunday**

Another pleasant day at sea, a repeat of yesterday's beautiful weather. It is 94 degrees with humidity to match. We made 185 miles yesterday. We had radar targets of two Chinese trawlers (I suspect) at 16 miles. I wouldn't have noticed them except that they broke radio silence on VHF, which is unusual for them. They don't use AIS, so it is unclear exactly who they are. From what a Polynesian told me, the Chinese bought the fishing rights to many island countries such as Tonga. The agreement, so I was told, precludes locals from fishing. The Chinese send in their fishing fleet and strip the waters over time. They build processing plants on the islands, and if the people want to buy fish, they must do so from the Chinese. The locals aren't used to working as hard as the Chinese expect, so Chinese workers are brought in from the mainland to work the plants. The locals then become unemployed, except for young women who earn money providing companionship to the Chinese workers. Not a pretty story, if it is true.

We set our clocks back 1 hour, so we are now –11 hours from GMT or –7 hours from Eastern Time. Samoa is –12 hours.

August 12   **At Sea – Day 6 – Tuesday**

Yesterday we made 205 miles. Today is another beautiful day, just like yesterday and all of the days of this passage so far. As required, we emailed via our Iridium phone a notification to the authorities in Samoa of our pending arrival.

Although we are not yet at the International Date Line (longitude 180 degrees), Samoa's calendar and clocks are set to correspond to New Zealand plus 1 hour. We decided to advance our calendars today (so we skipped August 11), which is why it isn't shown in the journal.

We hooked a beautiful wahoo late this afternoon. It fought hard for about 20 minutes. I brought it up to the boat toward Tom, who was standing on the swim platform ready to land him. Suddenly the great fish leaped in the air toward Tom. I was very concerned for Tom's safety, considering those razor-sharp teeth. The fish then settled back in the water and moved toward the port rub rail, ready to be ushered aboard. Sliding in the water next to *Argo*, we could see what a gorgeous creature he was; about 5 feet long, a beautiful, brownish, tiger-striped fish, magnificent to see in action in the water. Suddenly a lurch, the lure flew about 10 feet up into the air toward Tom again, and our dinner guest was gone. Oh, well. He was too beautiful for us anyway, but he was the biggest wahoo I almost caught!

SAMOA

August 13   **At Sea/Arriving in Apia, Samoa – Day 7 – Wednesday**

Another perfect cruising day. The sea came up a little overnight and is now in the 7 to 8-foot range on our beam, but it is confused and mixed with a long moment, so it is comfortable despite its size. *Argo* is running perfectly. We run the generator almost 24/7 so that we can keep the temperature and humidity comfortable onboard. The rugged peaks of American Samoa can be seen off to our port about 25 miles away. We're skipping it because of its ridiculously high immigration fee on motor vessels. Samoa is another 85 miles further west, and we should be anchored in Apia Harbor about 21:00 this evening. Neptune gave up one of his own this afternoon, a nice mahi-mahi.

We anchored in Apia Harbor at 21:00, safe and sound after a long voyage. We will be here about 5 days, then move on to Vava'U, Tonga.

August 13–21, 2014

Arrival: We arrived in Apia, Samoa, at 21:00 on August 13, 2014, after a lovely 6-day passage from Bora Bora. Although it was dark when we arrived and we were unfamiliar with the harbor, entry was easy and straightforward. The harbor is broad once inside the reef. It is completely open to the north, so it doesn't provide protection from the ocean's swell when the wind clocks around. We dropped the hook in 30 feet of water amongst a few sailboats at anchor. After a cocktail and a bit of relaxation, we buttoned her up and went below for a good night's sleep. The next morning, we contacted harbor control to begin the check-in procedure. Within an hour or so both immigration and health service came aboard. In early afternoon, we went ashore to check in with customs and quarantine services, both of whom we had to bring back to the boat for an inspection. Altogether there are four offices to check in with, four sets of papers asking for the same information, but no fees, which is very unusual. Everyone was friendly and easygoing.

The Islands: There are two large islands, Upolu and Savai'i, and several very small outer islands, only one or two of which are inhabited. Samoa has a population of about 185,000; 150,000 live on Upolu, and 35,000 live on Savai'i. Apia is the capital where the majority of the population resides. There are two authorities in Samoa, the civil government and the tribal or village chiefs. The civil government is elected and has legislative, executive, and judicial branches. The civil government is the final authority in all matters.

The islands are mountainous and of volcanic origin. The center of both islands is steep and rugged, strewn with lava rocks and overgrown with rain forests. It is very hot and humid most of the time here, making it a wonderful environment for vegetation of all kinds. The islands are ravaged by cyclones each year, consequently the high rain forest canopy that you might expect is instead a patchwork of banyans and other tall hardwood trees that are able to withstand the wind, along with vines and broad-leaf plants making up the lower layers of the forests. Coconut palms are truly the tree of life here in Samoa, and groves of them can be seen everywhere. There are two seasons in Samoa: the wet season (October to March) and the dry season. During the wet season, it rains in torrents each day, filling the ravines with raging rivers. Waterfalls cascade off the rugged plateaus from high up in the mountains, falling 900 feet straight down in several places. The two waterfalls that we saw were spectacularly high, with the water creating a bridal veil down the face of the black lava rock cliffs and falling into a beautiful cascade of small pools carved out of the lava over the millenniums and framed by coconut palms and giant ferns. In addition to powerful cyclones, Samoa is also subject to periodic tsunamis that ravage the east and south coasts.

Upolu is the larger of the two islands. Apia, the capital of Samoa, is located here and is the commercial and government center. The city has several large open-air farmers' markets, many restaurants, a movie theater, and shops of all types. It is clean, although it has no significant architectural buildings other than the recently restored 19th-century Roman Catholic Italianate-style cathedral, and a modern government building. Samoans are very proud of their little country and pride themselves on their friendliness. The Robert Lewis Stevenson plantation attracts a lot of interest. It is a surprisingly large, sprawling home with many verandas and surrounded by a fancy fence and imposing gate. Mr. Stevenson, who among other things authored *Treasure Island,* lived in the home for several years before succumbing to tuberculosis at the age of 44. He and his wife Fanny (a physician from California) are buried on the property, and our guide gladly took about 5 minutes to sing a cappella the funeral song composed by Mr. Stevenson himself for his own funeral. To me, that certainly demonstrated Mr. Stevenson's command of the moment! Both our guide's voice and the words of the song were quite lovely. After leaving the home, we stopped by a Bahia temple or house of worship. There are only a handful of these temples in the world, and, because one of our friends is a Bahia member, we thought we would stop by and check it out. The temple is of a modern architectural style and built of concrete in the shape of an inverted flower— maybe a tulip—with the stem end at the top and the petals as sides covering the worship area, which is a six-sided room similar in its simplicity to a Quaker Meeting Hall. The building is very plain with a lone small podium at floor level available for people to share their ideas, which, as I understand it, is the nature of the service. Outside, the building is landscaped in beautiful gardens, which, when mature, are likely to be spectacular.

As we continued our drive around the island we saw more village life: dogs, pigs, chickens, small children running about, and their parents lying on mats on the *fale* floor in the heat of midday. When we reached the south shore of the island, we visited To Sua, a private park that features beautiful geologic and coastal lava formations as well as a garden. The coast here stretches as far as the eye can see in both directions, and is a rugged lava stone matrix of arches and points against which the Southern Ocean pounds and upwells with spectacular effect. Away from the cliff and on firm ground can be found deep lava tubes that the sea replenishes with water from below, some of which are about an acre in size and perhaps 200 feet below ground level. The sides of the tubes were covered in beautiful ferns, and the water below was crystal clear. A stairway descends down the side of the lava tube to the pool so that the ambitious can swim in the pool for the price of climbing back up all those stairs.

Savai'i is the second largest island of Samoa, and much more rural and traditional than Upolu. We spent 2 days there, including the 1-hour ferry across Apolima Strait from Upolu. There are five tourist attractions on Savai'i: the lava field, the blowholes, the sea arches, swimming with turtles, and the traditional craft of tapas cloth making. The arches and blowholes occur on the southern shore of the island, and like To Sua on Upolu, are dramatic formations of lava where the island meets the sea. I have posted pictures on the website showing most of these attractions. The blow-holes are the most spectacular that I have ever seen. Given the right surf conditions, water spouts hundreds of feet in the air like a geyser. Our guide, whose name was Turkey, put a coconut into the tube just before a wave came in and it shot several hundred feet into the air when the hole blew. It was so interesting that we watched the surf and the blowhole for quite a long time.

As we drove around the island, we stopped at the home of a village chief and his family. The chief was reclined on the floor of his *fale* when we arrived. He was a handsome, self-assured fellow. Turkey asked if we could photograph his traditional Samoan tattoos. He happily complied, stood up, adjusted his lava-lava and proudly posed in the style of Arnold Schwarzenegger, resplendent with a girth appropriate for a chief of middle age. (A lava-lava is a single piece of cloth and, when used by men, is wrapped around the waist and extends to the knee and then is pulled up in front and tied in a knot to form a cover. It is the traditional dress for men in much of Polynesia. Men also have "Western" lava-lavas made of heavier fabric like a suit would be made of and it has pockets. Women use the same piece of cloth, but hang it above the breasts and tie it on the side as a dress. No one wears underwear, in case you were wondering.)

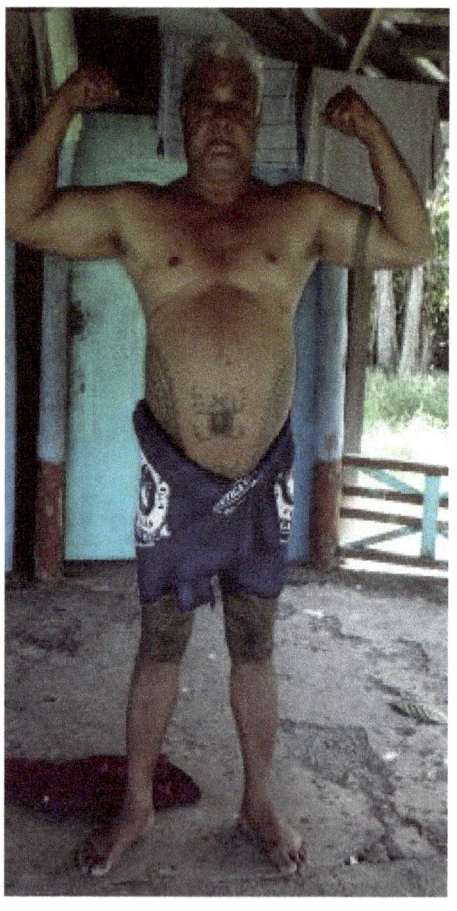

A few minutes later we entered another *fale* where his wife was making tapa, a traditional cloth made from tree bark. She took a 4-foot sapling stem of a particular tree and stripped the bark off, separated the moist inner bark from the weathered outer layer, and then pounded it into a 4 x 2-foot piece of coarse fabric. As it had several knotholes and other imperfections, other pieces of the same fabric were then glued over it with a glue made from tapioca root and pounded with a mallet until it was nearly uniform. After the patchwork was complete, it appeared nearly perfect and very pleasing in both texture and appearance. After a few hours drying, it becomes a thick, soft, flexible cloth that has been traditionally used to make clothing.

A Very Little History: People first came to Samoa about 1,000 years ago from Taiwan. They are the same tribe that populated Fiji, Tonga, Polynesia, Hawaii, and the other South Pacific islands. Europeans first "discovered" Samoa in the 18th century. Later, Britain, France, Germany, and the United States tussled over control of the islands during the 19th century in order to use them as a coaling station for their commercial and naval fleets. The United States formed alliances with local chieftains to secure its position and wound up with what is now called American Samoa. The Germans won Western Samoa, but lost it to the British during the First World War. The British turned over administration to New Zealand after WWII, and Western Samoa became independent in 1962. The citizens of American Samoa have voted to remain a protectorate of the United States.

Village Life: Eighty percent of the land of Samoa is owned by individuals, and the remainder is owned by the government, some of which is available for purchase. Private land is held within villages and is owned by the many extended families living there. The population of a village can be as small as a few hundred people or as large as a couple of thousand. Villages are governed by one or more high chiefs and a council of talking chiefs. A high chief is elected from a family having royal blood; that is, he is related in some way to one of the four ancestral royal families. The high chief is normally a male, but females may also qualify, particularly if there are no qualifying males. High chiefs are elected for life and are given a house adjoining the village *fale*, which is an open-air, oblong, thatched or (more recently) steel-roofed structure where gatherings are held. Talking chiefs are elected by the other families to represent and speak for them at council meetings held in the *fale*. Chiefs are elected based on their service to the family, village, and church.

This can take the form of helping the old and infirmed, giving food to village members, or helping others defray the expense of funerals and weddings, among other things.

The village is the center of life in Samoa. If a person commits a capital offense, that person may be expelled from the village and his house burned and property confiscated. If this happens, the individual is effectively a stateless person with no means of support. The chiefs handle matters such as property disputes, family domestic squabbles, teenage rowdiness, and other civil issues. In the case of rowdiness or spousal abuse, for example, the chiefs may impose a fine of as much as a thousand dollars or more, which the offender's family will have to pay if the individual cannot come up with the money. Younger men wishing to become chiefs help the council maintain order and carry out their mandates. Women have their own role, which is to keep the village clean and to decorate it with floral gardens, and to conduct money-raising events, the proceeds of which go to fund village projects. Women's groups have their own leadership hierarchy.

Each family owns part of the village land, and on each family's parcel are usually several homes and at least one *fale*. Often the homes are *fales* with little or no furniture and people sleep on mats or low plank beds with a futon-type mattress. They are built up on pilings about 3 feet above ground level, the sides are open and have thatched palm blinds that can be lowered when it rains, and mosquito nets assure a peaceful night's sleep. The roof is often thatched, but it can also be covered in steel sheeting. Some *fales* are painted and fancy, some are made of concrete, and some are old and dilapidated wooden structures. There are typically no rooms in a *fale*; it's just one large space. The temperature is so hot, and it is so humid, that open-sided *fales* are very practical during the day to keep the rain out and provide some shade. Behind or attached to the *fale* is often a modern-looking, four-sided home constructed of brick. There are usually several homes and *fales* on a site that may belong to different generations of a family. Newlyweds are usually given a plot to build a *fale* for their home, or they take over an older abode and the elders move to newer lodging. Somewhere in the front of the yard for all to see are the tombs of deceased ancestors. These can be quite large if the deceased was a high chief or a person who rose to prominence.

Driving around Samoa we saw a large percentage of *fale* made in the traditional way with people lying about on the floor on old tapa mats. No one looked like they were doing much, but they waved and were ready at the drop of a hat to have their picture taken. Many of the people in Samoa are quite heavy and likely to be tattooed with ancestral and culturally meaningful designs. The yards were full of breadfruit, papaya, taro, banana, and other edible plants. Perhaps the Garden of Eden was here. Dogs, chickens, and pigs roam about. Behind the *fale* would likely be a small, square-roofed structure with no sides; this is the kitchen. Food is cooked over an open fire, using banana leaves to steam vegetables. Coconut husks are used for fuel, and coconut cream is used in many dishes. It is obtained by first removing the husk and exposing the nut, then a well-placed strike of a stone along the lateral line of the shell will open it easily. The chef then scrapes the coconut fruit into a bowl in shreds. After he has collected enough shreds, he places the shreds on a fabric (like cheesecloth) made of the coconut husk and wrings the shreds inside the fabric until a milky liquid falls into a waiting bowl. The resulting liquid has the consistency of cream and is delicious. The leftover coconut shreds are fed to the hungry, but

197

wary, chickens. This makes catching them possible. As they brazenly come forth for the coconut, a quick grab results in one of the three main elements of the Sunday feast. The other two are fish and suckling pig.

Samoans are very religious people, and each village has one or more churches within its boundaries. Many of these churches are quite elaborate and grand, given the appearance of the surrounding village. Each afternoon at around 6 p.m. a horn sounds or bells ring, calling family members home for evening prayers. There is a curfew then, and under chiefs patrol the village looking for truants. Church attendance is mandatory on Sunday and subject to a fine if a person fails to attend. Each Sunday there is a morning service followed by the family feast, which is cooked by the men. Men do most of the cooking in Samoa. When people go to church, they wear their Sunday best. For women that is pretty standard finery including a big, fancy hat. For men it involves the lava-lava, which is the traditional, long wrap skirt. Normally during the week, they wear a working form of the lava-lava with or without a shirt. Shirts are usually cotton with a tropical print. On Sunday, despite the hot, humid weather, they wear an undershirt and

English-style white shirt and tie. You can see them walking along the side of the road to and from the churches. Once morning church services are over, they head back to the family compound for a feast with their extended family. After the feast comes a nap. When driving about the countryside, one can see resting on the floor of their *fales* heaving mounds of golden brown people snoozing blissfully in the midday heat. When naptime is over, it is back to church for 2 or more hours of evening services.

The village churches in Samoa are very big and impressive. All but two villages in the whole country have two or more churches inside their borders. There are the usual choices: Roman Catholic, Methodist, Jehovah's Witness, Seventh-Day Adventists, Presbyterian, and Mormon. Mormon is the fastest growing, and they have new facilities everywhere. I asked several people why that is. The answer? They have basketball courts, I was told. Perhaps this is as deep as it gets. Several of our drivers were Mormons, and I asked them about their experiences. Two of three had been foreign missionaries, and the offer of free travel abroad is probably very attractive to these young people. I asked both what was the distinguishing belief that differentiated them from, say, Catholics or Protestants. They didn't have any idea. Churchgoers are expected to tithe to the church. Once a month there is a special collection to support the minister or priest of the church, and if enough of a contribution isn't forthcoming from the flock, names of the laggards may be posted. The Protestant ministers that we saw lived in relatively lavish homes, with windows and air-conditioning. They drive fancy cars and are among the highest paid people in Samoan society . . . they take the prime cuts!

Families in Samoa are large, often 10 or more children. Land is inherited by males, and females normally join their husband's family and move to their husband's village after marriage. A high percentage of Samoan children leave the island as adults, residing in America, New Zealand, and Australia during their working years, and return to Samoa and the family compound after they retire. Children residing abroad are tapped constantly to help support their family at home, to provide the money to build a new home if needed, or to pay the travel costs of visiting Samoan family members. The ones remaining at home take care of mom, dad, and other family elders. Weddings and funerals are lavish and expensive affairs. These events can involve several days of feasting and a thousand or more invited and uninvited guests. People come from all over to eat during the events, and they will often take food away with them when they go home. Each nuclear family within the larger family will be tapped for several pigs, chickens, and pounds of fruits and vegetables. They will almost certainly be called on for a thousand or more dollars each, which is when the phones abroad will ring. These events can cost $10,000 or $12,000 on average! One of our Samoan acquaintances told us that if a brother's or sister's overseas phone has been disconnected or isn't answered, it is because they don't want to hear from the folks back home because they are probably tapped out! I don't think I would be far off the facts if I said that Samoa's largest export is its surplus population, and that its greatest import is cash from abroad.

On to Tonga: We checked out of Samoa on Tuesday and headed west around Upolu and south through the Apolima Strait toward Vava'U, Kingdom of Tonga. It was a beautiful day to start our 2-day, 350-mile passage, and the weather was forecasted to be very pleasant. We put out our lines and what do you know . . . we got a very big strike on the way through the strait. Tom didn't want to take it, so I did. It seemed huge: I battled it for at least 30 minutes. It was a strange fight, though, because it didn't run . . . it just wouldn't come in. I pulled and pulled, but I couldn't make any headway for about a half an hour. Then it began to weaken as I took advantage of every opportunity to reel it in. I had to be careful as I could easily break the line and lose my $20 lure! Gradually it gave way, and I could see that I was bringing something in . . . a tuna! I pulled it up, and there it was—a 15 to 20-pound bigeye. Very small for that species of fish and not capable of the sort of fight I experienced. I always wanted a bigeye, but then I saw the problem: a third of it was gone. A shark had grabbed its tail just as it struck my line and he was fighting me for the tuna . . . but I won most of it!

As has been said: "Keep your boat on the water and the water out of your boat!" Certainly, words to live by.

August 21 to September 22

Samoa to Vava'U: Our 320-mile trip down to Tonga from Samoa was a rough ride, with swells from the east in the 8 to 10-foot range. *Argo* handles high seas very well. Our stabilizers keep her from rolling or yawing very much, but the constant pitching and movement is unpleasant. It was a beam sea, and some of the swells were so large that we rolled to starboard as they began to pass under us, then leveled at the crest, and then rolled to port and slid down the back side of the wave sideways as it passed under us. Of course, we didn't leave Samoa without a weather forecast, but it was dead wrong. Unfortunately, a trough had formed and it was blowing around 30 knots for the whole voyage. No one felt well during the trip, and I got a good dose of seasickness to boot. It's passages like this that makes us think fondly of spending time in a plush hotel in Provence!

THE KINGDOM OF TONGA

The Kingdom of Tonga   **Vava'U – Ha'Apia – Tongatapu**

Arrival at Neiafu: We arrived at the town of Neiafu on the island of Vava'U at 07:00 and tied to the custom's dock. Before our lines were secured, the immigration, health, and customs agents were on the dock and ready for business. After filling out the customary forms and paying about $100 in various fees, we went ashore. It wasn't long before we had arranged telephone service, bought fresh vegetables from the farmers' market near the dock, and made a short walk down Main Street to see what Neiafu was all about. What we found was a ragtag collection of a few stores, three banks, a Western Union office, several bars, restaurants, churches, and souvenir shops. Neiafu is a waypoint for boaters who are either going south to Tongatapu and New Zealand, or westward to Fiji. The harbor is very large, clear blue, and deep. It can accommodate any size ship that can make it past the narrow channel in the reef at its entrance. When we arrived, there were about 30 boats on mooring balls in the harbor. At anchor in the western end of the harbor was Paul Allen's 225-foot yacht *Meduse*, one of several he owns. Along the waterfront was a selection of bars and restaurants; however, the Aquarium Restaurant seemed to be the gathering spot for most of the boaters. Mike, its American owner, was a congenial fellow who gladly provided information about the island and help with anything anyone needed.

Late in the morning we moved to an anchorage just west of town and anchored in 95 feet of water near *Meduse*. Rumor had it that some big shot like Bill Gates was coming, but no one showed up while we were there. Not to be outdone, we had our own personage to welcome aboard at Neiafu. Just as we dropped anchor, Mike from the Aquarium called on the VHF to tell us that our intrepid friend Reid had arrived and was at his dockside restaurant waiting for us to pick him up. Reid had flown 36 hours from Los Angeles to Auckland, then to Nuku'alofa, and finally on to Neiafu. He actually arrived a day ahead of schedule. With him were two bottles of vodka and three printer cartridges (that are unique to the United States). It was great to see our old friend.

Meanwhile back on *Argo*, Tom was diligently washing the sea salt off and readying her for company. Giving *Argo* a bath is a lot of work and takes an entire day. We are very lucky to have Tom onboard; Tom takes a great deal of pride in his work and makes this yacht shine like no other. He is a great asset to us.

The weather in Vava'U was in some ways a welcome relief from the searing heat and high humidity we had experienced since leaving Jamaica 6 months ago. For the first time, we didn't need air-conditioning. The Tongans told us that it was unseasonably cold: the temperature was consistently about 77 degrees, humidity in the high 60s, and the seawater temperature was 78 degrees. Despite this perfect combination, the wind blew at 20 mph for days, making the water a little too rough and cloudy to enjoy water sports or riding about in the dinghy. It's springtime in this part of the world, and transitional weather patterns bring more clouds and wind than usual. We were disappointed that Reid didn't have better conditions given the long trip he made to get here.

We found Neiafu to be a very pleasant place with friendly people who were helpful and kind. Many boating friends that we had met along the way were also there, so we spent a few enjoyable evenings catching up and hearing about their experiences. Altogether we spent 18 days at anchor diving, touring the island, talking with friends, whale snorkeling, going to church, feasting, and enjoying all that is.

The Kingdom of Tonga: The Vava'U Group is the northernmost archipelago of the Kingdom of Tonga. The kingdom is made up of three island groups: Vava'U to the north, Ha'Apia, in the center lying 60 miles south of Vava'U, and Tongatapu, the third archipelago that lies 60 miles south of Ha'Apia and is home to the kingdom's capital city, Nuku'alofa. Altogether the three groups stretch about 160 miles from north to south along the Tonga Ridge, which is formed by the meeting of the Australian and Pacific Plates in the South Pacific Ocean. Tonga is thought to be moving eastward at 25 cm per year and is gradually sinking into the ocean.

Unlike all the other islands of Polynesia, the Kingdom of Tonga has never been colonized by Westerners. Tonga is governed by a king who enjoys all the regalia that goes with monarchy: nobles, royal lands, money minted with the king's image on it, royal tombs, a palace, and of course, ownership of the key money-making enterprises. Originally the three island groups were each governed by a Tu'i Tonga, a man/god chief.

The Tu'i Tonga on Ha'Apia, with the help of the Wesleyan Methodists and the British Navy, attacked the Tu'i Tonga on Tongatapu and in the 20-year war overthrew him and established a kingdom modeled on the British monarchy. The chiefs who supported him were made nobles, and the Methodist Church and the British were granted special rights. The king named himself George I (all kings are named George, and today we have George VI). He proclaimed that all land was owned by God and given to him by God for safekeeping. Of course, he took the prime and largest cuts for himself, his cronies, and the Wesleyan Methodists. Even today all land in Tonga is owned by the king, but sometime ago the king granted title to 8-acre parcels to individual Tongan males. Women may not own land.

The country has a constitution that was established in the mid-1800s. Until 2006 the king was more or less an absolute monarch and ruled a nation of about 103,000 people. There were riots and the burning of buildings in 2006 as Tongans demanded greater democratization of the government, but it isn't clear that anything of substance has changed, although it now has a parliament.

There are estimated to be about 70,000 Tongans living abroad who send money back to their families in Tonga, and this constitutes the largest source of foreign revenue for the country. About 70,000 people live in the capital of Nuku'alofa, about 15,000 live on Vava'U, and the balance live on other islands. Land can only be titled to Tongans; however, squatter's rights come into play when a person moves onto land that no one is paying attention to and resides on for 10 years or more. The original owner loses title. A Tongan must appear in person on his land at least once every 10 years and chase any squatters off or risk losing it. If a palangi (a white person) wishes to acquire property, it can only be leased from a Tongan or noble, and leases must be approved by parliament and the king. Leases are easily obtained, and the lessee will eventually get a copy of the lease with the king's signature and the royal seal in wax at the bottom. Leases can extend up to 50 years.

As in Samoa, families are large (average 10 children), and those members that are ambitious are encouraged to migrate abroad and send money home. By and large I don't think Tongans are a very motivated lot, although they are very friendly. The country is poor, and the brighter people head for Australia, New Zealand, or the United States if they can get a visa, which is increasingly hard to come by. Most countries feel that they have enough islander immigrants, particularly as some Tongans abroad have been pushed into crime to meet the financial demands of their families at home. Title to land is devised on a primogenitor basis, so if you are not the firstborn male you might as well leave for greener pastures. Of course, at least one lucky soul is obligated to stay home and take care of mom, dad, and grandma, and keep an eye on the family's property. Despite their obvious poverty, few beg or go hungry. Tongans take care of each other and are deeply committed to their family. Tongans seem to be proud people; they have their islands, their heritage, and their religions. They also have a Western Union office in almost every village of any size, and its sign is the only one in good repair. Aside from having children, they raise pigs and chickens (*raise* is too strong a verb as they just let them run about and grab one for dinner as needed), cultivate small gardens of taro, kava, bananas, carrots, and whatever else will grow. Most of the land I saw under cultivation was done by human labor: no beasts of burden or tractors. Driving around the whole island I saw four tractors and one horse. Undoubtedly there are a few more, but most land is cultivated on small plots on a human scale. All this is supplemented by fish the men catch.

The climate here is more temperate than all the other islands we have visited, and for the first time we have seen fruits and vegetables that we are more accustomed to seeing at home. Each village has at least one church, and Sunday is an observed day of rest, religion, family, and feast. Their school system has managed to teach the English language to almost everyone over the last 25 years. The government provides primary school, and the religious sects, particularly Mormon and Wesleyan Methodist, provide secondary schools, although you have to belong to the church and tithe in order to send your children to the church's school. Driving around the countryside, you can see large noble estates, but most parcels are about 8 acres in size and are cultivated by a family for subsistence. The churches in Tonga are shamefully medieval in the power and wealth the clergy wields, and in the way people are forced to give money to them. The Mormons seem to be very aggressive and have built a facility at virtually every crossroad. We were told that they rebuild them every 10 years. Homes are very basic except for those of the local church ministers or government officials. Large houses (the size of a typical American suburban home) are either owned by nobles or church ministers. The villages are not kept up as they are in the other parts of Polynesia, and on the smaller islands of the Ha'Apia Group cyclone damage from last summer's storms is considerable.

Vava'U Group: Coming into Vava'U was very different from the other islands we had visited during the last 6 months. The island is not volcanic. It is a coral island rising abruptly about 300 feet from the ocean's surface to a flat plain that is covered in dense jungle. From the sea, the islands look like huge stone monoliths with dramatic cliffs; beaches are present only where the cliffs give way to a little bay or indentations in the rock. The water is crystal clear, and the bays and passages between the islands are deep sapphire blue and the islands colorful. Here, in the shelter of the islands and the warm waters of the mid-Pacific Ocean, humpback whales come to give birth and breed each year.

Whales: Vava'U is most well-known for swimming with whales. There are two or three outfitters who are licensed to take tourists on whale dives. A dive is actually a surface snorkel and is an all-day ordeal in which eight or so snorkelers accompany a guide, four at a time, into the water to swim next to a cow and calf (usually). Males are difficult to swim with because they are on the move and are often breaching or pushing each other around in an effort to attract the attention of a female (what's new?). Would-be swimmers wear wetsuits and ride around for hours in the open boat until an appropriate female and calf are spotted. Then the boat stops a hundred yards or so from the mother, and if she doesn't swim off, four snorkelers at a time quietly enter the water with a guide and swim over to within 15 or 20 feet of the whales. Females with newborns often rest for part of the day so as to let the little one nurse and safely play. As you swim toward the leviathan you can see how big these creatures are: 100-plus tons suspended just at the water's surface with the majority of the body hanging perhaps 100 or more feet below. You first see their giant black backs with a prominent spine. As you look downward you see the spine lead to the tail a hundred feet or so below in the blue water. The black upper body changes to a white underside with huge folds in its skin. The breathing hole is at the water's surface and is about one-third of the length of the body and behind the head. Forward of the breathing hole the head rests suspended in 15 or so feet of water and is a strange, but familiar, shape. The eyes are on the side of the head, well back of its huge jawline that is covered in barnacle-like growths. The little calf swims about its mother, turning and twisting as it goes, and then pausing for refreshment if desired. Calves drink about 50 gallons of a yogurt-type mother's milk each day and grow rapidly. The adjective *little* really doesn't apply, as they can be thousands of pounds within weeks.

My two most memorable animal experiences were swimming with a mother whale for forty-five minutes in Vava'U and having a large whale off the Oregon coast swim to our starboard side, roll over, and look at me as I was looking out the pilot house door on a warm moonlit night.

Rebecca

During our dives, we were within 10 or 15 feet of these huge, beautiful animals. On one of our dives we spent perhaps a half an hour within feet of a mother and calf. The baby came so close to us and was so frisky I thought it might injure us, not knowing its own youthful strength. After all the divers returned to the boat and were drying off, we watched the mother and baby at the surface of the water. I saw the mother's tail flukes rise high in the air, an indication of a deep dive. I assumed she was leaving. We were only a hundred yards or so from her. A moment or two later she erupted straight out of the sea, turning her immense body laterally over in the air, and then crashed down yards from our boat. It was awesome . . . spellbinding . . . breathtaking . . . like nothing we had ever seen or imagined. It was as though she was offering us one last glimpse into her world. After a few moments to collect our wits, we departed thankful for the experience and emotionally closer to our origins in the natural world.

See YouTube Video Swimming with Whales in Vavu'U, Kingdom of Tonga

The whale's world underwater in Vava'U is silent, tranquil, warm, and slow moving. Occasionally you can hear the whales sing. Sometimes you can see the males breaching, or pushing each other about in a contest of strength, or, more aggressively slamming each other with their giant heads in an attempt to prove dominance. For them this is not play, but the vital, essential business of life. It's also no place to snorkel!

Feasts: Like Samoans, Tongans love a feast. Aside from their private Sunday family gatherings, entrepreneurs offer feasts to tourists several days a week at different locations around the islands. We decided to go to one on Sunday at the 'Ene'io Botanical Garden. The proprietors picked us up in their rickety, old, filthy van and drove across the island through the little villages with the shiny new Mormon facilities to their seaside establishment. The owner, Halima, was celebrating his 69th birthday that day, so the feast was preceded by a speech in which he recalled growing up in the village and not knowing anything about the outside world, not even that it was round. He thanked providence for his good fortune to become the Assistant Secretary of Agriculture during his career, for his wonderful children, and apologized to his wife Lucy for being less than a perfect husband. With that, the feast was underway and one by one the eager guests proceeded to the buffet and began selecting from a variety of Tongan dishes, including suckling pig, curried fish, poultry, taro, breadfruit, curried vegetables, and other dishes. After the feast, I looked about and saw several pictures of Halima during his career, including one of him meeting Pope John Paul II in Rome in the company of other Tongan dignitaries, including HRH the King. He told me that he had actually met the Pope twice, and many other dignitaries from around the world as well. Not bad for a country not bigger than a small town in mid-America!

Our 25th Wedding Anniversary: We celebrated our 25th wedding anniversary here in Tonga. Rebecca found a nice resort established a few years ago by a sail boating couple from Switzerland who were apparently ready for life on the hard. Normally they are booked several weeks in advance, but somehow Rebecca got us in. Kathryn had called them from NYC to try to arrange a surprise, like a bottle of champagne or a local musician to play for us, but nothing like that was available in Tonga. We moved *Argo* to an anchorage offshore and dinghied in for a lovely dinner complete with a tablecloth and a beautiful flower centerpiece. Rebecca's dish was quite interesting: a whole red snapper split down the back from head to tail and baked. It was very artistic as it looked like a large, pink, spiral ribbon. It was delicious.

Diving the Shipwreck: Just west of our anchorage at Neiafu was a wreck that sunk about 20 years ago in 125 feet of water. This ship apparently had caught on fire, and the captain and engineer stayed aboard to try and save her. Both died when she sank. Wrecks are common in this part of the world. In Nuku'alofa, we counted nine wrecks in the harbor. In the third world, maintenance is not a valued practice on anything, much less a ship, and cyclones sweep through these parts every year. Many ships drag their anchor during big storms and wind up on a reef and break apart. Compounding matters, often the crews are made up of local men, and when a cyclone arrives they abandon their ship to take care of their families.

Tom and I dove the wreck on a sunny morning. I had never done that sort of diving before; it was a little spooky, given that two people lost their lives. The water wasn't very clear, but we could see her lying broken on the bottom. She was known as the *Clan McClellan*, a relatively large ship of a few hundred feet. We explored the decks above 100 feet in depth, seeing her railing and mast and thinking of the hopes that she carried with her and the tragedy of her demise.

Going to Church in Neiafu: Religion is the center of community life in Polynesia, much like it is in the American South. Here there is practically a church on every corner. One Sunday we decided to go to church and see what a service in Neiafu is all about. The church we visited was a Catholic church. It was built on the most prominent hill in the town and from the front looked like something you might find in Italy. The façade was Italianate in design, very ornate with painted pictures of Christ on the bell tower. It was built on a hill that required climbing about 25 steps to reach the entrance, and the climb made the church all the more imposing. Behind the facade was a more modest structure, sort of a pole barn with a white metal roof. Inside were pews and a couple of statues and shrines, very typical of a modest Catholic church. The service began when the choir started to sing, and that was something to behold and the real reason for our visit. The choir constituted at least a quarter of the people in the church, but the quality of their singing was second to none. The male singers were particularly noteworthy in that they possessed a deep, melodious voice reminiscent of the Russian religious music we heard in the old churches of Russia years before. They were terrific. A procession then began when the priest, following a small retinue of elders and officiates, made his way down the aisle to the altar. The church was packed, and people were standing outside. Men wore traditional lava-lavas with a ta'ovala skirt wrapped around their waists. The ta'ovala is a grass cloth traditional garb woven from mulberry bark as in the Samoan tapa-making process that I described previously. The women were, of course, dressed in their finest, and they too wore a sort of grass skirt over their Western dress, but much lacier and also made of tapa. Going to the church was a wonderful cultural experience for us.

A Drive-About: One of our friends, Adam, captain of *Spirit of Adventure*, mentioned that he had taken a dune buggy tour on the back roads of Vava'U. Rebecca and I thought it might be fun, so we arranged for a tour. The little company was run by a family of expats trying to eke out a living in Neiafu. We arrived at the appointed hour and met our guide Joshua. Joshua had grown up in New Zealand but had a Tongan father. His father owned some property in town, including a distillery of sorts, and at his death it became Joshua's. So, Joshua came back to Tonga to claim his birthright. Things weren't going all that well for him, but he knew the island well and spoke impeccable English, so off we went.

We should have known better—the cart was a death trap. I could hardly get into the thing, but away we rode over hill and dale, past the ubiquitous Mormon temple and basketball court, past the cemeteries with their huge quilts memorializing a recently deceased person, past the little hand-tilled fields of taro, eventually finding the cow path Joshua was looking for. This path took us several miles off the beaten track—through the dense jungle, past little subsistence farms, to some of the most beautifully natural and unspoiled sights we have seen. One such place was a gorgeous cliff overlooking the sea. The cliff had been eroded in a most unusual way by centuries of relentless pounding by the sea. About 50 feet above the sea was a huge circular hole about 20 feet in diameter in the cliff's outcropping. On the prominence above it roosted hundreds of fox bats—fruit-eating bats about a foot long that hung in the branches on the trees above.

Ha'Apia Group: The Ha'Apia Group lies about 65 miles south of Vava'U. We left our anchorage early in the morning and enjoyed a lovely cruise, one of the best we have experienced. It was a bright sunny day with calm seas and whales breaching along the way. Our trip took about 8 hours, and we arrived at Ha'ano Island late in the day. Approaching these islands takes great care and should only be done when the sunlight allows one to see all the coral heads and reefs. We cautiously entered the anchorage with all hands focused on any signs of danger. We were all very surprised by the geology of these islands compared to Vava'U; Ha'Apia Islands are flat sand atolls rising no more than 5 feet above the sea's surface and covered in jungle and shrubs. As I mentioned, surrounding the islands are extensive coral reefs, which makes them unpopular with boaters. When we arrived, we were the lone boat in the anchorage. After a pleasant and restful night at anchor, we went ashore the next morning to reconnoiter the little village of Ha'ano. Once ashore, we quickly appreciated that it had been terribly damaged by a cyclone the previous season. As we walked through the little village, we saw men rebuilding a water tower, and some of the people whose homes were destroyed living in tents. It was a very poor area in the best of times, but now it was devastated. After walking about and greeting the people we met, we decided to move along to the next island of Lifuka and the capital of Ha'Apia, Pangai village.

Tom's 30th Birthday: We thought that Pangai would have a little more to offer, and because it was Tom's 30th birthday we wanted to find a town with a suitable celebratory establishment. We picked our way through the coral heads and reefs and anchored a mile or so offshore. Our friends Jeff and Sherry on *Grasshopper* showed up in the anchorage shortly after we arrived to help celebrate, and we all went into Pangai village. The village itself was also heavily damaged by last January's cyclone, and people were living in very dilapidated circumstances. The town seemed all but abandoned. Dogs roamed the streets everywhere, which made us feel uneasy, particularly if they formed packs. As on other Polynesian islands, these dogs are a very sturdy breed and look to be part pit bull. On one street 10 or 15 of these dogs formed a pack and took off after a pig. They nipped at it and badgered it. Finally, as they became more brazen and aggressive, the pig must have sensed that the game could turn lethal at any moment, and with that, turned tail and outran the dogs in making its escape. As we walked farther along, the only human activity we saw was centered on a little food market run by Chinese proprietors. Older Tongans distrust the Chinese grocers because they sell alcohol to the young men, who in turn get drunk, rowdy, and fight. As we turned the corner toward the Mariner's Café, we heard a commotion and saw a serious fistfight erupt between two young men who had obviously been drinking. We wanted to get away from the fight and the men who were hanging around watching, so we hurried on to the café only to find it closed. A few minutes later the loser of the fight staggered by with the aid of an inebriated friend, his head bleeding profusely from a gash administered by his opponent with a wrench. As soon as the little crowd disbursed, we headed back to *Argo* where Rebecca made a wonderful birthday dinner complete with filet mignon, mashed potatoes, corn, and a fruit pie for dessert with candles for Tom.

The next day we moved south about 30 miles to the island of Ha'afeva. This island has a protected lagoon, like the Tuamotus. We entered the lagoon over a very narrow channel in the reef and anchored near the small dock the islanders use to bring in supplies. The lagoon's bottom was littered with coral heads and rocks, so Tom stood lookout on the bow pulpit and we picked our way around until he found a patch of sand and we dropped anchor. After settling down we found the area absolutely beautiful, but the wind was up and made for a rolling anchorage. Tom and Rebecca went for a swim, and we all took the dinghy for a spin later in the afternoon. The view from *Argo* was absolutely beautiful. We were surrounded by other islands and, more closely in, coral reefs. The ocean swells were crashing on the reefs, and off in the distance we could see the silhouette of the only active volcano in Tonga, which made for a spectacular vista.

As beautiful as it was, it was time to continue south toward Tongatapu and prepare for our passage to New Zealand. Our wonderful friends, Melanie and Curtis Hoff, were meeting us in Nuku'alofa. They planned on joining us for the final passage to New Zealand and the conclusion of our great adventure.

Tongatapu Group: These are the main islands of the Kingdom of Tonga and the site of its capital, Nuku'alofa. The city is on the south side of a very large bay that is open to the north. There are many reefs, coral heads, and islands scattered about, but so far, the charts have been accurate and we haven't bumped into anything yet. We anchored a little over a mile from the city's docks and inner harbor, which is in a shamble and littered with sunken wrecks. Several abandoned, rusting Japanese fishing vessels are tied to a dock and bear witness to Tonga's naval prowess; they confiscated the ships because the Japanese violated Tongan territorial waters. We anchored off Angiomotin Island at Big Mama's Yacht Club. Out front is a sunken bow of a large ship that went down here in a cyclone about 20 years ago. It acts as an artificial reef and attracts a lot of colorful fish. People come out to see the fish, enjoy the beautiful beach, and swim in the crystal-clear water. Mama is a very large lady, sort of like Aunt Jemima. She owns the Tiki bar, which looks inviting, but the food is horrible. At this end of the bay I counted nine partially sunken ships.

To get to the city, we took our tender about a mile and a half across the bay to the inner harbor, and then the inner-inner harbor, or boat basin. Instead of a proper, safe floating dock, they have taken scraps of old wood and hobbled things together to build a walkway and then floated it on old oil barrels. It is rickety and wobbly. The planks are unevenly spaced so that one could easily trip and fall through into the filthy water, or, if you get off center, as Rebecca did, one end of a plank could give way, and she nearly fell in. Once the dock is negotiated, the main road to town is near at hand, and the town center is about a 15-minute walk. Along the paved road are vendors selling fruits and vegetables, taro, watermelons, and firewood; hundreds of neatly stacked piles of cut wood for cooking fires are stacked next to the road. This is in contrast to optical fiber cable being installed along one of the main streets downtown.

Like the harbor, Nuku'alofa suffers from aesthetic deprivation. It is shabby and without many of the staples of everyday life that we had hoped to find here. They have a very fine farmers' market with all sorts of things we haven't seen on other islands, such as lettuce. I was looking around for a Tonga cap, and asked the local cap embroiderer where I could find one or if he could make one for me. He looked at me as though I were nuts. Who wants a Tonga hat? All their caps have American or other foreign sports team logos on them. Here, people identify with the West.

The next day we took a tour of the island. The first stop was the Royal Palace (19th-century Victorian-style summer home), then the Royal Tombs (it looks like a normal Tongan cemetery, where the soil is mounded over the body, but large stone statues of the deceased kings in European military garb stand over the graves). There were several beautiful coastal sites to see, including blowholes and natural arches, and finally the Ha'amonga 'a Maui trilithon, which is an ancient stone arch similar in some ways to Stonehenge, which marked the ceremonial center where the Tu'i Tonga presided. Every village has at least one Mormon school, basketball court, and meeting hall, and maybe a Catholic or Wesleyan Methodist church. There are also the odd Seventh-Day Adventist and Jehovah's Witnesses' meeting halls as well. In Tonga, the haves live well; the rest are serfs.

Ha'Amonga A Maui - gateway to the Royal Grounds of the Tu'iTonga circa 1200 AD

Leaving Tonga: Our friends, Melanie and Curtis Hoff, joined us in Nuku'alofa for the ride south to New Zealand. It was very symbolic in the sense that they came down to Stuart, Florida, and waved goodbye to us from the bridge as we left America, and now they were joining us on our final leg of the journey to New Zealand. Because the trip to New Zealand is long and fraught with the possibility of difficult seas, we offered them the chance to just meet us in Auckland, but they wanted to come along and we were very happy to have them. The Hoffs are boaters who have cruised the US East Coast extensively, so we all studied the weather files and decided unanimously to leave as soon as possible after fueling Wednesday at noon. Our passage involved threading the needle between three potential storms that were expected to form while we were at sea. A low was due to make its way across our course, bringing with it very high winds and high seas (13 feet), but if we left Tonga on Wednesday afternoon we felt there was a good chance that we could get south of it.

Tonga offers the possibility of buying tax-free fuel if we buy it on the way out, so Wednesday morning we hooved to a crumbling cement dock at the harbor (after helping an itinerant boater move to a mooring) and arranged to take on fuel. To get the tax-free permit we had to check out of the country with customs, which meant checking out with immigration (whose office was across town), then to the harbormaster's office on the other side of town to pay port charges (a real ripoff at about $200 USD for a week at anchor), then to the Total Petroleum facility with $14,000 in Tongan cash. To get the Tongan money, we had to go to the bank on Monday and convert our dollars. Lucky for us, in Tonga you can convert without charge up to $10,000 USD to Tongan per person per day. So, Rebecca and I each took enough US dollars and converted them so we could pay Total for the fuel. When we left the bank, my pockets were bulging with money and Rebecca's purse was stuffed. Although we were nervous, that's the only way it's done in Tonga! When we got to the Total office, the tax-free fuel price was the equivalent of $3.90 per gallon, which wasn't too bad (they sell it in liters, and we bought about 8,000 liters).

The fuel truck was due at noon, but arrived about an hour late (it's on Tongan time), and it took about an hour to fuel. In the end, *Argo* was full! We left Nuku'alofa on the incoming tide at about 14:30 on September 24 bound for Auckland, New Zealand, and the end of our voyage.

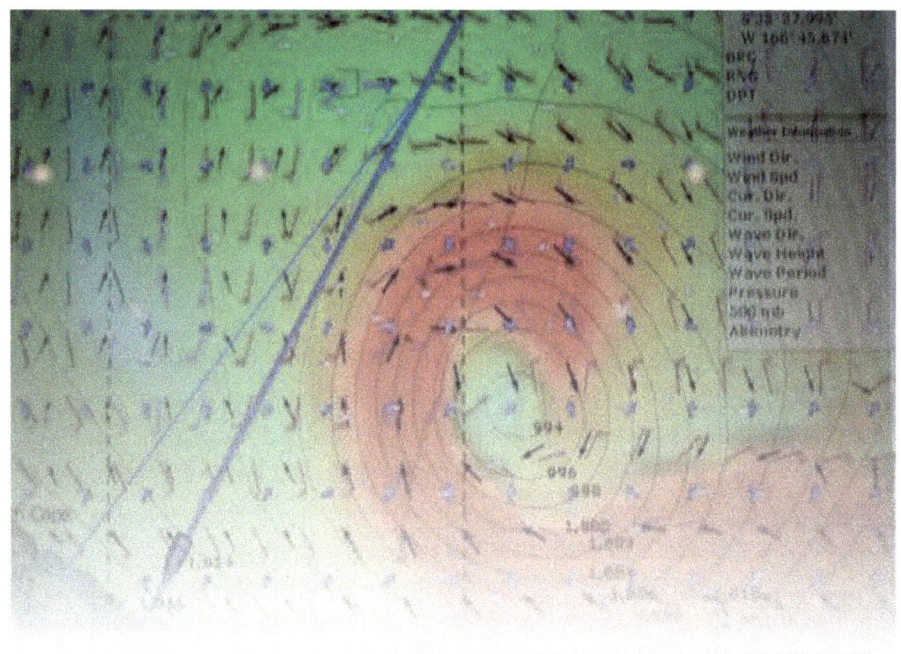

AT SEA TO NEW ZEALAND

September 21–29   **Encountering a Force 10 Gale**

At Sea in the South Pacific off the Coast of New Zealand: Leaving
Tongatapu required negotiating the channel between the reefs and 'Eua
Island to the east. The channel was boiling with an inrushing tidal current
the severity of which we hadn't seen since cruising Desolation Sound in
British Columbia in 2011. Once outside the channel we could see the waves
crashing on shore and the blowholes spouting huge mists of water in the air.
After about an hour we reached the open sea and the real show began; the
largest swells I have ever seen and only imagined came rolling toward us.

They were somewhere around 20 feet high on a moment of 12 seconds. They were massive mountains of water rolling at 30 mph under our keel. It was truly a spectacular, awesome, spellbinding sight! *Argo* was first lifted up by the waves, then she rolled over the top and came running down the backside. It really looked like a somewhat smaller version of the waves shown in the movie *The Perfect Storm*. Despite the size of the swells, our travel over them was pleasant due to their long moment. Swells of that size are things of beauty and amazement, and at the same time, terrifying. As we moved along, the seas subsided to a more normal state; we had 20 knots of wind and 8 to 12-foot seas on the forward port quarter for the balance of the day. We all took Meclizine to combat seasickness, and as a result we were all sleepy, but not sick. I slept like a baby as Tom stood the night watch. My crewmates, however, reported not sleeping so well that first night.

The next day things began to calm down, and by the second full day our passage was very pleasant. We downloaded a weather file from the satellite and confirmed that we were on track to avoid the worst of the storms that lay ahead. The current in this part of the ocean can be as high as 2 knots on our nose. It must be because of the upwelling of cold water from the Tongan Trench, which is one of the deepest parts of the ocean at 32,000 feet deep. We ramped up our rpm to 1,500 to try and maintain a speed of at least 8 knots, but often we would barely make 7 knots. We tried to maintain as much speed as possible to sneak past the rough weather emerging to our south; occasionally we made over 9 knots when the current slacked off. During the third, fourth, and fifth days, the ocean was like a lake, but our weather files showed the potential for rough seas as we approached New Zealand. We made plans to alter our course for the northern port of Opus if things turned sour. Meanwhile Rebecca and Melanie were cooking up some fantastic meals in the galley. Before we made landfall in New Zealand, we had to eat all our meat and vegetables or the Kiwis would confiscate it.

Force 10 Gale: Around 11:00 on September 29, with only 60 miles to go to Great Barrier Island, the radar picked up the image of a storm ahead. The seas were calm, the barometer was 1014, and the wind was only 10 knots. The forecasts had been very accurate during our passage, and we were updating them four times a day via satellite. We anticipated seas of 10 to 12 feet, which is no big deal for *Argo*; as it turned out, the actual weather we confronted was twice that forecast. I put a picture of the weather chart on the next page so you can see what we wound up facing. By 12:00 the seas had changed direction and were building as expected, and the wind was nearly 20 knots. By 14:00 the wind was about 45 knots +/–, and the seas continued to build. By 15:00 the winds were sustained over 45 knots and mostly in the 50 to 60 knot range, with top winds at 63.3 knots. Seas became tremendous at 20 to 30 feet at 8 to 12 seconds. They were huge, steep; mountains of water stair-stepped by the ferocious wind, rolling toward us at 30 mph, sucking the water up from beneath and leaving in its wake a deep and treacherous valley. The wind roared in a frightening howl, the ocean was a tumultuous, angry caldron.

I tried to position *Argo* to quarter the waves. Suddenly a massive rogue wave slammed over onto our bow, over the Portuguese bridge, and into the pilothouse windows. My adrenaline shot up. By now the wind was over 60 knots, and I began to contemplate an emergency scenario. At this point, everyone was in the pilothouse helping me evaluate options; lucky for us, Curtis Hoff has a PhD in marine engineering and many years of boating experience. His counsel was very helpful. I asked Tom to call the Coast Guard and report our position. Tom picked up the microphone and hailed the Coast Guard several times, but no response. Maybe our VHF radio was bad, so we switched to the other radio. Again, he hailed them for several minutes, but no reply. At that point, busily engaged in battling the storm, I asked Tom to call the US Coast Guard on the sat-phone and get the telephone number for the New Zealand authorities. We got the number and called the Marine police. They had been listening to our radio calls, but didn't respond because we had been calling the Coast Guard, which in New

Zealand is a voluntary organization similar to our Power Squadrons in the United States. I couldn't believe it.

Anyway, after that call we reported by VHF radio to Maritime Radio Great Barrier Island every hour until we reached safe waters 9 hours later. In the meantime, I focused on sea-keeping issues: guiding *Argo* in a direction and speed that prevented her from being broadsided by one of those giant waves, or falling into a trough and pitch-polling.

See the YouTube Video Force Ten Gale

"We were 250 NM behind Argo in our 60-foot Nordhavn... BELIEVE me it was NOT FUN. We got hit by a measured, 30-footrogue wave. These guys dealt with stuff that most folks never see IN PERSON. The video does not do justice to how bad it was. 7 days of pure mess, but worth the voyage. The boats performed fantastically."

-Adam Paskowitz

From the pilothouse, we could see the giants coming our way; at first, we could look up to the waves' crest above our roofline. It seemed as though they were going to crash into us, but then we would roll to starboard, be lifted to the top, see the combing crest, and watch the crest flow under us. We would then fall off the back of the wave, roll modestly to our port side, and slide down into the trough. *Argo* performed perfectly.

After a half hour or so we became concerned that by quartering the waves on our bow we were inextricably moving into the storm. By this time, we had been in the storm about 5 hours. We hoped the wind would subside and the storm would blow out to sea, but instead it was intensifying. We had to turn around and try to approximate a course toward land. We discussed the pros and cons of coming about in these dangerous seas, but in the end, we decided to take the risk. Turning is perhaps the most dangerous maneuver a captain can execute in a storm of this severity, but we had to do it. The sun was setting, and we didn't want to lose the light. We looked for a softening of the waves and found a moment in which to bring her about and put her stern to the waves. Although we were afraid she might be breached over the stern or take a wave broadside, that never happened. In fact, after the turn, *Argo* rode the seas more comfortably than before. We stayed on this course for about an hour. By now it was 19:00 and we had been in the storm for 6 hours, but we were much more confident in *Argo* and our ability to survive and ride out the storm. At this point I decided we had to return to our original course, which would take us to the outer fringes of the storm and eventually to Auckland, but this required another turnabout.

After executing the turn, we were finally on course for Auckland again. *Argo* was riding relatively well given the circumstances. The sun had set, it was pitch black outside, and the wind was screeching; we had 5 hours to go! An hour or so later Tom reported that the seawater pump for the hydraulic system had stopped functioning. Without this pump, the hydraulic system would soon overheat, we would lose our stabilizers, and we would be in serious, perhaps catastrophic, danger. Once again, I had to turn *Argo* stern-to and position her so that we could turn off the stabilizers before they closed down due to overheating. I found that *Argo* was most stable in this position. So, we turned on our spotlight to look at the waves, determined the exact wave direction, waited for the right moment, and initiated the turn with wide-open throttle. She made the turn between waves quickly, and we found a very stable position for her to assume. Tom sprang into action: he removed the strainer and the cover plate to the impeller. Everything was OK. Then he took the input hose off the heat exchanger, thinking that perhaps it sucked in some air and became air locked; again, everything seemed OK. So, we turned the system back on, and, thank God, it worked.

At this point we needed to turn *Argo* back into the waves and resume our course toward Great Barrier Island and safe anchorage still 5 hours away. Now it was pitch dark on the ocean. We were in the middle of this terrible storm, and waves were coming at us. *Argo* rode the waves perfectly, up and down, up and down. Once in a while a rogue wave would slam us near the stern and spin us off course, but *Argo* took the pounding and we moved relentlessly toward safe harbor. Every hour we called Maritime Radio to report our position. As we closed in on the Great Barrier Island, we asked permission to anchor. They reminded me that we had an appointment at 09:00 at the customs dock in Auckland the following morning, and they seemed reluctant to allow me to anchor in a bay near our position. The storm was still raging, and I had every right to seek safe harbor regardless of getting permission or not. Finally, we got permission, and 5 hours later at 01:30 we made Great Barrier Island and Katherine's Bay.

NEW ZEALAND

New Zealand   **Katherine's Bay**

Unfortunately, the bay was strewn with salmon farm pens, which may have been the reason for the reluctance of the authorities to grant us permission to anchor in that bay. With the storm raging around us, we dropped our anchor, had a drink, and fell into bed.

The next morning, we got underway at 08:45 and headed for Auckland, 55 miles away. Winds in the protected channel and Auckland harbor were still in the 30-mph range. We hove-to at the customs dock at 16:22, and cleared-in in an hour. The officers were very pleasant and issued us a 12-month cruising permit. They asked us how much the yacht was worth and calculated the fine due if we lingered longer: about $375,000! Then we tied up at our final destination, Viaduct Harbor Marina, at

18:00. After 14,000 miles of travel and 8 months underway, we didn't put so much as a scratch on this fantastic yacht! All of us are in awe of this boat. She took those huge seas with grace, and could take even more.

We were well prepared for the storm. We conduct engine room checks every hour during normal conditions and on the half hour during high seas (which permitted us to always discover problems before they became emergencies). We had installed storm plates on our large salon windows. We knew from experience how to deal with the problems and conditions we faced. Everything was tied down and properly stowed. Nothing was broken. No one was hurt. The outside of *Argo* and all of the equipment was undamaged and in perfect condition. It took a day or two for us to calm down, but we are all better seamen as a result of the experience. However, we do not want to experience it again!

Regarding the storm: it continued to rage for several days and intensified into a cyclone.

We spent a week in Auckland before returning home for a visit. Auckland is a wonderful, energetic city that is as delightful as it is expensive. The air here is crystal clear. We usually begin our visit to a new city by taking a tour, and our daylong private tour with the Hoffs was very enjoyable.

January 22, 2015 New Zealand: Auckland to Wellington

We arrived back in New Zealand on January 4 after a wonderful 2 ½ months back in the States. It was a busy time. We started off with a 1-week trip to New York City for a wonderful visit with our daughter and son-in-law, followed by a lecture I presented at the University of Michigan to economics students on the subject of "What it took for me to attain success in business." Next, Rebecca and I spoke over dinner to fellow boaters of the Power Squadron who invited us to present a talk on our transpacific voyage, which also was a lot of fun. One of the most rewarding events was our grandnephew Michael's Eagle Scout Award presentation ceremony: when young ones do well, it is especially gratifying for the family.

36-Day Drive around New Zealand

While we were home we received an email from Loren, a fellow who grew up in Ann Arbor but now lives in Auckland. He had seen Argo in the harbor and contacted us. We had a most enjoyable dinner with him and his partner, Donna, when we arrived back in Auckland.

While we were away, the boat in the slip next to us in Auckland provided Tom with some humorous entertainment; one afternoon the Voyager 56 cruising yacht arrived back in the harbor after a week or so out in the islands fishing. There were two couples on board, one member of which was the owner/captain who was on the fly bridge running the boat. He spun the boat around in the harbor and began backing into the slip next to us. He was moving the boat too fast. As the Voyager backed into the slip, engine roaring, smoke pouring from the exhaust, all hands took to their stations. However, something seemed amiss: it appeared that the party wasn't completely over and the crew seemed inebriated. Suddenly as it made its way halfway into the slip, the mate on the port bow fell off the boat into the frigid water. It was both dangerous and humorous. Tom was ready to jump in and save the bloke, and fortunately he made it to the dock without further mishap.

On another occasion, I talked to the owner for a while as he packed up their fish and washed down the boat. He was so happy and proud; he had just imported his dream car—a brand-new Corvette—and went on and on about what a fabulous car it was. As an American from the Detroit area, it was great to hear that our products are so well thought of. (An interesting factoid: only 550 left-hand-drive vehicles can be imported each year into New Zealand.)

New Zealand was formed by the upwelling of the Australian Plate as it overran the Pacific Plate about 30 million years ago. It lies on the Ring of Fire that encircles the Pacific Ocean, and so the islands are volcanic and prone to earthquakes, one of the most severe of which leveled Christchurch 4 years ago. New Zealand is the southernmost country in the world, lying between 37 and 47 degrees south—right in the middle of the "roaring 40s"—and is about 1,000 miles east of Australia and 1,000 miles south of Fiji. It is breezy here, if not downright windy. The air is extremely clean and clear. The sun shines with particular brilliance, perhaps owing to the hole in the ozone layer that lies directly overhead; sunscreen is a definite necessity. The islands are mountainous, and temperatures range from subtropical in the far north to subarctic in the far south. New Zealand enjoys four seasons, with summer occurring in January through March. The country is composed of two main islands that have a combined land area of 104,000 square miles and are home to a population of 4.5 million people. New Zealand GDP is about $125 billion or $30,000 per person. By comparison, Michigan's land area is about 97,000 square miles with a population of 10 million, a GDP of $450 billion, and a $45,000 per person average income.

The islands were first inhabited around 800 AD by the Maori, an Indo-Asian people who probably sailed from Indonesia or the Philippines. The European discovery of the islands occurred 800 years later when Captain Abel Tasman of The Netherlands discovered them in 1631 and named them New Zealand (in English it means New Sealand). Today the country has about 4.5 million inhabitants, most of whom live in one of its cities. Auckland is the largest city with a population of about 1.5 million, followed by the capital city, Wellington, with a population of 500,000. Of the population's makeup, 72 percent is white, 14 percent is Maori (indigenous people), and the balance is mostly Asian. New Zealand is a dominion of Great Britain and as such the Queen of England is the Chief of State with the Governor General her appointed representative. New Zealand has a parliamentary form of government with a unicameral legislature. The largest industry is agriculture, which is concentrated on sheep, cattle, wine, and lumber, followed in importance by tourism.

Traveling in New Zealand: To paraphrase Will Rogers, New Zealand may be free, but it ain't cheap. Everything is a little more expensive than in the United States, food in particular, which is surprising given that agriculture is the biggest industry here. The Kiwis have their own currency, the New Zealand dollar. Most of their foreign exchange is earned by agricultural exports. A bottle of New Zealand wine that we can buy in the United States for $20 costs about $50 here; a US $200/night hotel room costs about $350 here. Gasoline is around $6 a gallon, and car rentals are about $80/day. Of course, the near 20 percent sales tax doesn't help to keep prices low

January is a long holiday month for many Kiwis, so the roads are busy, as are the hotels and tourist attractions. We made our hotel reservations months in advance on advice that many of the choicer locations could be sold out during our planned travel time. The roads are two lanes across most of the country and they don't have shoulders, so if your left front tire rolls off the pavement you could be in serious trouble. The driver here is seated on the right side of the car, and traffic is reversed in direction relative to the United States; this takes a bit of getting used to, particularly around rotaries and at intersections. There are huge tandem trucks traveling the roads here, and they travel around the curvy, narrow roads at full speed. The result: New Zealand has one of the highest traffic fatality rates in the developed world. The posted speed limit literally means the maximum speed you are allowed to maintain, and they have hidden cameras placed about to take pictures of speeders. A person can get a ticket in the mail and not even know she has been caught until it is too late. Even 1 km over the speed limit can earn you a ticket, and 30 km over the limit is an automatic revocation of your driver's license. But given the narrowness of the roads and the curvy nature of them, I am ill-disposed to speeding anyway.

Auckland to Rotorua: We left Auckland January 9 and headed southwest toward the town of Otorohanga and the Waitomo Caves. Once outside of metro Auckland, we had about a 2-hour drive on winding country roads to reach the caves. The scenery was spectacular: steep, high hills with sharp ridges and deep gorges bearing witness to their violent creation in past ages. Green grass covered most of the land, although stands of conifers such as cedar, fir, and pine were abundant. In some places stands of giant eucalyptus grew, but everywhere the trees seemed much larger than in North America. It could be the long growing season, moderate temperatures, and brilliant sunshine, or maybe the rich volcanic soil. Who knows? But they certainly grow big trees here. Gradually as we traveled south the hills grew broader with large valleys. The valleys were green and lush and divided by tall (maybe 20 to 30 feet tall) hedges of an arborvitae shrub, in other places long windbreaks of Lombardy poplars or pines were all about. The rich grassland provides fodder for the large herds of sheep and dairy cattle, the largest we have ever seen. We were told of one farmer who milks 3,000 head on his 5,000-acre ranch, and of another who works 30,000 acres! Grassland here is cultivated like a crop. It is irrigated and fertilized to keep it green and full of nutrients for the grazing animals. There are no natural predators in New Zealand to harm the sheep or cattle. Everywhere there are beautiful stands of violet hydrangea, purple New Zealand phlox, and large orange flowers of a plant similar to an oversized Indian paintbrush.

As we drove westward across the North Island toward Waitomo, the flora became more verdant and lush with giant fern trees (Dicksoniaceae) abundant among the forests. These trees are about 20 feet tall with an umbrella-like expanse of fronds extending about 15 feet in diameter, with each frond being about 6 feet in length. They have existed for 300 million or more years and are thought to have been a primary staple of ancient herbivore dinosaurs. After a couple of hours driving, we arrived at the Waitomo Caves, a limestone cave formation in the center of the North Island. The cave we explored was very large and contained both stalactites and stalagmites and a very large cathedral room. Further down the path inside the cave we came upon the glowworms. The glowworms live on a part of the cave's ceiling above an underground river. The little worms emit a constant greenish light that makes the cave's ceiling look like a starry night's sky—pitch black with millions of little lights. To feed, the worms lower a thin strand of sticky, silky thread on which they hope to trap an insect that inadvertently wanders into the cave attracted by the worm's light. The whole experience was absolutely fascinating and beautiful. As we wandered down the steps deeper into the cave, we ultimately came to an underground river. There we boarded a small boat and made our way out of the cave, but not before encountering large concentrations of glowworms on the ceiling. It was dreamlike and otherworldly in both its beauty and its sheer strangeness.

Once back in reality, we continued our drive toward Rotorua. Along the way we stopped at a bird sanctuary that had several captive kiwis among other specimens. These are very rare animals, with only about 30,000 thought to exist. We were able to see the brown-spotted kiwi (rarest of them all), which is a large bird about the size of a small turkey. It looks awkward as it has no wings or tail, and its legs are placed far back toward its ample rump. It walks quickly about, poking its long beak into the soil in search of worms and grubs. A kiwi is agile, fast moving, and ill tempered. Its caretaker showed us a little scar she received while trying to care for it, confirming the fact that kiwis aren't very friendly.

An hour later we made it to Rotorua, home of the Maori culture. Rotorua is located on the banks of Lake Rotorua, the largest lake in New Zealand. The main attractions here are associated with the Maori culture, including a village located in the heart of a geothermal field. The little village was very interesting, with geysers, steam vents, and hot pools of water circling the 20 or so houses and stores in the town. It was both picturesque and unusual. Our Maori guide showed us how they cook all types of food in a community steamer powered by the water vapor escaping from vents from the earth; a completely frozen chicken is ready for the table in just 20 minutes! Likewise, they cook veggies in a bag immersed in a lovely aqua pond that is always at the boiling point. Around the corner from the village is a national park harboring a large stand of California redwoods planted in New Zealand around 1900. It was lovely to be among those spectacular trees and walk in the quiet, cool beauty unique to a redwood forest, which, as far as I am concerned, is as close to the home of God as we are likely to encounter on earth.

Rotorua is a fairly large country town, located on the shore of a lake in a flat, open valley. The town is based economically on agriculture and tourism. There aren't any shopping centers or big retailers here or elsewhere outside of Auckland; instead there are local shops located on a Main Street like we used to have in the United States. Our hotel was located on the lake, and although we carefully vetted it on the internet, we weren't aware that giant busses filled with Chinese tourists arrived every morning and disgorged into the lobby. They toured in groups, ate in groups, and crowded the elevators just like they do back in Shanghai or Beijing.

The next day we drove to the Waimangu Geothermal Area. This was a never-to-be-forgotten experience. The entry to the park is situated on the top of a mountain, and seeing the geothermal features required walking 90 minutes down a trail and along a fault fissure toward a lake at the bottom of the gorge. It was a crystal-clear day with brilliant sunshine and very warm temperatures. Our first stop was Frying Pan Lake (world's largest hot spring: 36 feet deep and 131 degrees Fahrenheit) with Cathedral Rock at its southern terminus. Then came the amazing aqua blue 176 degrees Inferno Crater Lake (intense aqua blue, –2.1 pH, largest geyser-like feature in the world, although the geyser cannot be seen because it is 120 feet under the surface of the water). Down the trail was Warbrick Terrace, a multicolored, fast-growing silica platform—the colors originating from sulfur, copper, magnesium, iron and silica, all modified and tempered by algae and bacteria of various types, and all growing in boiling water. Bubbling springs are everywhere, steam vents and mud pools, small geysers spouting, and hot and steaming water flowing like an ordinary creek down the valley floor—fault floor—to a distant lake. It was a great day walking amidst the powers that created our beautiful world.

On our fourth day, we drove 215 km to the town of Napier, located on the shores of Hawke's Bay. As we drove east, the grass changed from green to brown. The drive provided gorgeous vistas of flowering meadows, a distant snowcapped volcano, cultivated forestlands of giant pine trees, and rugged, steep volcanic hills on which trees such as oak, Lombardy poplars, palmettos, and giant lilac trees grow. Very large dairy herds could be seen grazing everywhere. As we got close to Napier, we could see that it lay in the heart of the North Island's wine and fruit-growing region. Napier is foremost a tourist destination, but like all smaller towns in New Zealand it is also a center of agriculture.

Following the 1931 earthquake, Napier was rebuilt in the Art Deco style. Today there are at least 100 beautiful Art Deco buildings in the district, and vintage cars of that era are available as an alternative to a walking tour. Floral gardens line the streets and the downtown shoreline. The residential areas of the town are either colorful seaside bungalows built along the shores of Hawke's Bay, whose beaches are black volcanic sand, or larger homes of an older vintage perched precariously on the hillside prominence that defines the original town site, something like Sausalito on San Francisco Bay. The highway leading south to the wine-growing areas is a boulevard lined on both sides with giant Norfolk pines. On the outskirts of town near where we stayed is located the fishing port and yacht marina. The warehouse district adjoining the working harbor has been partially transformed into an interesting wharf side casual bar and dining area that attracts locals for their afternoon social hour. Our hotel was just a short walk around the harbor and across from one of the beaches on the north side of town. It was a chic, modern hotel with lovely rooms and a nice restaurant.

We spent our first day in Napier enjoying the downtown and its Art Deco buildings. The next day we drove out to the Elephant Hill Winery, which offered fine wine and a gourmet lunch in a beautiful, artistic setting. A bottle of their featured La Phant Blanc (a blend of Pinot Gris, Viognier, and Gewürztraminer) cost $50 (wow!) and accompanied our selection for lunch: John Dory with a shrimp mousse encased in tempura batter attached to a zucchini neck. All of this rested on a couple of mandarin orange sections, and a few thinly sliced pieces of cucumber and radish, along with vanilla pearls in a drop or two of pomegranate sauce. It was very good to say the least.

After a couple of days in Napier, we drove 2 hours south to Wharekauhau, a 5,000-acre ranch and lodge located an hour's drive east of Wellington on the coast near Cook Strait. The drive was spectacular, with large herds of dairy cattle and sheep all along the way. The flora and topography was similar to that of beautiful Northern

California. After about a 2-hour drive from Napier we reached the little town of Fairview and began looking for our turnoff. We soon found it; a narrow strip of asphalt leading from Fairview, some 40 km of a winding one-lane road and little bridges leading to Ocean Beach and the site of Wharekauhau. After an hour or so of gorgeous countryside vistas we turned onto a narrow one-lane gravel road that descended 150 feet or more to a rock-strewn riverbed at its base. Then we saw it: a magnificent country estate like one might see in England or Scotland, located there in the midst of wild New Zealand. As we turned a treacherous corner and continued our descent down the hill, we became more and more excited with anticipation. We weren't disappointed!

Wharekauhau Lodge has 13 cottages for guests and a main lodge used for dining. Royals William and Kate stayed there last year when they visited New Zealand. Cocktails and canapés were served at 7 p.m. in the library. Dinner followed at 8 p.m. and consisted of a five-course gourmet meal exquisitely prepared by Marc Soper. Marc was so kind as to share a few recipes with us (although I doubt that we will be able to reproduce them). Arron (a Samoan immigrant who learned recently that he had inherited a Royal Chief 's title upon the death of his uncle) introduced us to a wonderful Pinot Noir (Pegasus Winery) that was as terrific as it was a surprise. For 3 days, we feasted on the most fabulous food one can imagine.

Our first full day was occupied mostly by a farm tour. As I mentioned, Wharekauhau is a 5,000-acre enterprise specializing in the raising of lambs for the table. They have about 10,000 sheep during lambing season: 3,000 ewes, 7,000 lambs, and a hundred or so rams. Lambs are born in the spring, which is August and September in New Zealand. Lambs are sold for slaughter in December after shearing. The poor little things have a very short life. Almost 100 percent of the meat produced in New Zealand is sold for export, most of it to the US market. Wharekauhau also has hundreds of head of beef cattle, mostly Spotted and Angus breeds. The Spotted is a fattier breed that when bred with Angus is intended to produce more tender and flavorful meat than Angus by itself. In any case, all the animals are fed only grass, which produces a lean and almost tasteless (my opinion) product. The farm employs about 30 people in all, and most live in housing provided by the farm. Two men and several sheepdogs control most of the livestock. The hands demonstrated their sheep shearing technique and the deployment of their dogs to round up the sheep. It was very interesting.

Our tour guide, Roger, took us down from the plateau where the lodge is located to the gravel road and the black sand beach below. Here you could see the effects of the violent, giant winter seas from Antarctica that rip ashore and slam the plateau. At the base of the plateau, in protected areas, are little rustic fishing cabins called batches that sportsmen use mostly as fish camps during the summer months. Roger owns one and told us of the various fishing methods employed here, two of which demonstrate the inventiveness and originality of the New Zealand mind. He asked me if I had ever heard of a Kon Tiki. Of course, . . . no. Roger's Kon Tiki is a Rube Goldberg contraption—a little 3-foot catamaran fitted with an airplane-type propeller, electric motor, and battery, and a fishing longline with 25 baited hooks. The Kon Tiki itself is tied to a reel with a mile or so of line (to bring it back to shore). The idea is to propel it out to sea about a mile, release the hooked line, wait an hour or two, then pull it back to shore and hope something is on the line. The reason for all this is that it is very difficult to launch boats here. The sand is very soft, and the beach very steep. Although boats can be launched, few people do it because it takes a bulldozer and a boat launching apparatus with huge diameter wheels tethered to the tractor with about a 30-foot steel arm. In these circumstances, the Kon Tiki has appeal.

After a few days at Wharekauhau, we reluctantly moved on to Wellington, capital city of New Zealand. Wellington is a big, modern, high-rise city located on Cook Strait about 12 miles above the South Island and situated in a relatively small notch in the mountains along the coast. The residential part of the city clings to the hillsides, and luxury seaside homes line the beaches and waterfront. The shopping district is located on Lambton Quay, a street that was once the water-front before an earthquake created more land. In the center of the city stands the Beehive, the ruling party's main office building and office of the Prime Minister. It is a very interesting building architecturally, a dome-like structure reflecting the modern concept of a capital building. Next to the Beehive is the House of Parliament, a conventional 19th-century classic building executed in gray marble and granite. Farther down the capital campus stands the Library of Parliament, a beautiful deep yellow stone Victorian edifice that looks very much like a cathedral. Across the street, but in line with the government buildings, stands the rose-colored, concrete, Anglican cathedral. Wellington is quite lovely, with a mix of creative modern architecture and classic older buildings. The city has made considerable investment in converting its former wharf harbor front into a beautiful and entertaining parkland that preserves the feel of the historical waterfront with the vibrancy of an exciting meeting and entertainment area. It features a walkway that tracks the entire bay coastline from the cruise ship terminal to the airport, altogether about 20 km; a lovely, walkable downtown area, a cable car that can take you up to the botanical gardens or to the campus of Victoria University, New Zealand's largest. Charming little neighborhoods with their own distinct identity formed because of their separation by the hills or rivers from each other. We really liked Wellington and found it to be a very enjoyable and livable city.

After three days in Wellington, it was time to board the ferry for Picton across the strait and begin our tour of the South Island.

Crossing Cook Strait (Jan 20): We left Wellington on the 8:30 a.m. ferry to Picton, a lovely little port on the north coast of the South Island just 13 miles across Cook Strait. It was a clear, sunny day with calm seas (which can get very angry during the winter season), making the 3-hour trip delightful. The ship weaved in and out of the picturesque islands, which are in reality the tops of mountains that extend from north to south in New Zealand. They are covered in green grass or forests, depending on the microenvironment, and the gorges in the steep hillsides provide little bays, some of which have a building or two marking a town's site. The ocean was a brilliant blue, and everything was clean and clear. It reminded us of our trip through Desolation Sound in British Columbia aboard *Odyssey* in 2011.

Driving to Abel Tasman Park: We disembarked in Picton and picked up our new rental car. From Picton we drove west for about 4 hours to the little town of Pohara on the Golden Bay, the western gateway to the Abel Tasman National Park. The two-lane highway took us through part of the Marlborough wine region on the north coast. The geography here is similar to Northern California, with broad valleys bordered by low mountains that are covered with forests. The famous vineyards of Cloudy Bay and Oyster Bay, among others, are spread out across the valley along with large cattle farms. The flat plain of the valley floor is broken up by windbreaks of high hedges, Lombardy poplars, or rows of pine trees. As we drove along we eventually came to the end of the valley, then ascended a windy, hairpin-curved road over the mountains to the next valley. The drive over the mountains provided stunning pastoral vistas: views of rivers flowing through the valleys and herds of animals grazing lazily in the warm sunshine. The roadside was carpeted in colorful wildflowers of orange, yellow, and purple. We stopped at the little town of Havelock for lunch, and as we entered the café we spotted a couple we knew: Leslie and Don Brown from Trueblue, a 65-foot Oyster sailing yacht we met in Papeete and again in Vava'U. What a nice surprise—they were touring the country by motorcycle! After a nice lunch including a bucket of green-lipped mussels, each the size of an egg, we were off again.

As we continued along, the highway began to skirt Tasman Bay at the City of Nelson, an artist colony and resort town at the eastern entrance to the park. The golden sand beaches were the largest I had ever seen, and people by the score took full advantage of the fabulous sunny weather and ocean surf. An hour or so more down the road brought us to Takaka a few more miles farther to our hotel in Pohara on the shores of the Golden Bay. Our hotel was a nice little spot run by a New Hampshire transplant and his partner. From this base we explored the park, but more importantly Cape Farewell and the Farewell Spit.

Cape Farewell and the Farewell Spit (Jan 21): Cape Farewell is the northwestern-most point on the South Island, and it is named for the countless seafarers who bade farewell to their loved ones as they went to sea. The cape itself is a beautiful promontory of greywacke rock, and the Spit is a finger of sand that extends 36 km north and encloses the Golden Bay by its eastern flank. The Spit is growing, as it has for thousands of years. It was formed by sand carried north by ocean currents from points south on the South Island's coast. The sand comes from the erosion of New Zealand's Southern Alps. The Southern Alps are made of rock that has been pushed up by tectonic plate forces as the Australian Plate folds under the Pacific Plate. The plates slide against one another, and the resulting fault is the boundary of the plates, which can be seen from space as a rift line falling on the western side of the Southern Alps and extending in a straight line from northeast to southwest. The fault is often the site of large lakes lying within the mountains of New Zealand. On the western side of the fault, the mountains are made of granite or dolomite from the Australian-Indian Plate; on the eastern side, the rocks are greywacke, sandstone, limestone, rock, and mud or seafloor strata from the Pacific Plate. Ancient creatures from the Cambrian are fossilized in some rocks, while others date from the Earth's original Gondwanan supercontinent 600 million years ago. The last ice age ended about 10,000 years ago, but for perhaps 100,000 years, massive glaciers 2 or 3 miles thick crushed the mountains and carved out New Zealand as we see it today. The glaciers ground the stone, and as the glaciers melted, rivers formed that brought the stone to the ocean's shore. The glaciers piled up huge moraines that radiate outward from the central mountains and look like mountains themselves. The ancient riverbeds of gravel, perhaps 400 feet deep, formed the plains that are the agricultural heartland of the country. The plains of the South Island are largest in the east and southern portions of the islands, and are narrower on the western side of the mountains. When driving around New Zealand, one of the most fascinating things I have found is that the geologic history of the world is all laid out before you, with different ages apparent around almost every turn. It is simply breathtaking!

Plate tectonics is forcing the mountains up about 1 inch per year, but erosion diminishes them by about the same amount. The tops of many mountains are huge gravel fields. As the mountains are eroded by wind and weather, sand is created, the mountain streams carry the sand to the Tasman Sea, and sea currents carry the sand north to Cape Farewell where a countercurrent causes the sand to be deposited, forming the Spit.

Our tour was conducted on a large bus especially customized to be a four-wheel drive, oversized dune buggy. Our tour lasted about 8 hours; we drove 30 km down the Spit to an old lighthouse. There the tour operators provided tea and snacks as we walked around the enclosure that once was home to the lighthouse keepers. We made several other exploratory stops along the way to examine interesting things like fur seals, the gannet colony, and to climb the beautiful dunes and explore features of the beach. Life along the Spit was very interesting, particularly the bird life, such as the oystercatchers and gannets. Touring the Cape Farewell Spit was one of the most interesting things we have done.

Driving to Arthur's Pass (Jan 23): The drive from tiny Pohara on the northern coast to Wilderness Lodge high up in Arthur's Pass was a 9-hour trip across the northwestern quadrant of the South Island. It started with a 20-km winding trip across the Arthur Range of Mountains, which are high and very beautiful with lush, verdant greenery. Wildflowers carpet the sides of the road, and large limestone massifs inspire awe as we whipped around hairpin curves avoiding giant, double tandem lorries. The scenery was remarkable. We descended the mountains into the Tapawera River Valley to find large dairy and sheep herds grazing on beautiful pastureland. We followed Highway 6 over hill and dale, through the valley for several hours until we reached the coast of the Tasman Sea at Westport. Along the way we picked up Simon, a young (24) lad from Salzburg who had left home after his mother died of cancer 3 years ago. His father died at sea when Simon was age 13. Simon had traveled first to Kazakhstan, then to India, Myanmar, Thailand, Cambodia, Laos, and Vietnam before coming to New Zealand. He was a very intelligent young man, but he said he had no reason to return to Europe (as he seemed to have no one to love or care for him there). He told us of his experiences twice being robbed of his backpack at knifepoint and being cheated by temporary employers or hostel owners. He asked me all sorts of questions about investing his inheritance of 20,000 euros. It seemed so sad to us that he wanders the world by himself without anyone to care about him or know where he is. One thing we did learn from Simon: backpackers don't shower much and Rebecca was forced to keep the A/C on full blast to provide relief for her delicate olfactory senses!

At Westport, we turned south and followed Highway 6 to Greymouth. This part of the South Island is covered in rain forest. Here they get plenty of rain, 6 to 7 meters per year. It rains 25 days a month, but fortunately we are traveling during a dry spell, so the sky is clear and beautiful. The road winds around the shoreline with the mountains and beautiful, lush fern forest on our left and the Tasman Sea on our right. The seawater is a beautiful gray-blue unlike any I have ever seen. Perhaps the sun reflects off the sand bottom or the suspended sand in the water being carried north as I described previously. As we drove south we came to the Pancake Rocks, a very unusual rock formation jutting out into the sea. The rocks look like chimneys or very thin stacks of pancakes. We spent an hour here, and it was fascinating. A picture is worth a thousand words, so I direct you to the picture gallery.

An hour or so farther down the road brought us to Greymouth, a major crossroad on the island: it connects Christchurch on the east coast with the west coast via both rail and highway. At this point we bade farewell to Simon and turned east up highway 73 toward the little town of Arthur's Pass and the Wilderness Lodge.

New Zealand Roads: In New Zealand there aren't any superhighways, just two-lane roads that were built in the 1960s. Both the scale of the roads and their engineering are very basic. The construction is gravel over bitumen. As the whole country is mountainous, rivers and creeks transect the land and bridges are frequently required. Bridges in New Zealand are almost always one lane, and a sign on the road tells you which direction has the right of way. The roads are narrow, and the bridges are often narrower. Roads are very curvaceous: straight sections rarely extend for more than half a kilometer. When driving up or down a mountain, the road follows every bend, twist, and curve of the mountainside, which can be steep, too, sometimes with 16-degree slopes. Some curves have signs reducing the speed limit to 10 km! That's how sharp the turns can be. Mountain scenery is fabulous anywhere, but these roads help the traveler get up close and personal with the mountains.

KEA - A NEW ZEALAND PARROT

The Wilderness Lodge (Jan 23): Arthur's Pass is the only pass across the Southern Alps in the central part of the South Island. The Alps are 10,000 feet or more in elevation, and the peaks are snowcapped all year round. They are beautiful, spellbinding, majestic peaks of rock. The western slope is forested and green, but the eastern slope and the Dunstan Range to the east are much drier and arid. In fact, 60 percent of New Zealand is arid or semiarid land. The drive from Greymouth to the Wilderness Lodge is almost halfway across the island. The lodge is a combination sheep station, cattle ranch, and eco-lodge. The sheep station raises Merino sheep, noted as the world's finest grade of wool. As we were shown about the station and shown several sheep, we were told that a human hair is 60 microns, carpet wool is about 25 microns, but Merino wool is just 18 microns or less, making it very fine indeed. It is used in Smart Wool and Ice Breaker brand garments.

257

When we arrived at the lodge we were met by Michael who manages the property and is the son of the owner; he was very friendly and helpful. The lodge offers hiking and kayaking as primary activities, and includes guided morning and evening hikes in the nearby beech forest. A five-course dinner is served after a social hour in the evening, and a full breakfast is prepared in the morning. The first day we took a half-day kayaking trip to a mountain lake and packed a picnic lunch to enjoy on the shore. The next day we tramped (in New Zealand you can tramp or trek, and you can also walk or hike) about the beech forest with a guide, and later in the day we drove to tiny Arthur's Pass village for lunch. We enjoyed the company of fellow travelers, Margo and Paul of Saskatchewan, who were very good company and experienced travelers with whom we traded travel recommendations. The third day was ostensibly my birthday; ostensibly because it depended on which hemisphere we chose to use as the time to be observed, so we chose both! (Rebecca loves to celebrate.) How lucky to celebrate a really big birthday literally at the top of the world (in the Southern Alps) and feeling that it is a metaphor for the way my life has turned out. Anyway, we tramped for about 90 minutes across a paddock (pasture) to the Mountain Gorge Trail, which took us up a riverbed and though a silver beech forest. The forest was graced with many types of ferns, moss, lichens, fungi, tiny colorful textured seedlings, and beautiful large trees. The riverbed was strewn with rocks and boulders with a light gray and uniform appearance through which a gurgling stream of cold, pristine mountain water runs. It was so lovely—I am running out of adjectives to describe the beauty of New Zealand—it is hard to imagine or describe. What a way to spend a birthday!

One night previously while we were having dinner, Rebecca became alarmed by the sight of not one, but two mice chasing about near the kitchen. She asked that something be done, but Alan, the guide, said that the forest was experiencing a population explosion of mice and nothing could be done. Mice were everywhere! Luckily, we saw no mice on my birthday and after a wonderful dinner and chorus of "Happy Birthday," the next day we departed the lodge for the Franz Josef Glacier, about 4 hours to our south.

The Franz Josef Glacier (Jan 27): Franz Josef is a little, alpinesque tourist town located south along the coast in the rain forest region. Tourists flock to see a glacier, and we were no exception. It was a 5-hour drive from the lodge, and it was also January 26 in the Western Hemisphere. Now it was my birthday for sure. We checked into a nice hotel that offered a second-story view of the rain forest and high-speed internet as well. Wow! Back in civilization. Rebecca lined up a surprise spa afternoon for me complete with massage, pedicure, and bar service. It was completely relaxing, and I topped it off with a cigar, champagne, and a wonderful dinner.

At the hotel in Franz Josef we bumped into a couple who had also stayed at the Wilderness Lodge while we were there. The lady told us that mice had gotten into her room and tried to open a bag of nuts she had near her suitcase. She apparently tried to rouse her husband to handle the problem, but he just turned over and went back to sleep. She thought she chased the entire family of mice out of the room, but the next morning she found one in bed with her! Later in the day when she arrived at the Franz Josef hotel she found another live mouse in her daughter's suitcase and was absolutely outraged! She wasn't too happy with her husband, either. We asked if she had requested a refund from the lodge, but she hadn't and didn't know the price of the room. When we told her, she immediately got in touch with the lodge and they refunded her the cost of the rooms. Her husband, a good-natured fellow, also took a hit.

White Herons: The next day we drove to Whataroa and the white heron bird sanctuary. There are only about 200 snowy white herons in New Zealand (an endangered bird), and they only nest along a 50-meter stretch of the Whataroa River deep within a virgin rain forest sanctuary. We took a tour bus to the river and then a hair-raising jet boat run to a boat landing 16 km into the sanctuary. Once off the boat, we walked another 500 meters or so through the rain forest until we reached an observation blind. From there we could see across the river to the white herons on their nests with many hatchlings under their care. These are beautiful birds with special mating plumage of delicate thin white feathers in full display. It felt like we were in a secret, special place in the wild kingdom reserved for just a lucky few, and we were glad to be a part of it.

The Glacier: That afternoon we took a 2-hour walk to the glacier. It has been receding about 70 inches a day, so in a few years it will exist only at the top of the mountain and may not be visible from below. At one time, it filled the valley and extended far out into the Tasman Sea. It has receded about a mile in the last 10 years. The little village of Franz Josef is literally abuzz with the sound of helicopters ferrying tourists for $329 a pop up to the clouds for a bird's-eye view.

The next morning, we broke camp and headed toward Queenstown, the tourist mecca of the South Island. But first we had a 2-day stopover at another Wilderness Lodge on Lake Moeraki, this time to explore the coastal rain forest.

Lake Moeraki Lodge (Jan 29): This lodge is owned by the same family that owns the lodge at Arthur's Pass. Gerry McSweeney, Michael's father and lodge owner, sought us out for a personal visit, perhaps owing to the mouse issue. Gerry is a very nice guy, and during our conversation asked me if I had seen the book on Michigan in the library. He then went on to name a few places in Michigan he knew of, such as the Mackinac Bridge and the Wolverines of the University of Michigan. I inquired as to whether he had ever traveled to Michigan. No, he said, but he had a guest from Michigan who had come to the lodge three times with his young wife Cathy . . . his name was Bo Schembechler!

The lodge was located in the rain forest, and Rebecca and I spent a few hours one morning on a tramp through the rainforest to the ocean. It was a walk we will never forget. The forest looked like a set for *The Lord of the Rings*—mystical and mysterious. It is damp, as you might expect a rain forest to be. The canopy trees are large, 1,000-year-old pine trees that stand 150 feet or more above the forest floor. In their limbs are mosses, lichens, and all manner of ferns and fungi. Lower down live the giant tree ferns, perhaps 20 feet tall, with their fronds spread out like giant umbrellas. Then beech trees and their seedlings, along with what we call ostrich ferns and other tropical plants and vines occupy the forest. Of course, many ancient trees have fallen and are now part of new life emerging from the forest floor, which is covered in sphagnum moss as thick as a carpet. Nestled amongst the plants are little flowers, or emerging ferns bright with a lighter shade of green. The name of the path we followed was the Monro Beach Trail, and after an hour of walking up hill and then down to the beach, we reached the Tasman Sea. This is a beach where penguins come to breed and raise their young during their mating season. However, the only life we saw were tiny sand flies, and they are as nasty as any swarm of hungry mosquitos.

Our Drive to Queenstown (Jan 31): The next morning we got up and went after bidding farewell to Gerry and Ann and the guests we had visited with during our stay. Our drive to Queenstown was 265 km. It began with a 2-hour trip through the rain forest of the Mount Aspiring National Park, a World Heritage Site, on the west coast of the South Island. The scenery was once again spectacular. At about the 90-km mark the road turned inland as it crossed the Southern Alps. On the western slope, the vegetation is verdant and lush. As we ascended, we reached a point where the vegetation turned tawny brown and shrubs replaced trees. Some of the mountainsides were barren and very steep. As we drove along, huge sweeping vistas of rock ledges and outcrops on the mountains came into view. The mountains enclosed surprisingly large lakes, some of which were over 50 km long (Lake Wanaka and Lake Hawea) and are the faults marking the point of contact between the Pacific and Australian Plates. As we progressed, we entered the Otago region of New Zealand, noted for its beauty, and, like Napa and Sonoma Valleys, well known for its thriving fruit and viticulture industry. Occasionally we would see high fences enclosing a paddock (pasture), within which were red deer that are being raised for the venison market. They are much larger than our white-tailed variety, and are offered on the menus throughout New Zealand.

Queenstown (Feb 1): After about 6 hours of driving through some of the most spectacular scenery on earth, we arrived at Queenstown, located in the middle of the Southern Alps. The little town is situated on Lake Wakatipu, a crystal-clear lake about 60 km long and surrounded by mountains of differing shapes including rock massifs, striking pyramidal shapes, and high mountains that slope to the lake. The lake itself is in the basin of the rift formed by the Pacific and Indo-Australian Plates. Some of the mountainsides are arid, some are forested, some are semi-rain-forest, and some are covered in shrub: it all depends on the microclimate. The town itself hangs on the hillsides around a bay: it is a lovely setting featuring a spectacular view of the snow-covered, rocky peaks of the Remarkable Mountains.

Queenstown is a resort for vacationers from Wellington and Auckland who flock here particularly during the winter ski season and the summer holiday period in January. The hills are covered with very nice holiday homes, and the area near the lake has copious numbers of small hotels and condos. The town is also a sort of Fort Lauderdale for Chinese kids from Beijing, who can take direct flights to Christchurch and then hop local planes to Queenstown. The 18 to 30-year set likes to party hearty here during the Chinese New Year's celebration in mid-February. They love the town center with its shops and restaurants that cater to the inexperienced.

We stayed in a lovely hotel right on the banks of the lake facing the Remarkable Mountains and their unforgettable vista. At many hotels breakfast is included with the room tariff, and that was the case with this hotel. Rebecca and I came down to breakfast the morning after we had arrived and sitting near us were four scruffy-looking men in their late 60s; they looked "rode hard and put away wet." Tattoos, long stringy gray hair, earrings, and clothes that looked as though they were carefully selected for a particular "look." Then I remembered that we passed a huge number of cars and busses parked in a field near a stage that had been set up by a hillside that could be used for an amphitheater. Hundreds of people were waiting in the hot sun for the show to start. What was the attraction? None other than Three Dog Night (e.g., "Just an Old-Fashioned Love Song"), and yes, these dudes were sitting right next to us for breakfast talking about stage lighting!

Milford Sound and the Fiord lands: The next day we took a tour to Milford Sound, which is really a fiord because it was created by a glacier not a river. Our trip was by bus, which we chose because we were told the drive to the sound was very dangerous, but apparently our advisors were not familiar with what we had already driven through. Anyway, we took the bus tour, which included overnight accommodations aboard a small ship designed for fiord tours. The bus drive was about 6 hours and provided a trip with out-of-this-world scenery. Queenstown is surrounded by mountains. As we traveled south, the landscape broadened; the mountains spread out to a broad glacial plain. The fields became flat and the mountains subsided into rolling hills except at the boundary of the plain. Large herds of sheep, cattle, and deer were contentedly grazing on lush green pastures on hillsides and mountain slopes. It was a perfect, if not a heavenly, pastoral scene.

After several photo and comfort stops, the bus finally made it to the Milford Sound National Park, a World Heritage Site. The afternoon was cloudy and rainy, but at the time we didn't know it was perfect for seeing the fiords. As we ascended the torturously curved roads into the clouds only 3,000 feet above sea level, we entered the world of the glacier and some of the most spectacular formations on the planet. Huge mountains perhaps 10,000 feet above sea level had been literally carved, cut, and ground into the sharp gorges and fiords that we entered. The mountains rose vertically from the floor of the canyons or the sea straight up to the clouds. Rain fell, and that which fell onto the mountains was transformed into veils of falling water in hundreds of falls over miles of vertical mountain massifs. When the rain stopped, the waterfalls disappeared.

We spent the night aboard the *Mariner*, a 100-foot vessel designed to accommodate 100 tourists on just this sort of tour. The ship took us about 3 miles out into the fiord, stopping at different places, such as when the captain positioned the bow into one of the giant waterfalls so that the water tumbled onto the ship. Later the ship anchored in a little bay and dinner was served. Our tablemates, George and Mary, were from England, and he was head of Britain's 15 nuclear power plants. He had just retired. It was interesting to talk with him about the controversy surrounding nuclear power: Germany's recent decision to close off all of its plants, China's plan to build hundreds of them, and Japan's Fukushima disaster. He feels the technology is safe but Japan is a closed society in many ways, including the fact that Japan does not participate in international professional groups nor do they permit oversight bodies to help them manage their reactors. This led to the disaster and coverup.

The next day the sun came out and revealed a spectacular day. We were able to see the glorious mountain scenery, but this time in the full sun. By late afternoon we had arrived back at our very nice hotel in time for a lovely meal in their very fine restaurant.

Queenstown has a downtown area, perhaps a bit more developed than most, yet still typical of New Zealand towns. There are no shopping centers like we have in North America, rather their city centers are like the main streets we used to have: small shops, for the most part locally owned, with all sorts of businesses occupying storefronts. Of course, there are lots of restaurants and bars in this resort city.

Queenstown to Christchurch (Feb 5): The drive to Christchurch was a long one, about 400 km across the backbone of New Zealand. I thought it would be mostly mountain roads, but it turned out to be smooth sailing once we got over the Southern Alps. Unlike the green rain forest and lush grassland along the western coast, the Otago and Canterbury regions are semiarid grasslands that look a lot like Northern California in some places and like Nevada in others. As we drove eastward, the mountains turned into large rolling hills with the most interesting formations, then to flatlands created by the glacial rivers millenniums ago. High in the mountains were the large sheep stations, and as the angularity of the land subsided, cattle herds predominated. New Zealand has about 75 million head of cattle, and 45 million head of sheep.

Christchurch is the largest city on the South Island with a population of 350,000. In both 2010 and 2011 it suffered magnitude 8 earthquakes. The damage was horrific: the entire city center was destroyed, including priceless Gothic Revival buildings, modern 15- or 20-story office buildings, and hotels. Many large buildings are still standing, but are surrounded by fencing to keep people away from them in case they fall. The Anglican cathedral, which dominates Cathedral Square in the center of town, is now partially destroyed and in ruins. The residential areas were not spared: about 20 percent of the homes were destroyed. In the Fukushima earthquake Japan suffered a loss equivalent to 3 percent of its GDP. In the case of Christchurch, New Zealand is estimated to have suffered losses valued at 10 percent of its GDP. Despite the destruction, Christ's College, with its beautiful Gothic Revival buildings constructed of gray stone walls and limestone windowsills and doorsills, remains. These buildings adjoin the beautiful and world-renowned botanical gardens that lie beside the Avon River as it meanders through the city. We enjoyed the morning walking through the gardens and the afternoon walking around the rest of the center city.

The next day we took the Tranz Alpine Train across Arthur's Pass to Greymouth and back. While this was a somewhat redundant trip given that we had spent several days in the Pass at Wilderness Lodge, it afforded one last look at these fabulous mountains from a different perspective.

Christchurch to Marlborough (Feb 8): It is a 4-hour drive north along the rocky, picturesque coast to the little city of Blenheim, heart of the New Zealand wine industry. Here are thousands of acres of grape vines under cultivation, producing the famous Sauvignon Blanc grape among others. Names like Cloudy Bay and Oyster Bay, so familiar to we wine drinkers, dot the countryside. Touring and tasting the produce occupied us for most of a day, and we learned, among other things, that the first vine was planted here in 1979. In just 35 short years a colossus was established.

We stayed at the Straw Lodge, a small, 21-acre organic vineyard and B&B in the middle of the valley. Trudy and Barry Gainford bought the farm last year and work it with their son-in-law. They immigrated to New Zealand 21 years ago from South Africa. Barry is an optometrist turned grape farmer, and he and his son-in-law (formerly an accountant) now run the operation. Their first harvest was last year. Barry grows Sauvignon Blanc and Pinot Noir. Of the 21 acres, 16.5 are used for farming, and the other acreage is used for roads and buildings. Each cultivated acre produces about 1 metric ton of grapes, which he can sell for about $18,500. Barry told me that he can bottle the wine and sell it for around $20 to $30 a bottle, and it would cost about $4 a bottle to have it processed, including the grapes, processing, and the bottle itself. Each bottle contains 1 kilo of grapes, so his property could produce about 16,500 bottles of wine. The profit is potentially much higher before considering marketing expenses. So, the whole key to higher profits is to leverage some sort of marketing plan for his small winery in conjunction with other growers.

One morning Trudy asked me if I had ever heard of "green eggs and ham." What father hasn't heard of that? I thought it was just a fantasy of Dr. Seuss, but Trudy told me there is a breed of chicken that lays a greenish egg, called an Aracuna chicken, and Trudy had a few. She brought me the egg and compared it to a brown egg, and indeed it was a greenish blue. It was about the size of a duck's egg and very delicious, I might add. So, indeed, I had green eggs and ham that morning at the Straw Lodge!

During the day, we toured the little towns in the area, lunched at a winery, and tramped a trail along the Queen Charlotte Sound. It was a lovely time and very interesting. Our tour of the South Island was now complete, we rose early the next day, enjoyed a wonderful breakfast at the Straw Lodge, drove to Picton, took the ferry back to Wellington and the highway north toward Auckland.

Kingsgate and Lake Taupo (Feb 12–14): Our first stop that night was in the town of Kingsgate on the Whanganui River at the Sea of Tasman coast, after a 3-hour drive. It was a good-size town with an interesting main street. On the cliff across the river overlooking the town stood a very large, brown stone tower about 130 feet high that commemorates the soldiers of WWI, captioned "The Great War."

The next day we drove about 4 hours northeast to the town of Taupo, situated on the coast of New Zealand's largest lake. It was a very interesting drive across tortured ground that is the fault rift marking the boundary of the Indo-Australian Plate and the Pacific Plate. As we neared Lake Taupo we could see one of three snowcapped volcanoes that mark this site as a World Heritage Site. Eventually we could see all three volcanoes lined up in a row, with Lake Taupo in the same rift line as the volcanoes. It was one of the most interesting and gorgeous geologic sights I have ever seen, and desolate as well. Two of the three volcanoes are cone shaped, about 7,000 feet high, and formed of a purple-brown rock. There was nothing living on the sides of these mountains. The third volcano was much bigger and was crowned with eight glaciers. It was massive. Surrounding them was hundreds of square miles of colorful arid landscape. It is seldom that one can see one of the active sites that is currently forming our planet.

We stayed at the Lake Taupo Lodge, a lovely five-room hotel that has hosted Barbra Streisand, Burt Reynolds, and other celebrities. Lake Taupo and environs is one of the premier trout fishing spots in the world, with rainbow and brown trout so large they look like salmon. I am hoping to return in April for a taste of New Zealand fly-fishing.

A Few Miscellaneous Observations:

- Most homes are small and unpretentious. I would guess 1,400 to 2,000 square feet.

- There are no billboards along the roads of New Zealand, making it even more beautiful.

- There are a lot of Japanese cars. As in Jamaica, the Japanese sell their off-lease vehicles here at a reduced cost. (Samoa actually switched from left-hand to right-hand driving to take advantage of the Japanese used car market.)

- There are a lot of foreign kids backpacking and doing summer work in New Zealand. They can easily obtain a 1-year work/travel visa here. Unfortunate don't do this in the United States.

- The Kiwis are fond of the words *pop* as in "pop in for a moment," or, "I'll pop around this afternoon," and the phrase "sort it out" as in "call your insurance agent and he will sort it out for you."

They often use the word *sort* when there is nothing to sort out, as in: "I left the key in the room." The hotel clerk replied, "That' I'll sort it out." The Kiwis pop and sort all kinds of things all day long!

• Kiwis established a blanket prohibition against personal liability accident liability and instead established a no-fault system to cover accident-related costs. This had some unexpected ramifications. For example, tubs and showers are slippery, pedestrians are in real danger as drivers literally will run you over if you are in the way.

February 20

Our previous entry was posted from Lake Taupo as we were heading back to Auckland on the last leg of our 5-week tour of New Zealand. After driving on two-lane roads through the beautiful farmland of the central North Island, passing the thermal fields, volcanoes, and geologic wonders of the island, we drove back to Auckland and spent a week walking the city and enjoying the Chinese New Year's Festival held in the center city. Hundreds of students from China come to New Zealand over this holiday to enjoy a respite from the Chinese winter, like their American counterparts in Ft. Lauderdale. These are rich, young, and beautiful people of the People's Republic; Prada, Gucci, and Versace are on full display, along with a certain arrogant aloofness that seems common to the young and privileged regardless of their state of origin. In Auckland City Center the Chinese government sponsors a huge cultural festival featuring colorful classical dances, ancient traditional puppet shows, and food from all over China; it was all very interesting.

March 2

We flew back to the States to attend the wedding of the daughter of two of our dearest friends. The wedding was held in Beaver Creek, Colorado, and attended by many of our lifelong friends. It was quite an adjustment having traveled across many time and altitudinal zones. We shared a luxurious apartment with our daughter and son-in-law, spent a day or two skiing, dined at beautiful restaurants, and spent an afternoon snowmobiling in the alpine splendor of the Rocky Mountains. It was a great time.

After the wedding, we returned to Ann Arbor to attend to the renovation of our home and to file our tax returns. On the bright side, we had been invited to speak to the historic Detroit Yacht Club on Belle Isle, and our Rotary Club in Ann Arbor. These events were a lot of fun, as it gave us a chance to meet other boaters and to show our friends in Ann Arbor exactly what we had been doing over the past year. Unfortunately, in the midst of a hurried visit home, Rebecca's father began to quickly fail; regrettably, 2 weeks later he passed away.

April 9   **Hauling Out for Maintenance**

I returned to New Zealand on April 9 to move *Argo* about 25 miles north of Auckland to Gulf Harbor Shipyard at Whangaparaoa, and to oversee the maintenance work that was scheduled. She was slow and not very agile on her short passage north after 6 months in the Viaduct Marina. As we later learned, Viaduct Harbor is notorious for heavy marine growth and when *Argo* was pulled out of the water it was evident that she had become home to a shocking number of crusty bivalves. This is all to be expected as boats need to be hauled about every 12 to 18 months to remove marine growth from their bottom and through-hulls. After she was cleaned up, *Argo* received a new coat of bottom paint and her propellers were coated with a special paint to inhibit marine growth and to make them more slippery. At the same time, other repairs were made, including a hull waxing and cleaning the two forward fuel tanks of a silicone sealing substance that had fallen into the tanks during the boat's construction and posed the potential of clogging fuel lines. This required a technician to remove the access covers from the tanks, don a hazmat suit, crawl inside the tanks, and scrub all the surfaces by hand. Before he started, all the fuel on board was removed and polished in special centrifugal filters. After all this work, *Argo* was beautiful from top to bottom and the travel hoist came to lift her off her supports and put her in the water, ready for our trip north to Fiji. All of this took a couple of weeks.

As the work was coming to an end, I escaped to the Lake Taupo Lodge for a few days of fly-fishing in one of the world's greatest trout habitats. The area is designated a UNESCO World Heritage Site because of its beauty and geological importance. Three cone-shaped volcanoes lie on a flat plain of ancient volcanic debris. The largest volcano is snowcapped most of the year, and the other two lies on a path a few miles apart in line with Lake Taupo. Lake Taupo is a freshwater lake about 240 square miles in size, and occupies the sunken caldera of an extinct volcano that exploded 26,500 years ago. The eruption, perhaps the largest in history, is known as the Oruanui eruption and ejected about 1,170 cubic kilometers of material into the atmosphere. Scientists speculate that this eruption may have started the last ice age. Today the lake is the tranquil home to huge brown and rainbow trout (brought over about 100 years ago from stock obtained in Scotland

and California) that feast on crayfish and spawn in the Waitahanui, Tongariro, and the Tauranga Taupo Rivers. My fishing adventure began on the Tauranga Taupo River. My guide drove us to his cabin on the river that he leases from the Maori, where we put on waders and spent the day tramping along the banks and in the river casting for elusive trout. It was a beautiful day spent in a rocky, forested area that is as pristine as second-growth forests can be. The old-growth forests of New Zealand with their huge Kauri trees were chopped down during the last century, and the current forest is only a fraction of what it once was, but is nevertheless quite lovely and the trout seem to flourish here. We fished using wet flies and strike indicators, casting out to deep pools where the big fish lie. Unlike our ocean fishing practice of using heavy line and steel leaders to bring big, toothy fish aboard *Argo*, here we used very light line and tackle to give the fish a fighting chance. These fish are big and strong, and put up quite a fight as they try to escape by dancing down the river on their tails. It is easy for them to break the line or throw the hook, so some measure of skill is required to sense their taking of the fly and to gently bring them to the net. It didn't take long before I had a 5 to 6-pound rainbow on the line. Getting it to the net and then removing the hook so that it could be released to go about its life unharmed required a fair degree of finesse.

The next day we drove about 90 minutes to the mountains above Napier to the Waipawa River. This river is also a very famous trout stream that we fished using a raft to transport us to various spots along the river. Our float lasted about 6 hours. Our fishing was very productive; I caught at least 15 large fish, all educated and then released. The river worked its way toward the ocean, cutting a gorge through limestone cliffs that hundreds of millions of years ago were part of the ocean floor on the Pacific tectonic plate, and before that, part of the original continent of Pangea. As we floated by limestone cliffs, we could see fossils and large volcanic rocks embedded in them from ages past. Above the cliffs were sheep and cattle station pastures; grass is grown as a crop as earnestly as we grow corn. The largest sheep and cattle ranch in New Zealand (75,000 acres) that had previously been owned by a prominent family for generations was recently sold to a Chinese person.

The next day I drove back to Auckland, past huge stainless-steel pipes glittering in the bright sunshine carrying geothermal energy that the Kiwis use for heat and electricity. On the way, I picked up Rebecca at the airport. She had remained for an extra 2 weeks in Michigan to help her mother following her father's death. Tired but anxious to see *Argo* again, we drove the 50 or so miles back to Whangaparaoa.

The next morning the travel lift was coming to put *Argo* back in the water. We were planning to take her up to Fiji over the winter, so her launch was occurring with great anticipation. The wind was up, and it was a cold, rainy morning. As the lift strained to carry her to the well, I prepared to go onboard to pilot her out of the well and on to her assigned dock. The lift lowered her gently back in the water, and I climbed aboard. I fired up the engines to make sure the air had been purged from the systems and that the cooling systems were working well. I gently tested the thrusters, and they seemed to work although we were in such a confined space all I could do was to hear them rumble to know they were working. Soon I was given the authorization to back out of the lift. It was a very tight area with small boats all around and concrete pilings near at hand. I put her in dead slow reverse, and she answered by slowly pulling out of the well. The current or wind caught, and she began to drift sideways, so I moved the thruster to port. *Argo* moved to starboard! I thrusted again thinking I must have pushed the lever in the wrong direction. I touched it, and she again moved to starboard. Now she was rubbing against the concrete, and she was moving close to another boat astern of us. I was becoming anxious. So, I put her dead forward and used the stern thruster to move her in the proper direction, but again she answered opposite to my command. Now I was flummoxed! She was now catty-cornered and being scratched by the moorings. The shipyard launched a boat to act as a tug and push us straight in line with the well. I put her in forward and used the thrusters in reverse to settle her back into the sling. Unfortunately, she had become scratched by rubbing on the concrete pilings and needed to be hauled again to repair her hull.

As we analyzed what had happened, we found out that the thruster propellers were taken off for cleaning. We called the thruster manufacturer in the United States and asked if it was possible to install the thruster propellers backwards. It turns out that the manufacturer's technician, the same person that repaired the hydraulic equipment in Bora Bora, took the thruster blades off for cleaning and reinstalled them backwards.

Repairing the scratches on *Argo's* hull didn't seem like a big deal, but every day in the shipyard costs hundreds of dollars, not to mention the repair cost itself. My view was that the technician should pay for it, since it was their fault. Fortunately, the boatyard required all workers to have insurance. Although it took weeks to get in touch with him and for him to admit that he caused the problem, his insurance eventually paid for all the repairs. Meanwhile I had another even more serious problem arise.

The first morning after the accident, I arose to complete my ADLs; I was shocked to find blood in my urine. Alarmed, we went to the local hospital (of course it was a

3-day holiday weekend), but nothing could really be diagnosed there. The next morning more blood, so we quickly arranged to return home and I was scheduled for an examination at the University of Michigan. There we learned that I had bladder cancer, an excision of the lesion was performed within 10 days and followed by 6 weeks of immunotherapy. After the last dose, we had a 6-week break until the next biopsy, and we hoped during those weeks to bring *Argo* up to Fiji and cruise those islands until I had to go back for further tests.

In the meantime, repairing *Argo* had turned into a nightmare. There were three insurance companies involved, and no work could be done until a survey was completed and everyone was in agreement on moving forward. That took weeks. A captain on another Nordhavn referred me to a retired fiberglass/gelcoat expert who agreed to act as a general contractor to arrange and oversee the repairs. Matching gelcoat color is very difficult, because it has to be a custom color formulated to match an original color that has faded over time. Once applied, you have to wait for it to dry. If it isn't right, it has to be sanded off, making the spot bigger. After three or four companies attempted a fix, the spot grew in size to a sizable disfigurement of the bow. Finally, after 8 weeks, someone was able to match my ultra-finicky contractor's standards and the repair was perfect. *Argo* was then refloated, and ready for sea with the thruster blades properly installed. All of this was an unimaginable stress when combined with my cancer treatment.

In the meantime, fall in New Zealand was approaching, and our weather window for heading north was closing. My cruising permit was also running out. A foreign yachtsman has a 365-day permit to cruise New Zealand waters. If we had to stay longer, we would have to pay hundreds of thousands of dollars in taxes just as though we had bought the yacht in New Zealand: it's the equivalent of the New Zealand sales tax, which is in the 20% range. Of course, at this point I was in Ann Arbor literally fighting for my life. I hired Paul to captain *Argo*, and he and Tom took her back to Auckland for provisioning. While backing into the slip, which was a very difficult maneuver, the ship's hydraulic system failed again (the same part that failed in Fiji), dumping all her hydraulic fluid in the bilge. She lost her thrusters, making it very difficult to maneuver in a tight harbor. Because of Paul's excellent ship-handling ability, *Argo* avoided another potentially serious accident. After several days of repairs and thousands more in expense, *Argo* was underway for Fiji.

BULA! FROM FIJI

July 8–15, 2015   **Flight to Fiji and the Westin Denarau**

Our flight from LAX to Nadi, Fiji, was about 11 hours. The Fiji Airways isn't as fancy as other airlines, but it was adequate. The nice thing is that it leaves L.A. at 10 p.m. and arrives in Fiji at 9 a.m. the next morning. You can get a reasonably good night's sleep on this flight. Because I had to be back in Ann Arbor in 5 weeks for more cancer treatments, we decided to hire a captain to bring *Argo* up to Fiji from Auckland. Unfortunately, she was delayed in her departure from Gulf Harbor because of weather, so we stayed at the Westin Resort at Denarau while we waited for her arrival. Fiji is a major vacation destination for Kiwis and Aussies, and it was booked solid because of school holidays in New Zealand and Australia. When we arrived, the weather was cool and windy, so we arranged tours of the area and went to a Fijian cultural night at the hotel.

The main feature of the cultural night was the firewalkers. The evening began with a presentation of historical warrior dances followed by a dinner cooked Fijian style. Rocks were heated by a large fire, a pit was dug, food was wrapped in leaves or foil and placed in the pit and covered first with banana leaves and then with the heated rocks. The feast included a variety of meat and fish along with taro, cassava, and other vegetables. Despite all the festivities, the food really wasn't very good. Once dinner was over the rocks were rearranged and the warriors walked barefoot on them. This is called fire walking and is quite a spectacle. Historically the Fijians were a war-like people who avidly practiced cannibalism, and their cultural shows recall some of this heritage. One can only speculate that after barbequing their victim, warriors fire walked in a final triumphant act.

The next day we toured Nadi, the largest town in the area. The town supports the international airport that was built during WWII by the United States to accommodate large airplanes; now it is the only airport capable of handling jet airliners. Nadi offers two sights: the Hindu temple and the farmers' market. The impressive Hindu temple was very colorful and quite interesting. One thing that caught our attention was the number of religions that are practiced in such a small country, including Islam, Hinduism, Buddhism, and of course a variety of Christian denominations.

When *Argo* arrived at Port Denarau (Nadi's embarkation port for many tourists going to resorts by ferry), she was quite a sight, especially since it was the first time we had ever seen her come into port. She looked beautiful, and her cosmetic surgery was invisible.

Denarau is a very nice, new development with shops, restaurants, and a yacht club. Trying to figure out entry formalities can be very time consuming, confusing, and frustrating, so we hired an agent to sort it all out for us. Total costs and fees for entering Fiji were about $325 USD. Almost all countries seem fixated on taxing alcohol; Canada is particularly obnoxious, but Fiji takes the cake. Here they reserve the right to mark each bottle of booze aboard a yacht and tax the owner on what has been consumed while in Fijian waters!

See YouTube video: Argo delivery-Nordhavn 68

Fiji is an island nation made up of 322 islands, a hundred of which are inhabited. Most of the population (under 900,000) lives on the largest two islands, Viti Levu and Vanua Levu. The islands are volcanic in origin and lie 1,100 miles directly north of New Zealand and 400 miles west of Tonga. The smaller, more remote islands of the Lau Group lie 200 miles east of Viti Levu and are sparsely populated. People of the Lau Group live a traditional way of life. Visiting these islands requires permission of the village chief, which can be obtained after completing Savusavu, a ceremony of respect and supplication requiring the presentation of kava, which comes from the yaqona bush. Kava is a root that when washed and pressed by hand in a large bowl produces a magenta, muddy-colored drink that yields a numbing, relaxing effect. Kava is reputed to be an aphrodisiac for women, but it puts men to sleep. Generally speaking, women do not like their men to drink kava. West of Viti Levu lies the Yasawa Islands, where fancy resorts accommodate the tourists of Australia, New Zealand, and increasingly China. Between two of the islands lies the Blue Lagoon, made famous by the Brooke Shields' movie bearing its name.

Argo is now moored next to *Dragonfly,* a large yacht owned by the founders of Google (not sure if it is one or both owners) at Denarau Marina near Nadi. We must be in the high rent district. Anchored out in the bay is an even larger yacht owned by a Russian. Eli, our agent here who is handling the formalities of that yacht too, told us that the couple lives aboard with a dog. They have two veterinarians, two nurses, and a security detail on board for the dog. Recently the dog had some sort of eye problem and they flew the thing to Honolulu in a private jet with its full entourage! Nice to know how the other 10^{-100} percent of the population lives!

July 16   **Underway from Denarau**

We left Denarau Marina the next morning and headed for Waya Island and the Octopus Resort. It was a glorious day. Paul, our captain from New Zealand, was staying aboard for a few days as our guest. The first 20 miles or so were just beautiful, then the wind and waves picked up. By the time we got to Waya Island both Rebecca and I were a little seasick, having been on land for about 8 months. The bay at Waya was too rough to anchor, so we decided to head north to Naviti Island in the Yasawa Group.

The Fijian Islands are difficult to navigate because the charts are poor and the islands are surrounded by reefs and coral heads. Passages here should only be attempted during daylight hours and then only between 10 a.m. and 4 p.m. when the sun is high overhead and obstacles in the water can be clearly seen. From a seafarer's standpoint, it is difficult sailing. The trade winds blow relentlessly around 18 to 25 knots, so the seas are rough and choppy. It was sunset when we finally anchored at Soso Village Bay, a protected anchorage on Naviti Island. The bay was surrounded by mountains covered by tall brown grass like the rest of western Fiji. There was a small village at the end of the bay nestled in a coconut grove along the beach. Locals passed us, waving and yelling "Bula!" as they returned from work aboard their outboard-driven skiffs. Along the beach, we could see campfires burning as the sun set. We anchored in about 60 feet of water with the wind blowing around 25 to 30 knots. Katabatic winds were a concern in this anchorage. Later in the evening a cruise ship anchored at the outer edge of the bay, probably seeking refuge in smooth water for its passengers.

Rebecca made a lovely dinner despite not feeling 100 percent: chicken cacciatore along with local French green beans, a vegan chocolate cake with a hint of cayenne pepper, all served up with a lovely red Saumur. It was delicious and perfect for a tired crew.

July 17   Soso V Bay to Turtle Island Underway from Denarau

The next morning brought brilliant sunshine. The wind was still up, so a choppy ride was in store for us as we weighed the anchor and started the 22-mile passage to the Blue Lagoon near Turtle Island. This is the place made famous by Brook Shields and the movie of the same name. We picked our way past the reefs and coral heads and found a nice anchorage near the beach amongst a few sailboats and coral heads. We dropped the tender and made our way to the resort's iconic tropical beach restaurant for lunch. This was a lovely little resort with about 20 rooms spread out in little bungalows along the beach. It seemed to be popular with Kiwis and Aussies. It was the only developed area within view of our boat.

During the afternoon, we tidied things up aboard *Argo* and then relaxed. We grilled New Zealand lamb chops for dinner served with couscous and a wonderful fresh fruit salad.

July 18   **Blue Lagoon**

This is a beautiful spot, not really a lagoon in the sense that we discovered in the Tuamotus, but actually a widened passage between several islands. These islands rise out of the cerulean blue water as big, steep hills perhaps 2,000 feet high, covered in tall brown grass this time of year, with palm trees growing along the shores and in valleys. There were three villages on the beaches of different islands. We were anchored just off a very long gold sand beach with reefs all about. After breakfast, Rebecca and I went ashore and walked a few miles on the beach, then returned to the resort around noon for lunch. It took almost an hour to get our order, which was just a couple of sandwiches, and when I inquired as to when we might get them we were offered an apology and told it would be soon: the cook had gone to lunch!

All of us exercised in one way or another that afternoon. Around 5 p.m. we went ashore for Happy Hour at the Tiki bar and talked with several sailors who had made the Pacific crossing at the same time we did. We hadn't met them before, but they recognized *Argo*. Among them were Craig and Carol who hailed from Seattle. They had summered over in Fiji and didn't go to New Zealand as many sailors do to avoid the cyclone season. They said they don't want to take that risk again. It was great fun to share stories and learn from their experiences. They had crossed the Pacific on a raggedy 40-foot sailboat that had almost no amenities. They had an old-fashioned ice box rather than a freezer or refrigerator, but they seemed to be having the time of their life.

July 19   **Crossing Bligh Water to Volivoli**

It was a crystal-clear day with a very comfortable weather forecast of light winds and moderate seas, so we decided to weigh anchor and cross Bligh Water to Volivoli on the northwest coast of Viti Levu. It was a 50-mile crossing that would take about 6 hours. Bligh Water is named after Captain William Bligh (later Vice Admiral) of the HMS *Bounty* (which was a Cutter, and Bligh was a lieutenant and its only officer at the time). He and 18 loyal crew members were cast adrift in a small launch (by mutinous members of his crew) in 1789. In one of the all-time greatest feats of seamanship (Bligh learned navigation from Captain Cook), he sailed the boat 3,618 miles across an open, hostile ocean from Tahiti to Timor. He passed right through this Fijian channel, which the British named after him. Apparently, he didn't stop at Fiji because of the fierceness of the Fijians and their reputation for cannibalism. Local Fijians anecdotally claim that their ancestors chased him at sea, but failed to catch him.

Our course from Turtle Island to Viti Levu was almost a straight rhumbline, save for picking our way around a few reefs and coral heads. Although navigation is very hazardous, we found our MaxSea chart software to be almost accurate, but a sharp eye was always needed for the possibility of unmarked hazards. We traveled only between the hours of 10:00 and 16:00 when the sun was high and the reefs could be seen. We arrived at the channel through the reef at Viti Levu at 16:30. The chart was a little off, and we needed to correct our course to port to avoid hitting the reef, so in this case traveling only when the sun was high was a safety essential. Once inside the passage between the reefs, we turned to port and followed the channel inside the reef a few miles past Malakai Island to Volivoli Point and the protected bay where we anchored. Once settled, we had the chance to sit outside around our table in the cockpit and enjoy a libation and a glorious sunset.

Rebecca cooked up wonderful steaks and vegetables, topped off with a vegan fruit and coconut cake. Delicious!

July 20   Volivoli Beach

It was a beautiful day with the trades generously blowing from the east. Volivoli Beach is located on the northwest coast of the big island of Viti Levu. We went ashore to reconnoiter the little resort; Paul wanted to make travel arrangements to Denarau and we wanted to know about dinner reservations and local sights. We spent most of the day cleaning the salt off *Argo* and making minor adjustments and repairs. Paul was very generous with his knowledge of boats and helped with some maintenance items. Tinkering took all day, and that evening we all got aboard our dinghy and went to the resort's restaurant for a night out. One cannot be too dressed up for these affairs as you have to climb out of the tender into knee-deep water and walk on the beach to the resort. It was a lot of fun.

July 21   Diving on Golden Dream Reef and Goodbye to Captain Paul

At 08:15 we boarded the dive boat and headed off to scuba dive on Golden Dream Reef. Golden Dream is a series of coral heads on a much larger reef, which is at least a square mile in size. We dove about 5 miles offshore. The tide was incoming, which is apparently when the coral blooms, and Golden Dream is all about the beautiful yellow flowering corals. It was windy and little cold, and choppy waves made it a difficult dive. Nevertheless, we stepped off the dive boat into the sea, got our bearings, and then descended to a depth of about 100 feet. Immediately we could see the coral cliffs covered in golden fan corals. Swimming between bommies or coral heads was much like being in a labyrinth of flowering columns. It certainly was a golden dream.

July 22   **Rakiraki Town**

The wind was blowing, and it looked like poor cruising weather for the next few days so we arranged for a taxi and went to the market in Rakiraki Town. It was about a 20-minute trip along the King's Highway that circles the island and then over very rough gravel to the heart of town. The island is clearly volcanic: in the distance were huge mountains that were once part of a volcano's cone. The foothills in the foreground were either formed when the caldera collapsed or originated when lava flowed. Now the hills are home to subsistence farms with fields of sugarcane. The farmhouses are neatly painted and well-maintained masonry structures, with goats and cattle milling about. Near Rakiraki Town is the sugar mill. The town itself looks like most third-world small towns: masonry block two-story buildings brightly painted with very high sidewalks of differing elevations. We were looking for the market, which we found located on one side of the square, with the shops and restaurants occupying the other three sides. Most businesses, including the markets, are run by Indians. Fiji's climate and fertile volcanic soil can grow almost anything, so we found all kinds of things that we were looking for, including their delicious pineapples. There was a bakery offering hot bread, so we stopped by for a loaf. There were all kinds of activity around the square, including busy pedestrians in colorful clothing, particularly the Indian women with their beautiful exotic saris, men conducting business, busses picking up passengers for trips to other towns, shoppers moving in and out of the storefronts. It was exciting to be in the middle of such vibrant and colorful activity once again.

July 23   **Day Tour to the Village of Navala**

The Volivoli Resort helped us make arrangements for a guide and driver for a tour of the broader area. The next day we were picked up at 08:30 in front of the hotel along with our four bags of trash. Getting rid of trash can sometimes be an issue on a boat, so our first order of business was for our guide, Sunny, to take us to the dump. Unlike our dumps, third-world trash heaps don't have anything useful in them. People here are poor, don't buy much to begin with, and consequently there isn't much to discard.

Our touring objective was the village of Navala located high in the mountains above the city of Ba. It took about 3, mostly tortuous, hours to get there, as many of the roads were gravel and in poor repair. Our route took us south on the King's Highway past many small villages and thousands of acres of sugarcane fields. Local tribes own the land and the cane fields, which are tended by the village men. Field workers retain half the earnings from the sale of the cane, and the other half goes to the village. From what I could tell, a worker keeps about $50 USD per day if things are good. Cutting sugarcane looks like such hard and thankless work that I wanted to experience what an average field hand experiences, so I got out of the car and went into a field to ask if I they would teach me to cut sugarcane. The field hands were delighted to talk with us and allowed me a privileged glimpse into their world. My impressions were correct: it is tough work in sweltering heat!

We moved along past the sugarcane mill at Rakiraki and numerous little villages until we turned onto the gravel mountain road leading to the village of Navala, which is famous for its traditional thatched roof, bamboo, and palm leaf huts. It is the only historic place of its kind left in the islands; every other village makes their domiciles of modern materials like clap wood, corrugated steel, or concrete block. Navala lies in a little valley high in the mountains surrounded by steep hillsides covered with tall brown grasses punctuated with black volcanic rock outcroppings. Here and there were green shrubs and an occasional mango or other tropical tree. Navala is laid out in the shape of a Christian cross with 125 huts housing 850 residents. They have an elementary school with a dorm where the children sleep when school is in session, but they come back home each day for meals. I guess this gives the parents the opportunity to make more kids! The village also has a new Catholic church, as religion is a key aspect of village life. Drinking water comes from an artesian well up high in the mountains, but bathing is done in the nearby rivers. The men go to the sugarcane fields around 06:30 each morning except Sunday; the women prepare the noon meal at a house located in the cane fields each day, and the men return home around 16:00 in the afternoon. The cane fields are part of over 19,000 acres owned by the chief (village). When speaking on official matters, the chief often speaks through a spokesman or assistant chief, who is the person we met. The assistant chief sits at the chief's right hand during council meetings. When visiting, we had to obtain permission to enter the village in advance. We were met by the assistant chief who conducted the kava ceremony in his hut next to the chief's hut and collected the F $25 per person fee plus a F $25 touring fee. The ceremony involves the presentation of a gift of kava, the recitation of ritual words, cupped-hand clapping by the men in attendance, and the sharing of a bowl of kava. Women sit behind the men and must be fully covered. Several village women were in the room with us, and little children peeked in from the doorway to see what was going on, but were shooed away as soon as the adults saw them.

The kava ceremony is a ritual that formally welcomes guests into the village as members of the village family. Guests are extended the privileges and protection of the village and may anchor in the bay, fish, swim, come ashore, and hike about so long as they observe the courtesies of Fijian life. Kava is drunk by downing a full cup at a time. Kava numbs the tongue and lips and is said to cause drowsiness and laziness when consumed in larger quantities. After the ceremony, Michael gave us a tour of the village and then we returned to his hut where the ladies had spread out a cloth and offered trinkets for sale.

While in Navala we learned that the Fijian Health Ministry is promoting tooth brushing, two children per family (down from double digit procreation), and the wearing of flip-flops. It turns out that many people in the islands traditionally go barefoot. Unfortunately, there is a parasitic worm that often burrows into people's feet from the soil, causing them to become disabled. Flip-flops can put a stop to this condition.

On our way back to Volivoli Resort, we stopped at the grave of the "Cannibal King" Chief Udre who holds the Guinness World Record for eating the most people. He kept a stone for each corpse he ate, and these stones were placed under and around his sarcophagus in Rakiraki. At his death in 1840 the pile added up to 999. He apparently believed that if he ate 1,000 corpses he would gain immortality. Who knows, perhaps he achieved it anyway.

July 24   **Crossing Vatu-I-Ra Channel to Savusavu**

Since our arrival 2 weeks ago, the winds in Fiji have been fierce. This was disappointing as we had hoped to visit the Lao Island Group during this cruise, but the waves were 8 feet +/– at a 6 to 8 second moment, very steep and box like. If we went to the Laos, it would require beating into these uncomfortable head seas for almost 200 miles, so we changed our plans and decided to head 82 miles northeast across Vatu-I-Ra Channel to Vanua Levu Island and the little port of Savusavu. This is a 10 or 12-hour journey from Volivoli for *Argo*. The Vatu-I-Ra Channel has got to be one of the all-time worst channels to cross. It separates the two biggest Fijian islands of Viti Levu and Vanau Levu by a narrow gorge in the sea bottom through which pass the trade winds and the ocean swell that has developed across the Southern Ocean all the way from Antarctica. Winds average 35 knots with gusts to 47 knots, and they gain velocity on the lee side after having been compressed as they pass through the channel. As we passed through it, the seas were high and very steep, but fortunately the main channel is only about 15 miles (2 ½ hours) across before coral reefs provide a little protection. We felt some trepidation about the passage inside the reef, given the accuracy of our charts and the experience of many sailors who found uncharted coral heads the hard way, with their boat! A week before, a 70-foot sailing yacht with a crew of six onboard went down not far from here. As we progressed along our course we used our Furuno CH-250 directional sonar to search the depths in front of us, which gave us some measure of confidence. However, keeping a sharp eye is always important as I spotted a patch of unsettled water that turned out to be a very large uncharted rock just slightly off our course to starboard. Lucky for us I saw it! There were three narrow passages through various parts of the reef. One of them, Nasonisani Passage, was particularly difficult. The surf was rolling into the passage from the south pushed by 40-knot winds, and when the waves hit the reef they exploded high in the air. As we neared the channel we could see monster rollers boiling in, but by then we were committed and there was nothing to do except to push through. *Argo* rose at least 10 feet on the first wave and then fell off in seconds, plowing the bow under the next wave and causing green water to roll up to the pilothouse windows. Then she rose again, only to fall into the next wave. It was quite a violent few minutes, all the time we were praying that nothing went wrong with the boat or that we wouldn't encounter an uncharted coral head. Eventually we went through the pass and made Savusavu harbor at sunset in 25 knots of wind; we anchored at the head of the bay in 75 feet of water. The harbor was completely filled with sailboats waiting out the heavy weather. After settling in, we enjoyed a couple of rums and a nice dinner.

Anchoring is a necessary skill when you're doing the kind of cruising we're doing. The first thing you need is a good anchor. We have a 350-pound plow type anchor fixed to 600 feet of ½ inch high-strength steel chain, which weighs about 3 pounds per foot. We generally let out chain equal to five or six times the distance from the bow to the bottom. For example, in calm weather and with a depth of 50 feet, we would let out 250 +/– feet of chain. In that case we would have a total weight at the bottom of about 1,100 pounds. When anchoring, we lay out the chain first, then put *Argo* in reverse until the anchor digs in. Once it bites, we are hooked and she doesn't move even when the wind comes up.

July 25   Savusavu

Savusavu is a one-street town built on a creek with a bay on one side and steep, verdant hillsides on the other. It was a Saturday, and the town was filled with people shopping in the stores and the farmers' market. We started the day with a trip to the farmers' market, then the supermarkets, then the various stores to entertain ourselves. In the late afternoon, we joined some other sailors for a trip to the Planters' Club for drinks. Our sailor comrades told us about Curly and his seminars on Fijian waters held Sunday afternoon at a local restaurant.

July 26   Curly Carswell

Curly is a salty old mariner of New Zealand extraction who has lived in Fiji on a houseboat in the Savusavu Creek for over 40 years. He is a silver-haired, bearded fellow who knows the ins and outs of these reefs like nobody else. He conducts a seminar ($10 USD) once a week for arriving boaters and tells tales of the islands and provides waypoints through the reefs to places we all want to see. He sprinkles his lecture with stories of boats that have gone aground or yachts that have been totally lost on the hazardous reefs. Curly reported that so far this year four boats have gone hard aground. He is a very knowledgeable and charming character indeed. We spent 4 hours listening to his tales and getting his waypoints, and he helped us plan our trip to Taveuni Island and Viani Bay.

July 27   **Market Day in Savusavu**

We spent the next day preparing and provisioning for our trip to Viani Bay, home to one of the best dive sites in the world—the famous Rainbow Reef. We needed to freshen our stores and get last-minute waypoints from Curly, otherwise it was a lazy day that seemed to evaporate like a dream.

July 28   **Passage to Viani Bay**

It was a rough start after we weighed anchor at 08:30. The short passage out of Savusavu Bay was pleasant enough, particularly as we passed the Jean-Michel Cousteau Resort near the point separating Savusavu Bay from the Koro Sea. As we passed through Point Passage things deteriorated quickly. Large rollers were boiling into the bay across the reef; *Argo* plowed through with her customary power and stability. Once out into the sea the waves soldiered in from the east in 5 to 6 second intervals and were about 6 feet high, while the wind blew at a steady 25 knots: it was unpleasant indeed. As we progressed up the coast toward Viani Bay and Taveuni Island, we could see the lush, green-forested hillsides of both Vanau Levu and Taveuni Islands. This is the wind-ward side of Fiji, so it experiences more rain and thus has more vegetation. It was picturesque to see the green and brown hills rise out of the blue ocean.

As the day wore on, we eventually gained some shelter from the lee of Taveuni and life became more pleasant. Around 15:00 we approached Viani Pass to make our way through the reef. This is a very dangerous time during any passage: reefs are coral and rock outcroppings that pose the potential of poking a hole in the bottom of any boat. One can expect to encounter strong currents (from the ocean rushing in and out with the tides), and waves of substantial size and power can develop. From the pilothouse, we could see the reef's beautiful blue and green waters in the distance along with breaking waves. The desire to get to the safety inside the pass can be very beguiling, but there was more danger to come as we couldn't tell precisely how the boat would handle in these circumstances or if there was an uncharted rock or coral head on our course. At any rate, we entered the pass without difficulty and soon passed the reef and entered the placid waters leading to Viani Bay. The bay was quite large with several boats at anchor in various places. Only a couple of Fijian dwellings were visible. The hills surrounding the bay were high and steep, some with green foliage, some with tall brown grass, and some turned black from the burning of grass by the locals.

After settling in we went on the internet to find a dive resort and make arrangements to dive on the reef the next morning. Then cocktails, dinner, and a movie.

July 29   **Rainbow Reef**

The next morning a boat picked us up at our anchorage at 07:00 and took us to Dolphin Bay a few miles around the point near where we entered the pass. We wanted to dive the famous Rainbow Reef, one of the top dive spots in the world. The boat took us to a little dive resort located on the bay; it was a shabby place, but very iconic South Seas. Guests live in tents and shower using a bucket of water. Every building has a sand floor, but the food and service are superb. All of the guests were either European or American and were among the most traveled and well-informed people we have ever encountered. The owner, Roland (a German), was reputed to be the best dive operator in the region, and our dive-master Susan (also German) was excellent. Once we got our gear organized we headed to the dive boat and met our boatman, a colossal Fijian named Apex. We were glad to see him; he could pull anyone out of the water with one hand! After a 15-minute boat ride, we arrived at the first dive site. We dove in 100 feet of water, first on the channel side then on the lagoon side. Corals flourish in areas of swift current, and there is such a variety of corals here, all having different shapes and color, earning its name the Rainbow Reef.

The reef was spectacular. After jumping off the dive boat and descending to depth, the current pushed us along at about 3 miles per hour. Looking about the ledge, we saw countless schools of fish, fantastic colors, and shapes in a world parallel to ours but much different. There are the familiar elk horn, brain, mushroom, fan, and other types of corals, and of course there was a large variety of fish, many with the most amazing and dazzling indigo, red, green, olive, white and brown. As we flew along the reef enjoying the spectacular scenery, all of a sudden, we felt a current from above pushing us toward the dark blue infinity 1,300 feet below, but we moved past it.

We returned to the dive resort around 14:00 and enjoyed lunch with our fellow divers. The cook had prepared a watercress salad, pumpkin squash fritters, and a chocolate crepe dessert. It was delicious. We were back on *Argo* around 16:00.

July 30   **Tour of Taveuni Island**

At 07:00 Apex picked us up for our trip to Taveuni Island across the Somosomo Channel. Taveuni is known as the Garden Isle, and indeed it was as lush and beautiful as any island we have seen. The island seemed to be one huge mountain, perhaps 50 miles long, 4,000 feet high, and 25 miles wide. It doesn't have a peak per se, but rather almost the whole island is a ridge of the same height. The lower third shows the patchwork signs of agricultural activity, but the upper two-thirds is all rain forest. Aside from enjoying the beauty of the island, we were scheduled for three stops: Tavoro Falls at the north end of the island, the International Date Line marker, and the little villages that dot the coastline. Our guide was Kamal, a farmer and part-time guide for the Dolphin Bay Divers. Kamal is the third generation of his family in Fiji; his grandfather was a laborer brought here by the British to work in the sugarcane fields. His father was a laborer in the coconut plantations. Somehow Kamal was able to acquire a freehold of land, build a farm, and raise three children who are now all college educated. Quite an achievement. He now grows kava, which is a 4-year crop and very profitable. He is in the process of planting 1,000 sandalwood trees. It takes 25 years for a tree to mature, and if of good quality can be sold for $100,000 each. Kamal apparently has patience, foresight, and big dreams.

On our drive, Kamal stopped by the home of the grower of the saplings he wishes to buy to complete his 1,000-tree inventory. When we arrived at the home of the grower, we had to wake him from his afternoon nap, which is customary for Fijians. When I was introduced to him, the first thing he told me was that he was the pastor of the Seventh-Day Adventist Church. I congratulated him as he seemed very proud of this accomplishment, and then I noticed that he was wearing a T-shirt that read "Love Your Bank." You can't make this sort of thing up! He showed us about his little yard. He has one sandalwood tree growing in the yard, and from this tree he grows saplings that he has planted on his farm and also sold to other people. I asked how he got in the sandal-wood business. Apparently, he learned about the business from his brother who had researched it on the internet. They learned what a sandalwood tree was worth in India, which inspired them to start growing it for themselves in Fiji. Sandalwood is used in making soap and fragrances.

Kamal told us how the average Taveuni Fijian lives. Basically, they go to their fields in the morning and tend their crops until lunchtime. They return home for lunch, take a nap, and that's it. After dinner, the men sit around and drink kava, a nonalcoholic beverage that nevertheless has a numbing effect on the mind and body. The men stay up past midnight and then fall asleep only to repeat this routine day-after-day. Women do the wash by hand, clean the dwelling, and tend to the children. Men often do the cooking. From what we could see, the Fijians live an impoverished life by our standards, but they are clearly a happy lot. They basically live off the land, own a few animals for food, and collect the income that the tribe earns from renting its land to other people like the industrious Indians, who run and own most of the businesses in Fiji. Fijians, however, own 90 percent of all the land in Fiji.

As far as tourist sights are concerned, the waterfall was perhaps the most beautiful I have ever seen. Long, slender, cascading sheets of water falling 100 feet or more to a beautiful blue pool, surrounded by red rocks and lush, tropical plants; it was idyllic.

The Rotary Club in Taveuni has constructed an attractive and informative site to illustrate the International Date Line, which passes through the area. You can stand on one side of the line and half your body will be in today and the other half in yesterday. Very interesting. We traveled on a two-lane cow path for a mile to find it.

July 31   **Viani Bay to the Blue Lagoon**

El Nino is apparently causing comparatively poor weather conditions here. The winds are higher than normal, making the seas rough and unpleasant. Because of the islands, wind is focused and compressed between the island channels and then accelerates out the other side, turning normal 18 to 25 knot trade winds into 40 to 45 knot blows. The trades are one thing, but katabatic winds add to the mix. Today a tropical low pressure formed over Vanuatu and the Solomon Islands and is moving toward Fiji, bringing high winds and heavy rain Sunday through most of the week. For that reason, we decided to move again to the Yasawa Islands and the Blue Lagoon to wait out the weather. It has a protected harbor, usually with other boaters for company, and a resort, beach bar, and restaurant on shore. It is a nice spot. Getting there required a 1 ½ day trip around the lee or western side of Vanau Levu and across the Vatu-I-Ra channel once again. The trip on the lee side of Vanua Levu was pleasant and relatively calm as we suspected, but by the time we got to the channel it was a mess, with very high winds and big seas. Luckily the crossing was only a 2-hour ordeal, and we made the Blue Lagoon 29 hours after we departed Viani Bay. Once again, we found *Argo* to be simply the best: she powered through the seas, giving us a relatively good ride in spite of 10-foot beam seas on an 8-second moment.

August 1   **Arrival at the Blue Lagoon Bay to the Blue Lagoon**

After an all-night run from Viani Bay we arrived and dropped anchor in 50 feet of water. Salty and tired, we lowered the tender and made for the beach for cocktails and dinner. The resort was small and intimate. Only three couples showed up for dinner that night, but the resort scheduled a men's singing group to perform Fijian music accompanied by guitar, ukulele, and a homemade bass composed of a stick and string pressed on a large wooden box for amplification. It all sounded very good. Dinner was great, too, particularly the banana cream pie made with the special coconut cream and sweet finger-sized bananas that you can only get in these islands.

August 2–6   **The Blue Lagoon**

We were at anchor in the wind and rain for several days. The wind was up to 45 knots in the anchorage, and *Argo* was moving around accordingly. On occasion, we went into the resort for dinner, and the furious conditions were rather unsettling as we headed to shore in our tender.

One day we decided to venture out in the dinghy across the bay to another island and a small subsistence farm that sometimes sells fruits and vegetables to yachters. Salie, a local village woman, guided us to the farm. We crossed the bay that was wind whipped and turbulent and then rounded a point and preceded into second bay. Altogether it was an uncomfortable, wet, 30-minute ordeal. We were looking for a small mangrove area at the shoreline inside of which was a small river. We took the river to its end and anchored the boat to the shore, climbed the mud footpath up a hill to a place where three small buildings, a couple of goats, and a flock of chickens were located. Mattie, Salie's auntie, met us with a handshake and "Bula!" and agreed to sell us some food. She led us down the other side of the hill along a well-worn footpath through the jungle about a quarter mile to her hand-cultivated fields. Along the footpath was a 3-inch rubber irrigation line that fed water to her gardens. The cultivated fields were small, perhaps a quarter acre each. She grew melons, beans, carrots, spinach, lettuce, cassava, taro, bananas, papaya, cucumbers, tomatoes, and squash. She also raised goats, chickens, and a steer. As we placed our order she went about the gardens with a knife harvesting. It was great fun to see how native Fijians live, but we had to deal with the boat ride back!

The next day we talked with Ivan, the owner of the resort. He is a 73-year-old Australian ex-truck driver who bought the Nanuya Resort 3 years ago. Education is wonderful, but when you see what a practical, industrious person can do for himself and other people it is simply amazing! For 15 years, he and his wife had been active in charitable work to aid the Fijians. When this resort became available for purchase, they decided to buy it, in part to help the three villages in this area. For 3 years, he and his Fijian workers have been renovating it. The resort needs a lot of electrical power not only to run the desalination plant, but also to run hair dryers, the laundry, cooking appliances, lights, TVs . . . the works. It's a lot of electricity. One of the most interesting things we discovered was that Ivan had installed an American-made solar power system to provide power for the whole resort, including making fresh water. High on the hillside overlooking the resort was a vast array of solar panels that replaced a generator that used to provide power. The generator burned almost $130,000 a year in fuel, whereas the solar power system cost about $800,000 to construct. Ivan figured it had a 9-year payback period when all costs were considered. Next to the solar arrays were newly cultivated and irrigated fields of pineapple and other vegetables. Now the resort grows some of its food, makes its own water, and generates all its own electricity —all without paying for oil or incurring any costs other than maintenance. From what I could see, solar power is going to make a tremendous difference worldwide in terms of reducing pollution and also the demand for oil.

The way of life in Fiji is changing. Most of the people live in villages. They have lived for a millennium or more in a non-cash economy. They didn't need money because they could literally catch a fish or grab a piece of fruit off a tree when they were hungry. Their clothes were made of easily obtainable materials. They wanted for nothing. Then came the cell phone and now the internet. Now they need cash to pay their phone bill. One night we were returning to *Argo* and walked down the beach to our dinghy. It was a beautiful starry night. I noticed a Fijian man sitting on a coconut tree log on the beach at the water's edge in the moonlight. It seemed idyllic; an isolated Garden of Eden far from the cares and hustle-bustle of the developed world. Then I noticed—he was talking on his cell phone. There is no escape; there are no corners of the earth any longer, not even in Fiji.

The next day was beautiful and calm. Rebecca and I packed up the tender with beach chairs, books, and snorkel gear and headed for the beach. It was a rare and beautiful time for us. In all the cruising we have done, we rarely get a moment like that.

August 7–9   Denarau

Tuesday morning, we awoke to a dysfunctional watermaker. We were at anchor far from the water supply, so we had only 3 days or so to get the thing fixed before our water tanks would run dry. We tried all the simple things that we knew how to do, but a 50-mile trip to Denarau was in the cards. We called our agent, Eli, to see if she could line up a slip and a technician in Denarau for us. Luckily, she found a 2-day berth for us and she scheduled a technician to meet us at 15:00 on the dock. In the meantime, we called the factory in the United States to sort out the possibilities. Fortunately, we had all the parts we needed on board. After we docked, we took the machine completely apart and examined its innards. The high-pressure pump needed a rebuild, and after a technician completed that job, everything was up and running again. It is always a great feeling to actually fix something.

Across the dock from us was berthed our Swedish friend, Kaj, on S/Y *Amelit*. We first met Kaj in Panama, then again in Fatu Hiva, Papeete, and Gulf Harbor. During our last night in port we enjoyed a lovely cookout on *Argo* with Kaj, talking about our various ports of call and the experiences we have shared (he later came to the U.S. and bought a used Nordhavn 75-footer).

August 9–14   Musket Cove

We moved 12 miles south of Denarau the next morning to Musket Cove Marina on Malolo Lailai Island. Getting into the bay was a little tricky with all the reefs about, but we knew we were on the right track when we passed *Dragonfly* (Google's yacht) on the way in. It was as windy as heck, so we anchored in the bay until the next morning when we moved to the little marina. In the meantime, Dragonfly's tenders replete with professional crew sped by Argo with noisy abandon, throwing waves and water in a most inconsiderate manner.

Musket Cove is a cool little spot with cottages, a beach, restaurants, and a golf course. *Argo* was stern tied to a dock that was constructed on one side of a waterway formed between two islands that were perhaps 100 yards wide. We brought *Argo* into the narrow waterway, and located our appointed 30-foot space on the dock. We turned her nose into the sand across from our dock and started to back her into position. We dropped the anchor so as to hold her off the dock and then continued to back her in and tie her off. We then tightened the anchor chain to make her secure. At that point, *Argo* was right beside a genuine thatch-roofed Tiki bar with a classic beach sand floor. Fantastic!

Musket Cove is a popular resort complete with a nine-hole oceanfront golf course. We played the golf course one morning; it cost $10 USD for nine holes. Although it wasn't the best golf course we ever played, it certainly was picturesque and the cheapest. We spent a few days here, walking around the island and seeing the lovely vacation homes owned by foreigners. Before leaving for the United States to resume my medical treatment, we talked with Tom about future plans if I couldn't return immediately. He assured us that he "had our back," which was very comforting indeed. We planned to leave *Argo* at Musket Cove with Tom aboard, and then to move her before the hurricane season.

RETURN TO CALIFORNIA

August 18   **Returned Home**

We returned home for another resection of my bladder to see if the immune therapy had been successful. Unfortunately, the tumor progressed despite the therapy, and our worst fears had been realized. We were very concerned that it could have metastasized, as bladder cancer is one of the deadliest forms of cancers. Every expert that we spoke with recommended the same thing: don't take any chances with this time bomb, get it out, have a cystectomy. A cystectomy is really a nasty experience. The only silver lining, if there was one, was that the University of Michigan is one of the best places to be treated for this type of cancer. So, we went ahead and scheduled it for October 16.

While I was contemplating my future after the resection, the phone rang. It was Tom. What a kind gesture, I thought, calling all the way from Fiji to see how I was doing. As I was thanking him, he interrupted me. He said that the reason for the call was that he was quitting and would be leaving the boat in 2 weeks to take a job as a deckhand on a larger yacht!

Wow! What a shock! It felt like a punch in the gut! I was bewildered emotionally. What a deep, personal disappointment! He was our friend and shipmate. We shared wonderful times, lived together for almost a year, and yet he left us stranded in a moment of dire need. We were truly and deeply hurt. What else could go wrong?

I explained to him what had happened to me and that I couldn't come to Fiji for months to take care of *Argo*. I reminded him of his commitment to us. The boat was in the middle of nowhere, with no one to care for it or protect it from vandals, that it needed to be moved soon because of the coming cyclone season, and that he had signed an employment agreement in which he specifically agreed not to abandon the vessel in a foreign port. That didn't move him. Rebecca and I begged him, pleaded with him, offered him more money, promised to promote him to captain and recommend him to other yacht owners . . . all to no avail. With a $3-million investment at risk, Rebecca and I were beside ourselves!

We sat down to consider alternatives. I really couldn't postpone my upcoming surgery to return to Fiji and move *Argo* myself. We had two alternatives: hire a captain and crew and return the yacht to New Zealand or have them bring it to the United States. In any case, it had to be out of Fiji and the cyclone area of the South Pacific within a month or two (as it turned out, Fiji was hit with one of the largest cyclones in history later that season). Because there was no way to assess my future, we decided to bring *Argo* back to the United States and put her up for sale. The dollar's exchange value was so high that foreign buyers were virtually out of the market and only a US citizen would be a likely buyer.

We located Paul, the New Zealand captain who brought the boat up from Auckland 6 weeks earlier. I explained our situation and asked him if he could hire a crew and take the boat via Hawaii to Los Angeles. Fortunately, he was between engagements and thought he could get a crew assembled. Within a week, he had a crew confirmed. We agreed upon terms and fees, I wrote up a contract for Paul's signature, confirmed our arrangements with our insurance company, and wired money to his bank. Paul told me that the two crew members he hired both held captain's licenses as well as engineering certifications and he had traveled with both people before. It looked like a very competent, excellent crew. After all the papers were signed and plane tickets purchased, things began to move along. Paul and I agreed that *Argo* would first go north to Hawaii, lay over a day or two depending on weather, then cross to California before the gale season started in the North Pacific. Fortunately, Tom agreed to stay a day or two longer so that he could help Paul get *Argo* to Denarau. Fortunately, our agent was able to get a slip for one day so that the crew and provisions could be brought aboard. *Argo* seemed ready for its nearly 5,000-mile voyage.

As *Argo* left port, another calamity befell her. The hydraulic system failed again, spilling thick hydraulic fluid into her bilges. Her stabilizers were unusable, and so a sea voyage to Hawaii was out of the question. The point of failure was the same actuator that had failed in Auckland and Bore Bora. We immediately called the manufacturer. This time ABT sent a new actuator to Denarau at my expense.

Since there were no slips in Denarau, *Argo* lay like a dead duck at anchor in the outer harbor. Until the actuator was repaired, she couldn't raise her anchor and in the meantime, we were paying for a crew of three who had to go back and forth to the harbor for food and supplies using the ship's tender. We prayed that the weather would hold and that she would remain safe and secure. On the fourth day of this trial, parts finally arrived. The crew completed repairs, raised the tender, and finally got underway for Hawaii. She arrived there on October 3.

Before landing in Hawaii, I called the U.S. Customs and Immigration Service to get the boat and crew cleared into the United States. I provided all the documentation required and the Customs officers met Argo at the dock when she arrived. After interviewing the crew, the service called and asked me, among other things, how much cash was aboard. I told them we had two hidden safes on board. One safe on the bridge was to hold a relatively small amount of money so that thieves could be appeased if we were ever robbed. We knew that $2,500 was in the upper safe, but we weren't sure how much was in the lower hidden safe. In any case, it could have been more than the de minimis $10,000 allowed. Unfortunately, before the ship left Fiji, Tom, without my permission, gave Paul the combination to the upper safe, which I found annoying. No one knew about the lower safe. Anyway, I told the customs officer all this and he sent the crew off the boat while he opened the safes: $2,500 was in the upper safe (the correct amount), and about $9,000 was in the lower safe. At that point, everything was in order and the crew was allowed back aboard and they entered the United States.

The next day, October 4, we received a call from the harbormaster in Hawaii. Apparently, when he arrived at work that morning there was a message on his phone's voice mail. Paul's wife in New Zealand had called asking him to go to the boat and find Paul. He immediately went to Argo and found Paul unconscious on the cockpit deck covered in blood, with blood spatter on the carpets and in other places of the boat. He immediately called for an ambulance and the police. Paul was taken to the hospital with three broken ribs, a broken jaw, an orbital floor fracture, and numerous broken teeth. He was admitted and remained in the hospital for several days.

Then the police went to work; one of the crew members was quickly rounded up. He was still drunk from the night before, aimlessly wandering around the docks. The other crew member, the perpetrator, was later arrested in Honolulu and jailed. The police report told the story from the perpetrator's point of view: Paul had badgered them day and night about taking care of the yacht. He apparently wanted them to keep their feet off the furniture and avoid scratching the woodwork. These two guys had spent their entire careers on oil rigs and service boats, and were not gentle people. They had no idea how to care for nice things. After 2 weeks in close quarters at sea, and a night of drinking in Honolulu, the bigger, younger crewman had had enough and decided to repay Paul by beating the hell out of him.

Weeks later the perp's sister came to Hawaii to get him out of jail. Somehow, she got hold of my phone number and called me with a very aggressive attitude asking how I could have left her brother penniless and stranded in Hawaii; after all, he had a wife and children to support back in New Zealand. I simply asked her to read the police report. We didn't hear from her again. Later we learned that authorities from New Zealand flew to Honolulu to take him into custody. Eventually he lost his licenses and was jailed in New Zealand.

Meanwhile, we needed a whole new crew. The harbormaster told us that no one could board the yacht unless a hazmat company was hired and completely cleaned *Argo*, removing all signs of blood. Of course, we complied, and that was expensive!

Another problem presented itself: Weather was closing in and if *Argo* wasn't underway soon, she could be stuck in Hawaii until spring. That would also be quite expensive. I was beside myself with anxiety, both about the boat and about my upcoming operation.

I immediately started searching for a solution to this new and unexpected problem. First, I called our friends at Nordhavn Yachts in Dana Point, California. Luckily Devin, the teaching captain that helped us learn to cruise on our first Nordhavn 55-footer named *Odyssey*, was available and agreed to help us out. Wow! That was a godsend! Devin, his father, and another crew member were on a plane for Hawaii the next day. When they arrived, they rented a car, went to the grocery store to provision for the 2,500-mile run to Los Angeles. Paul crawled out of the hospital 3 days after he was admitted and went directly to *Argo* to meet the new crew and help them as best he could get fueled and become situated on the yacht. *Argo* got underway for Los Angeles on October 7, which in itself was a minor miracle.

I called Devin on the sat-phone almost every day to see how things were going. Storms were brewing both north and south of him. A hurricane was forming off the coast of Los Cabos and would send rough waters to the north, perhaps directly at *Argo*. At the same time, strong early winter storms were coming in from the north. Even if he didn't directly encounter a storm, the waves they send out could produce a rough and unpleasant ride. Devine threaded the needle and maneuvered Argo between the various fronts. Meanwhile, I was getting emotionally and physically prepared for my surgery.

We followed *Argo* at sea via her satellite tracking device. Twelve days after she left Hawaii, and 3 days after my surgery, *Argo* arrived safely and without incident in San Pedro Harbor. She was home safe and sound.

EPILOGUE

We returned to *Argo* after Christmas and moved her to Ensenada, Mexico, for the winter.

There was no money in the upper safe, but the lower safe was untouched.

"We had no serious illness on the trip – just strained back muscles and a cold. Thankfully no surgeries or IV's required."
-Rebecca

Paul returned to New Zealand, and then went to Vanuatu where he had a friend who was a dentist. After more than a year, he was still hurting. We have no knowledge of the other two crewmen.

We haven't heard from Tom.

My cancer surgery was very difficult, but successful. Managing the issues associated with it, however, seemed too difficult at the time to allow us to continue sailing the oceans, so we sold *Argo*.

Our crossing of the Pacific was fantastic beyond belief.

"Dream as if you'll live forever, live as if you'll die today."

– James Dean

Robert R. Tisch

CLOSING THOUGHTS...

Unlike a master of the universe flying 30,000 feet above it all, we plodded along at 8 knots for 10,000 miles, which affords a person a unique, and humbling perspective of the earth. During weeks at sea in slow motion and solitude, we came to feel the rhythm of life on our planet. We gained a new appreciation for the size of the earth, the relativity of time, the homogeneity of modern life, and the impact we as humans are having on the environment.

It's a Small World:

We began our voyage thinking of the world abstractly in terms of its size, but if you travel relentlessly day and night at even very slow speeds, eventually a lot of miles flow under the keel. By sailing just 200 miles a day, in a month you will have gone a quarter of the way around the earth. The distance from Tokyo to Dublin is a mere 9,000 miles, and the span of North America is just 2,500 miles from New York to LA. Once we actualized this, we gained an insight into how the explorers and our ancient ancestors migrated and discovered the world, and we felt an unexpected kinship to them.

The Relativity of Time:

The earth is round, has a circumference of approximately 24,000 miles at the equator, and rotates on its axis at 1,000 mph. Since it makes a 360^0 rotation in 24 hours, each increment of that rotation is measured in minutes and seconds that correspond to the miles the earth has rotated from the 0^0 meridian, and this corresponds directly to the tick-tock of our clocks and watches. As we calculated our position on the globe each day using degrees of longitude and latitude, we were constantly aware of time and what it means. As the earth spins, the gravity of the moon and sun exert forces that create tides and influence currents. As each day came to an end, just as the sun came close to setting, the wind and waves rose as if in parting tribute to our ancient god's recline. As darkness enveloped the sea, phosphorescent life forms rose to the ocean's surface in a daily migration that is the basis of life on our planet. When the sky darkened and night fell, the stars appeared and rotated overhead as the earth spun on its axis. The cosmos came alive with shooting stars from distant galaxies, making us aware that we, the earth, are part of a much larger universe of matter that is virtually timeless. Time and its relentless passage were ever-present in our minds, as was the realization of our place in the order of things.

As we progressed and moved south of the equator, the Southern Cross rose above the horizon, marking our entry into the land of Polynesia. After weeks alone on the ocean, making landfall on a strikingly beautiful and verdant island was a wonderment. Spellbound by its beauty and astonished by its isolation, we were captivated at the thought of the violent forces that convulsed these islands up from the seafloor 25 million years ago. Soaring into the sky, the eroded cones of their long extinct volcanoes not only bear witness to their origin, but also to the relentless power of wind and rain to carve them into their present beautiful form. For 24,999,000 years these islands existed in splendid isolation spawning the fish, the corals, and the Garden of Eden that was our inheritance. Then, about 1,000 years ago, human beings came to the South Pacific. They lived here untouched and in harmony until 1770, just 247 years ago, when Captain James Cook arrived replete with religion, technology, and European civilization. Cannibalism was still gruesomely practiced as late as the mid-20th century. Walking the hills and beaches, and gazing at the volcanic megaliths that form these islands, one cannot help but be struck by the brevity of human history and the acceleration of the impact of our economic activity over the last 50 years. In that short, infinitesimal span of time, we human beings have unknowingly, yet compulsively, put the entire chain of life at risk.

Modern Life:

The idyllic, slow and breezy pace of life in the South Pacific existed until a few decades ago. People who 10 years ago fished for a living in nearby waters and lived lazily with their six or more children in a hut on a remote island are now trying to earn money to pay their cell phone bill and connect to the newly installed internet. To earn money, they have shipped their children off to foreign lands expecting a monthly stipend. They have sold their birthright, their fishing rights, to the Chinese who hire them to work in the canning plants until they fish out the waters with their long lines and huge nets. This is happening with frightening rapidity. Consumption and materialism are quickly changing the world, and people of the South Pacific are not immune. Children are moving to the cities for an education and employment; remote areas are left to the old and less able. TV, the internet, and cell phones are accelerating this assimilation everywhere. From hamburgers to T-shirt monograms to architecture—ideas are spread and adopted around the world with the speed of light. It is obvious that a once distinct and unusual culture is now subsumed into the homogeneity of the modern world; yet the eclectic mix of old and new is fascinating to see and exciting to experience.

The Environment:

Evidence of Asia's prosperity is everywhere as plastic and other refuse floats across the Pacific and lands for the most part north of the equator. We have seen the beautiful beaches in Panama and Central America completely covered in refuse of every kind; from toothbrushes to dishpans to diapers. And the same is true far out at sea, where we encountered large rafts of flotsam that have drifted on the wind thousands of miles from the Yangtze River and other places. Particularly surprising to me was the impact of the diesel engine on the ecology of the oceans. People used to fish using one line and one hook at a time and this practice was sustainable. Diesel engines, which came into wide use after WWII, enabled man to dominate the oceans like never before. Today, fishing vessels operate for months at sea and pull massive nets and long lines of 50 km or more. No longer are prey species the only target, modern methods are indiscriminate, scooping up everything in their path. Many islands that we visited have been fished out! Worse yet, a fish monger we met tests the large bluefin tunas he receives with a Geiger Counter, because since the Fukushima Daiichi disaster many fish have tested positive for radioactivity. Herring, Alaska salmon, and other fish are also being found with high levels of radioactivity and cancerous lesions in Alaskan waters. Even the population of sea birds is collapsing as long line baited hooks catch both fish and birds. Scientists report that the PH of the ocean has risen, threatening the ability of plankton and other species to survive. All of this is driven by population pressure and the impetus to survive and make money, to buy lunch as it were. Ignorance plays a big role. Most of this eco-pressure has occurred within the last 30 years; not even a twinkling of time!

The ocean and its living creatures are so beautiful, such a joy for us to discover, that we must not let them perish. However, I am afraid the oceans have been taken for granted, and as big as they are, are being devastated. **Everything that we put on the land will someday wind up in the oceans.** But for the earth and the universe, it means nothing. It is part of the process of life and evolution, and I doubt we as humans can do anything about it, although I hope we do.

A truly awesome experience!

In crossing the Pacific, we found the beauty of life everywhere—in the flora and fauna, in the mountains and beaches, in art, archeology, and in the remarkable, interesting human stories of struggle and accomplishment. We couldn't have spent the time of our life better. It was a truly awesome, eye opening, and unimaginable experience.

Our advice: Go forth, have fun, and live your dream.

Randy and Rebecca Tisch

ABOUT THE AUTHOR

Robert R. (Randy) Tisch and his wife, Rebecca, reside in Ann Arbor, Michigan. They began their boating career on the Great Lakes in 1992, and circumnavigated Lakes Superior, Michigan and Huron. After selling their businesses in 2009, they purchased their first trans-ocean cruiser, and have traveled since over 50,000 ocean miles from Alaska to Newfoundland, and from Newfoundland to New Zealand. Randy holds a USCG Captain's license.

During his professional life, Randy built a successful investment management practice and ultimately sold it to a public company prior to beginning his ocean cruising experiences. Rebecca is a pediatric ophthalmologist.